PROFIT

WITHDRAWN

Coin Collecting

By David L. Ganz

©2008 David L. Ganz

Published by

krause publications

An Imprint of F+W Publications

700 East State Street • Iola, WI 54990-0001
715-445-2214 • 888-457-2873
www.krausebooks.com

Our toll-free number to place an order or obtain
a free catalog is (800) 258-0929.

Library of Congress Control Number: 2007942695

ISBN-13: 978-08969-629-1
ISBN-10: 0-89689-629-3

Designed by Kay Sanders
Edited by Arlyn Sieber

Printed in China

Dedication

To Kathy, with love. You are as passionate about your embroidery as I am with my coins, tokens and medals, and we remain an MS-70 match.

and

for Clifford Mishler, who took a chance on a greenhorn in 1969 and made him (me) the Washington correspondent for *Numismatic News*.

and

to Chet Krause, who testified at the 1973 Bicentennial coinage hearings in Washington, D.C., and offered me a summer job in 1973 as I waited to get into law school, and then hired me until I started on my real career path,

and

to Dave Harper, who turns out to be a reader since childhood, and the best editor a writer and columnist could hope for.

Acknowledgments

No book exists in a vacuum, and in this field, we all build on the writings of our predecessors. The research that went into this book was done over several years – long before a book was even contemplated – and the Internet was the main research tool.

Jim Halperin of Heritage Auction Galleries in Dallas made the illustrations possible. He put his staff to work and offered his firm's extensive auction archives, which made illustrating this book a snap. He also provided assistance in correcting the provenance of rarities. Christine Karstadt of Stack's Rare Coins in New York City gave encouragement and assistance with photographs.

Julian Leidman, whom I have known for more than 30 years, including the time he served as a director of the Professional Numismatists Guild and I as its general counsel, shared his recollections of the many rarities that passed through his hands, some of which are written about. Karl Moulton provided invaluable assistance in locating auction catalogs and prices realized from a bygone era. I thought the results would prove interesting, and Karl was able to provide some original items that existing numismatic libraries, including my own, lacked.

Arthur Friedberg of The Coin & Currency Institute Inc. in Clifton, New Jersey, has been a friend for more than 35 years. I worked with him professionally on the 1982 Olympic coin legislation and earlier when the Friedberg family decided to sell its Brasher doubloon in Auction '79. Arthur is acknowledged here for his assistance with auction catalogs and prices realized, and as publisher of the book *The Investor's Guide to United States Coins* by Neil S. Berman and Silvano DiGenova, which first used the Solomon Brothers guide so effectively in 1986 and again in the completely new 2007 edition.

Neil S. Berman, whom I have known for more than 25 years in good times and better times, provided assistance with auction catalogs and prices realized as well as commentary on his book with Hans Schulman.

I am deeply indebted to Bob Harwell of Hancock & Harwell in Atlanta, whom I have known since the early 1980s when we allowed our shared passion for fine wine to turn into a personal importing business, for the Dukes Creek collection data and information about the Arthur

Montgomery and Fisher collections. His generosity was helpful in the overall charting and analysis. Information about gold coins from the Bareford sale in 1978, which subsequently became the Dukes Creek collection, made this book richer in pricing data.

Dennis Baker and NumisMedia in Aliso Viejo, California, my friend for many years dating back to his tenure as editor of the *Coin Dealer Newsletter*, is owed the most hearty of thanks for the yeomanlike way in which he has provided pricing data for the market basket for the past seven years. Dennis gave freely of himself and his company in pricing coins in a variety of conditions. This book would be poorer without his research.

My dear friend Dr. Donald Kagin of Kagin's in Tiburon, California, whom I have known since the early 1970s, was kind enough to share generously his recollection and records on the 1894-S dime.

Thanks also to following:

-- Randy Thern of F+W Publications for believing in the project.

-- Donn Pearlman, with whom I served on the American Numismatic Association Board of Governors, for assistance in gathering 1913 nickel photos from one of his best ever public-relations items.

-- My dear friend Burt Blumert, who first appointed me general counsel to the National Association of Coin & Precious Metals Dealers in 1981 and called me with a recent story about a 1946 war nickel. You have my continued admiration, Burt.

-- Francis "Frank" Campbell, American Numismatic Society librarian. Without his assistance, this book would be the poorer. I have been an ANS member since the early 1970s – first as an associate, now as a life fellow. Frank cheerfully provided assistance in locating older auction catalogs and data on a variety of numismatic rarities and helped find obscure answers to difficult questions.

-- Mark Van Winkle of Heritage Auction Galleries, who shared research necessary to disprove the existence of one or more rare coins in a pedigree chain.

-- Wayne Homren, who edits *E-Sylum,* a wonderful weekly online journal of the Numismatic Bibliomania Society. Wayne deserves kudos for his assistance in obtaining the Charles Benson catalog from 1880, and Karl Moulton deserves kudos for supplying the catalog and prices realized. Write whomren@coinlibrary.com to apply for a free subscription to *E-Sylum.*

I joined the American Numismatic Association in 1967, became a life member in 1972 and legislative counsel in 1978, and served as president from 1993 to 1995. The association's library is one of its crown jewels, and for this book, ANA research librarian Amber Thompson, master of library science, located a Frossard catalog from 1884 and its prices realized, as well as a Kreisberg sales catalog or two from the 1960s and '70s on the 1838-O half dollar. This book would be the poorer without her help.

I double and triple checked some facts using the online edition of *The New York Times*. That was made possible by the Bergen County Library Cooperative System, available to residents of Bergen County, New Jersey, where I have served as a county supervisor (or freeholder, in local parlance) since 2003. Jennifer Rachaner, indefatigable campaigner and my freeholder aide, helped put it all together for final proofing. Her assistance is greatly appreciated.

At the last minute, I decided I needed a new photograph of the finest known 1894-S dime and reached out to John Feigenbaum, president of David Lawrence Rare Coins in Virginia Beach, Virginia. John has my gratitude for the 1894-S dime photos and information. Kim Ludwig, also of David Lawrence Rare Coins, gets kudos for sheer grit in working through the computer glitches to get the digital images.

Mary Hermann, art director for Heritage Auction Galleries, gets special mention for her outstanding work with the photos. But if I ever see an art and photolog again, it will be too soon. Thanks are due to: The Goldbergs, Beverley Hills, CA,, Larry & Ira Goldberg; Don Pearlman; Burt Blumert; Larry Hanks (1838-O Half Dollar); Prof. Mike Duffy; Bob Harwell.

We have four cats at home. Helpful Hannah (whose real name is Mimosa Rosa, nicknamed Mimi) often stopped by and parked herself in front of the computer screen. Their cat mom, my wife Kathy, often came to the rescue and, in any event, helped enormously with first edits and typing some of the corrections.

Last, in 1960, Beverlee Ganz took a 9-year-old boy to the Rockville Centre, New York, public library to find some of the answers to questions occasioned by his finding a 1906 Indian cent in grade very good in pocket change. Thanks, Mom. Reading those books led to a lifetime hobby and this book.

The following persons gave generously of their time to help track down pedigrees listed in this book. My heartfelt thanks for sharing your numismatic knowledge and recollections of events long, long ago.

David Akers
Dennis Baker
Neil Berman
Dr. Mark Blackburn
Mark Borckardt
Bryce Brown
Ted Buttrey
Frank Campbell (ANS Librarian)
John Danreuther
Beth Deisher
Sheridan Downey
Arthur Friedberg
Jeff Friedman
Ken Goldman
Ron Guth
Jim Halperin
Larry Hanks

Reed Hawn
David Harper
Wayne Homren
Dr. Donald Kagin
Julian Leidman
Stu Levine
Andy Lustig
Dwight Manley
Norm Pullen
Maurice Rosen
Tony Terranova
Amber Thompson (ANA Librarian)
Scott Travers
Luis Vigor
Dale Williams
Doug Winter

Permissions and Credits

Photos
Heritage Auction Galleries, Dallas.
David Lawrence Rare Coins, Virginia Beach, Virginia.
Stack's Rare Coins, LLC, New York City.
Teletrade, 18061 Fitch, Irvine, CA 94614-6018
Burton Blumert (1946 War Nickel)
Some photos are by David L. Ganz.

Pricing
Dennis Baker, Numismedia, Aliso Viejo, California.
Farmland Data, Prof. Mike Duffy, Iowa Stage University

Preface

Coin collecting has been my passion for nearly a half century. I have been hooked since 1960, when I found an Indian cent in grade "very good" in pocket change and learned that my 1-cent investment was worth 25 cents. The economics of it told the story of how pocket change could lead to a small fortune for a 9-year-old boy on a limited allowance. Hours of household chores yielded the same result as a few moments of numismatic diligence.

After several trips to the Rockville Centre, New York, public library, I was armed and ready to search pocket change for a small fortune, which is exactly the maximum that you can expect if your expectations are limited by an allowance the size of a Washington quarter. There had to be a better way, and I found it at the County Federal Savings & Loan Association bank. Each Saturday, armed with two $1 bills, I would arrive in time for the bank's 9 a.m. opening, go to the head teller, and ask for four rolls of "pennies" – 200 coins. I would then retire to the carpeted waiting area, where I would happily sort them on the floor or on a cocktail-height table and take out one or two coins per roll for my blue Whitman album. I would then carefully re-wrap three of the four rolls and exchange them with the teller, who oddly insisted on counting them.

On a typical Saturday, by the time the bank closed at noon or 1 p.m., I would have three or four or, on a good day, five new coins in my collection. Every one of them helped form the basis of a collection that has grown over time into a major pastime, a wonderful hobby, and a truly outstanding investment.

Around 1965, my parents sent me as an exchange student to live in Mexico City with a host family that was well connected in Mexican society. In fact, Emilio Suberbie was a *consejero* for the Banco de Mexico and, in the quaint English expression of my Mexican family siblings, "signed his name to all the pesos." It wasn't all of them – there were notes signed by other advisers, too – but some. Before long, his son, Emilio Suberbie de Mendiola, arranged for me to visit the Casa de Moneda of Mexico, the oldest continually operating mint in the Western Hemisphere.

I began writing about coins in 1965 for *The Coin Shopper,* a monthly house organ of Gateway Coins in Fort Worth, Texas, and thought up the clever title of "Under the Glass" for my monthly column of about 250 words. The magnifying glass is an accouterment used by virtually every collector, and the name stuck.

Two years later, I wrote about that visit to the Mexico City mint in a 1967 issue of *The Coin Collector,* a monthly periodical published by the Lawrence Brothers of Anamosa, Iowa, and submitted it as an expanded "Under the Glass" column, for which I was paid the munificent sum of a penny a word. The column stuck, and in 1968, Krause Publications acquired *The Coin Collector,* merged it with another periodical, re-named the newspaper *The Coin Collector & Shopper,* and began running the column monthly. The following year, I attended my first American Numismatic Association convention, held that year in Philadelphia, and bought my first "expensive" coin, an 1883 Hawaiian quarter in uncirculated condition. I bought it from dealer Tom McAfee for $19, paying $1 down and $6 a month for three months – a good investment for both of us.

1883 Hawaiian quarter.

McAfee made a customer who, for the next 20 years, progressively bought more expensive coins, all paid over time between one ANA convention and another. One time, I was just making my final payment on a $3,500 Hawaiian nickel pattern in circulated condition when McAfee suggested that I should think about upgrading to a better example at double the price. This I did promptly.

McAfee made that 1969 sale of an 1883 quarter in grade brilliant uncirculated (there was no 11-point uncirculated grading in those days) for $19. It was a pretty coin, but there were better ones; McAfee had uncirculated specimens for as low as $12 or $15 and for as much as $25. The coin was a nice compromise, probably a grade MS-63+ or MS-64. McAfee did not grade the examples; he priced them. I liked the price and the coin's appearance.

In 1980, when the coin market was running amok, McAfee recalled this quarter and bid $2,000 to re-acquire it. It wasn't for sale then. It was deaccessioned when I sold my Hawaiian collection in 1994 to finance the down payment on a house. The price it brought was the approximate price of a grade choice uncirculated (MS-63) coin.

In 1969, I moved to Washington, D.C., and started college at the Georgetown University School of Foreign Service. I began to offer spot Washington news coverage for *Numismatic News*, and in January 1970, my "Under the Glass" column began to run regularly. It's still there today, though there was a long hiatus when the column appeared in another weekly periodical.

While writing for *Numismatic News* and other hobby periodicals, I found myself drawn to reporting on the economics of numismatics. I covered auction sales, did extensive price comparisons, and wrote extensively about the market. For more than a dozen years, I wrote the column "Coin Market Perspective" for *Coins* magazine, a sister publication of *Numismatic News*.

The 1982 edition of *A Guidebook of United States Coins,* commonly called the "Red Book," contained an article I wrote about planning your rare-coin retirement. It used a study by Salomon Brothers, a Wall Street investment banking firm, in comparing coins to other assets. Salomon, like my article, used an essay that had appeared in a Federal Reserve Bank publication about investment choices.

I wrote about Salomon Brothers until the annual survey ceased publication (the story is included in this book), but I kept up the survey on my own for the succeeding years. The results are startling but satisfying. Like my collection of Hawaiian coins, which were sold to buy a house, it shows that coin collecting can be profitable also a lot of fun.

– New York City
March, 2008

Contents

Introduction

There are 130 million Americans who collect coins. The overwhelming majority of them collect the new 50 State Quarters. There is a hard-core group of probably 750,000 who collect rare coins for profit, not fun, and yet another group with numbers somewhere in between who have yet to discover how much fun it is to collect coins and how profitable it can be. This book is intended to create some excitement for collecting coins for profit, as opposed to just for fun, though it tells you how to do that as well.

It's OK to acquire coins from pocket change; it can be profitable. Even today, rarities such as the 1946 silver war nickel error coin (value: $10,000) can be found in dealer "junk" boxes. They are worth going through. Coin errors, particularly among the state quarters, are collectible. More problematical, but not without profit potential, are the U.S. Mint's modern commemorative coins. The key is their aftermarket, and its study permits generalization about the potential of a series and its individual issues.

Tennessee and California 50 State quarters.

But it also shows there are opportunities to be had among other coins, and in that sense, this book is different. It will talk about a 1794 silver dollar (mintage: 1,758) and graph price examples over an extended time. But it will also examine a more common 1795 Draped Bust dollar, which is more likely to be purchased by a collector and held longer. The 1795 coin – indeed all of the coins in the Salomon Brothers market basket – represent a broad class. For example, the 1795 silver dollar can be substituted with any silver dollar struck from 1795 through 1798.

Some coins not originally included in the Salomon survey but meeting its general criteria are also examined. Among them are some gold coins and the 1909-S "V.D.B." cent.

Each chapter on coins has at least one photograph, a graph, commentary, and analysis. There are also chapters on grading and investment strategies.

From 1978 until 1990, an annual survey by the white-shoe investment house of Salomon Brothers compared the investment return of rare coins to stocks, bonds, and a bevy of tangible and intangible assets. These included gold bullion, silver, old-master paintings, foreign exchange, and other assets with reportable daily prices. These were compared to farmland sales, the consumer price index, and stocks and bonds to see which provided the highest rate of return.

The comparison shows how rare coins fare against the consumer price index and Dow Jones industrial average. It also shows how coins compare with each other – a 1921 half dollar in grade MS-63 versus a 1794 half cent in grade extremely fine, for example.

Data is shared for coins when extended backward because of the lack of a homogeneous marketplace and precise records in previous times. In the 1930s, for example, 1860s half dollars in uncirculated condition commonly sold for under a dollar (some were 45 cents), so they were unlikely to appear as individual lots in auctions.

Until the 1960s, weekly and monthly periodicals were rare, though *The Numismatist*, published since 1888 and the American Numismatic Association's official journal since 1891, is a good source for pricing data. But even there, a researcher is reduced to picking out advertisements from merchants of the era. Chapman, Zug, Zerbe, and others lived on the prices they charged – evidencing the marketplace.

For the most part, what was rare then is rare now. There are exceptions. The 1903-O silver dollar was rare, despite a high mintage for some 60 years, until a hoard was found in the Treasury Department vaults in Washington, D.C., and released to the people, bursting the price bubble.

I have always found *A Guidebook of United States Coins* ("Red Book")

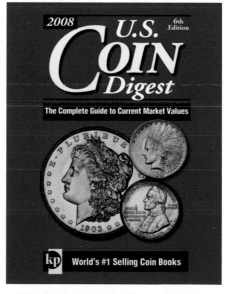

The book *U.S. Coin Digest* provides annual updates on coin values.

Ads and auction reports in periodicals like Numismatic News can be sources for historical data on coin values.

to be a great source for historical evidence of the marketplace. That's one reason why there is a secondary market for the book; early editions carry a premium of several hundred dollars. It also captures an annual snapshot in time. Today, the book *U.S. Coin Digest* (2008 marked the sixth edition), edited by David C. Harper, serves a similar purpose. But before this guide, there was the Red Book – period. When I was a kid collecting coins in the early 1960s, the July 1 unveiling of the annual Red Book was second in importance only to getting a good seat for the fireworks. I anxiously looked to see how Indian cents were doing (never that well for the grades I could then afford).

Other important historical sources are auction prices from Stack's Rare Coins (since 1935) and ads in *The Numismatic Scrapbook Magazine* (also starting in 1935) and later periodicals like *Numismatic News* (1952), *Coin World* (1960), *Coins* magazine (circa 1962), and *COINage* magazine (circa 1964).

All of these sources were checked, and thousands of entries were made in a spreadsheet for the pricing component in this presentation. This was done because of the need to augment or supplement the Salomon market basket, which ignores important segments of the market.

In addition to the Salomon Brothers coins, selected gold pieces are also included, as well as several other denominations not adequately covered in the Salomon study. The important collection of Harold Bareford is also discussed. Bareford's collection was sold by Stack's in October 1978. It was noted for its quality. Bareford's nearly $14,000 worth of purchases between 1945 and 1954 yielded more than $1.3 million at the gavel in 1978. Bareford's collection is used as a lead-in to gold coins, which were not · covered in the original Salomon Brothers study.

Following are the other additional coins covered by reason of their value, the story they tell, or other interest:

-- 1794 Flowing Hair silver dollar.
-- 1909-S "V.D.B." Lincoln cent.
-- 1913 Liberty nickel.
-- 1838-O Liberty Cap half dollar.
-- War nickels (1942-1945), plus the 1946.
-- 1804 Draped Bust silver dollar.
-- 1894-S Barber dime.
-- 1933 Saint-Gaudens gold $20.
-- 1993 Thomas Jefferson commemorative silver dollar.

Following are the Salomon coins (dealt with collectively):

-- 1794 Liberty Cap half cent, grade extremely fine.
-- 1873 2-cent piece, brilliant proof.
-- 1866 nickel 5-cent, with rays, brilliant proof.
-- 1862 silver 3-cent, brilliant uncirculated.
-- 1862 Seated Liberty half dime, BU.
-- 1807 Draped Bust dime, BU.
-- 1866 Seated Liberty dime, BU.
-- 1876 20-cent, BU.
-- 1873 Seated Liberty quarter, arrows at date, BU.
-- 1886 Seated Liberty quarter, BU.
-- 1916 Standing Liberty quarter, BU.
-- 1815 Liberty Cap half dollar, uncirculated.
-- 1834 Liberty Cap half dollar, BU.
-- 1855-O Seated Liberty half dollar, BU.
-- 1921 Walking Liberty half dollar, BU.
-- 1795 Draped Bust silver dollar, BU.
-- 1847 Seated Liberty silver dollar, BU.
-- 1884-S Morgan silver dollar, BU.
-- 1881 Trade dollar, proof. (Much published data erroneously refers to this coin as uncirculated. The 1881 is a proof-only issue.)
-- 1928 Hawaiian commemorative half dollar.

My 48-year love affair with numismatics has been fun and profitable. Although not every investment in coins is a collection, experienced numismatists have found through the years that virtually every collection is an investment. This book shows how to have more fun collecting and provides the tools for making good investments of time and capital spent on collectible coins.

Chapter 1

Charting the past and future

The Salomon survey in perspective

Salomon Brothers, once Wall Street's darling white-shoe investment banking firm, released its first study of tangible assets – including rare coins – in 1978. To the surprise of many on Wall Street and elsewhere, rare coins as investments substantially out-performed equities and bonds. The coin market exploded as a result of the survey and a variety of other economic factors.

That classic examination, and the dozen that followed it each summer, were closely watched by many investors and collectors, who wondered how an objective examination of the rare-coin market would fare. A number of other tangible assets were also brought into the comparison, which was organized by investment banking partner Robert S. Salomon as a means of creating impetus for alternative investment vehicles, rather than the traditional stocks and bonds.

Over its lifetime, Salomon Brothers' survey compared rare coins to the Consumer Price Index, stocks, bonds, collectible postage stamps, Chinese ceramics, farmland, gold, silver, old-master paintings, foreign exchange, diamonds, and even U.S. Treasury bills. For tangible assets, a variety of reliable sources were tapped for information.

Results of the annual survey, which considered a marketbasket of some 20 type coins (silver dollars and subsidiary and minor coinage, but no gold coins), were consistently impressive, showing that over long periods, rare coins had a solid track record of increases.

Gold coins were omitted because private gold ownership was relatively new and it was feared that it would skew the results. It was felt gold could be accounted for by including bullion as a separate category. Although that is true for common-date gold coins – an uncirculated (MS-62) Saint-Gaudens gold $20 will virtually track the bullion market price – it is less accurate for rare gold coins.

Values for rare gold coins, such as this 1927-S Saint-Gaudens $20, are not tied as closely to their bullion value as the values for more common gold coins.

The first survey, in 1978, showed stocks grew 2.8 percent annually over the previous 10 years. Bonds rose 6.1 percent – the precise change in the Consumer Price Index – during the same period. That meant bond buyers saw no growth after inflation and equity buyers suffered a loss. It is taken as proof by Wall Street that the bond market indeed doesn't always grow but can sometimes be stagnant. (Over the long run, stocks remain good investments.)

Salomon Brothers was able to chart the entire market, or various indices, over the entire decade. For amateurs, using the year end as a measuring device showed that the Dow Jones industrial average actually declined from 1968 (906) to 1978 (816). Moody's Aaa-rated bonds returned 8.04 percent in 1968 versus 9.63 percent in 1978. But during the same time, the Consumer Price Index moved from 33.40 to 60.60, an 81.4-percent change, which meant bonds eked out a modest return over inflation.

By contrast, rare coins in that first survey showed a consistent 13-percent annual return, the same as old-masters art, which had not yet exploded to the stratospheric proportions that made front-page news in the 1990s.

Heading the list were Chinese ceramics (19.2-percent return) and gold bullion (16.3-percent compounded annual rate). China had just re-opened trade with the West after years of being buttoned down in a communist economic system, contributing to the rise in Chinese ceramics' popularity. Gold was relatively new to the free market; private gold ownership in the United States had only seriously begun in 1975. The meteoric rise of 1980 had yet to be recorded – as well as the precipitous decline in later years, which left gold bugs scratching their heads. Gold has since rebounded.

Still, what gave the study mettle was that it was created by a highly respected Wall Street firm. It was therefore viewed seriously by those not in collectibles fields. Just how seriously was seen in a government study. *The New England Economic Review*, published by the Federal Reserve Bank of Boston, focused on the study in an article titled "Are Stocks a Bargain?" in May 1979. It concluded that stocks were well off their historical rate of return and hence were in fact a bargain.

To compare rare coins to other investments – such as farmland, stocks, bonds, stamps, Chinese ceramics, and other tangible assets – Salomon Brothers

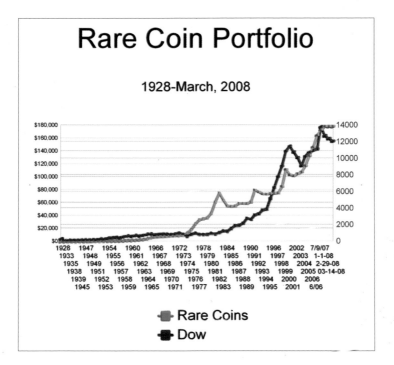

Rare Coin Portfolio

1928-March, 2008

Legend:
- Rare Coins
- Dow

requested that a marketbasket be built. The portfolio would be similar
to the Dow Jones industrial average – 30 key stocks that broadly represent all industrial stocks – and the Standard & Poor's 500, a still broader
stock index. These marketbaskets give good general pictures of what is
transpiring in the investments represented and how they contrast over
the years, but they are hardly perfect. The Dow Jones industrial average,
which has been around for more than a century, provides one focal point
for stocks. But some prefer to look at the Nasdaq and its stock index.
There are certainly indices other than the Salomon survey that have been,
and will be, used to examine coin price trends.

Over time, the Dow's composition has changed as companies have
merged, gone out of business, or been bypassed by time. The original 12
stocks in the index were American Cotton Oil; American Sugar; American Tobacco; Chicago Gas; Distilling & Cattle Feeding; General Electric;
Laclede Gas Light; National Lead; North American Company; Tennessee Coal, Iron and Railroad; U.S. Leather preferred; and U.S. Rubber.

General Electric is the only company from the original 12 that remains
in today's 30-stock index, as of February, 2008, the other 29 are 3M; Al-
coa; American Express; American International Group; AT&T; Bank of

America, Boeing; Caterpillar; Chevron, Citigroup; Coca-Cola; DuPont; Exxon Mobil; General Motors; Hewlett-Packard; Home Depot; Intel; International Business Machines; Johnson & Johnson; JPMorgan Chase & Co.; McDonald's; Merck & Co.; Microsoft; Pfizer; Procter & Gamble; United Technologies; Verizon Communications; Wal-Mart; and Walt Disney Co.

By the year 2001, Salomon Brothers itself ceased to exist independently. It became part of Smith Barney, which in turn became part of Citigroup.

The coins used in the index have changed, too, through the years – not by date, type or denomination, but by grade in some instances. The reason has as much to do with the mechanics of reporting as it does with changes in grading terminology.

Early on, for example, value guides didn't list prices for every grade and condition for every coin. The 1794 large cent in grade extremely fine, for example, contained in the Salomon marketbasket, wasn't even listed in the 1947 edition of *A Guide Book of U.S. Coins* ("Red Book") by R.S. Yeoman. The maximum condition was grade fine. So in carrying the data back to the 1930s, the task becomes much harder. In other instances, "brilliant proof" was selected for coins like the 1873 2-cent piece and 1881 Trade dollar with no further guidance. Proof-63 pricing was selected as the historical equivalent.

All of this makes a long-term examination and comparison difficult but not impossible if you're willing to settle for long-term trend lines and themes rather than pinpoint accuracy, which is nearly impossible.

Like the Dow Jones average, which doesn't represent all publicly held companies or even all significant stocks that trade on the exchange, each coin in the Salomon portfolio is broadly representative of the marketplace, and to that extent, its trend line symbolizes the actual market. Salomon chose Stack's Rare Coins of New York City to select the coins in the index and monitor their performance.

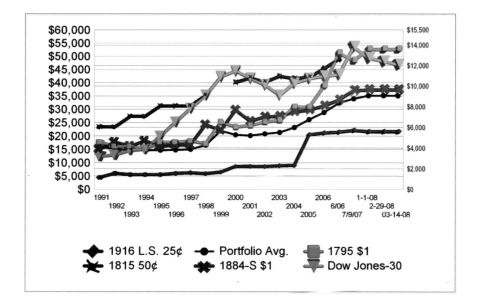

| | 1916 L.S. 25¢ | | Portfolio Avg. | | 1795 $1 |
| | 1815 50¢ | | 1884-S $1 | | Dow Jones-30 |

The coin firm's Harvey G. Stack said the index was not formulated to show that rare coins were investments per se. Instead, the coins selected for the index were typical of those that might be found in the holdings of a serious collector, but that collector wouldn't necessarily seek only the best condition possible. A substantial amount of capital would be tied up in these coins, but they did not necessarily constitute an investment, except to the extent that any purchase might retain or increase in value over time.

None of the 20 coins included in the marketbasket was of gem quality; most were choice uncirculated, the equivalent of MS-63 on most of today's numerical grading scales. Some were proofs, such as the 1873 2-cent, the 1866 Shield nickel, and the 1881 Trade dollar. They are examined as if they were proof-63.

If gold coins had been among the original components, they would have made for an even greater rate of return. One need only look at the collection of Harold Bareford, a New York attorney who acquired an extraordinary collection of gold coins one piece at a time from 1945 to 1954 at a cost of around

1795 Draped Bust dollar.

1807 Draped Bust dime.

1815 Liberty Cap half dollar.

$14,000. When his collection was sold at auction in 1978 by Stack's, it realized more than $1.3 million.

Although not initially revealed because of fear of market manipulation, the list of silver dollars and subsidiary and minor coins included in the Salomon survey were first made public by Neil S. Berman and Hans M.F. Schulman in their book *The Investor's Guide to United States Coins* (The Coin & Currency Institute, 1986). They amplified the analysis in a new edition of *The Investor's Guide to United States Coins* (The Coin & Currency Institute, 2007) by Berman and Silvano DiGenova, with special statistical research by Dr. Jason Perry, a financial economist with the Federal Reserve Bank of Boston.

The Salomon coins were revealed as the following:

-- 1794 Liberty Cap half cent, grade extremely fine.

-- 1795 Draped Bust dollar, uncirculated.

-- 1807 Draped Bust dime, uncirculated.

-- 1815 Liberty Cap half dollar, uncirculated.

-- 1834 Liberty Cap half dollar, uncirculated.

-- 1847 Seated Liberty dollar, uncirculated.

-- 1855-O Seated Liberty half dollar, uncirculated

-- 1862 Seated Liberty half dime, uncirculated.

-- 1862 silver 3-cent, uncirculated.

-- 1866 Seated Liberty dime, uncirculated.

-- 1866 Shield nickel, brilliant proof.

-- 1873 2-cent, brilliant proof.

-- 1873 Seated Liberty quarter, arrows at date, uncirculated.

-- 1876 20-cent, uncirculated.

-- 1881 Trade dollar, proof. (The Berman-DiGenova book, like others, mistakenly lists this proof-only issue in grade uncirculated, but the pricing listed is correct.)

-- 1884-S Morgan silver dollar, uncirculated.

-- 1886 Seated Liberty quarter, uncirculated.

-- 1916 Standing Liberty quarter, uncirculated.

-- 1921 Walking Liberty half dollar, uncirculated.

-- 1928 Hawaiian commemorative half dollar, uncirculated.

For a dozen years, the first week in June was a time of great hype in the coin market. That's when the Salomon Brothers' annual report of the rare-coin market was released in the form of a four- or six-page newsletter. The dates and grades of the coins included in the survey were never mentioned.

By 1989, the results were still impressive. "Conclusion offered: during the succeeding 12 month period of time, rare coins offered a return of more than 30%," the Salomon survey reported. That result ranked coins behind only old-masters paintings and Chinese ceramics.

1834 Liberty Cap half dollar.

By the following year, I wrote, "Little wonder, then, that Wall Street is smiling on the rare coin industry, whose one year ranking in the survey showed a 14.6 percent annual return, and a ranking of fourth."

For 1991, however, the investment banking house bowed to pressure from the Federal Trade Commission and decided to withdraw rare coins from its chart of tangible assets.

"When we began publishing our annual report on investment returns a dozen years ago," the Salomon report said, "we expected that the assets in the survey would generally fall into two classes of investments – financial and tangible – and that returns from these categories would diverge."

Claiming that Stack's did "too well" in selecting a model portfolio, Robert Salomon announced that rare coins would be replaced by stamps. In the process, it was hoped that the survey's results would no longer be used by telemarketers to sell rare coins to the gullible.

1847 Seated Liberty dollar.

1855-O Seated Liberty
half dollar.

Salomon Brothers changed its survey to cover three types of investments: financial assets, tangible assets, and collectibles. Those interested in rare coins were the subject of an intriguing comment in the Salomon report. It characterized collectibles purchases as "conspicuous consumption" – a desire to show others that you've reached a particular financial plateau or are capable of acquiring an item someone else desires but can't afford. "They are a means of proving to others the financial capability of the buyer, i.e., conspicuous consumption," the report said.

Foreign currency, by contrast, is not consumed; it is financial. In 2001, that investment was less than stellar but still respectable. Salomon termed foreign exchange (10.5-percent average growth) the fifth best investment, just after coins during one period measured.

Rates of Return and Change

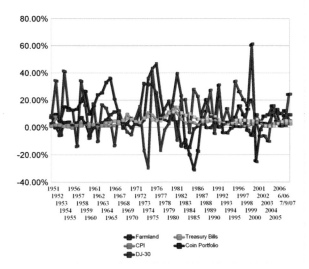

1862 silver 3-cent.

The Salomon coin survey went on for a dozen years, until 1991, but it is possible to extrapolate data and reach back to the 1930s and forward to 2008. Doing so shows rare coins are superior investments with phenomenal rates of return not approached by other financial or tangible assets.

No wonder, then, that Wall Street started to dabble in the rare-coin market. It created numismatic "funds" or limited partnerships (actually, securities, anyway you look at it), which offered a mutual-fund type of approach to eliminate the investor's need for numismatic knowledge. The investor could rely on the purchasing manager's numismatic knowledge and the overall upward trend in the marketplace.

The Salomon Brothers Survey of Tangible Assets, and its inclusion of numismatic items, helped transform a hobby into a cottage industry and later into the dynamo that it is today. Does it precisely parallel how thousands of different coins have gained or lost through the years? The answer, obviously, is no. Nor does the Dow Jones industrial average, the Standard & Poor's 500 index, or any other marketbasket approach to statistics in their respective fields.

The 1987 stock-market crash saw the largest single drop in the Dow Jones industrial average – either numerically or as a percentage – in history. But a few stocks still gained substantially on the day of the crash. So, too, is it with coins. No one claims that the Salomon coin portfolio is perfect, but it constitutes what a serious collector might have accumulated in an era when price appreciation was generally moderate and gains from a collection were realized over a lifetime.

The gains and losses recorded on the charts and graphs in this book differ slightly from the actual percentages and rates of return found in the Salomon Brothers examination because the method of compiling prices for the chart differ from the raw auction data used in the compilation of the Salomon review. But because the same basic approach was used for every year going back half a century, the rate of return is a reasonably accurate measure of the coin market's status.

1866 Seated Liberty dime.

1873 2 Cent.

1866 Shield nickel with rays.

1884-S Morgan Dollar

Portfolio Coins
Average Annual Change 1928-2008

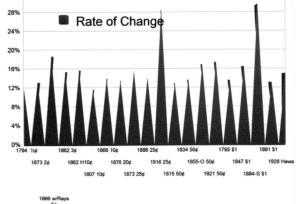

1881 Trade dollar.

An accompanying chart shows the combined values of the 20 coins found in the Salomon Brothers list, as reported by Berman-Schulman, and their pricing history from about the late 1920s to the present. Pricing for 1928, 1933, 1935, and 1938 is based on advertisements for coins in *The Numismatist, The Numismatic Scrapbook Magazine,* auctions, and the old Wayte Raymond *Standard Catalog of U.S. Coins.* These sources were used together with *Numismatic News* (starting in 1952), *Coin World* (starting in 1960), and auction catalogs from Stack's and other auctioneers of the period. As a check, the Red Book, mingled with some other price guides, was looked at for price interpretation.

Readers of *Numismatic News,* where my "Under the Glass" column first appeared in 1969, are familiar with my reports – first annually and, since 2005, twice a year – on the state of the numismatic economy. Since 1999, Dennis Baker's NumisMedia™ has been the source for the impartial pricing I used to build my models, graphs and indices.

Although there may be a lack of historical information on the coin market, that's not true for other financial instruments. The *Statistical Abstract of the United States* (2007 edition), which the U.S. Department of Commerce has published since 1878, puts this in perspective in the accompanying table.

Total returns of stocks, bonds and Treasury bills, 1950-2005

Period	Total return after inflation	Capital gains	Dividends and reinvestment	Total return after inflation	Treasury bills total return	Bonds (10-year) total return
1950-1959	19.25	13.58	4.99	16.65	2.02	0.69
1960-1969	7.78	4.39	3.25	5.14	4.06	2.35
1970-1979	5.88	1.60	4.20	-1.38	6.48	5.94
1980-1989	17.55	12.59	4.40	11.85	9.13	13.01
1990-1999	18.21	15.31	2.51	14.85	4.95	8.02
2000-2004	-2.30	-3.38	1.54	-4.67	2.66	8.41
Average	11.06	7.35	3.48	7.07	4.88	6.40
2001	-11.89	-13.04	1.32	-13.68	3.32	5.51
2002	-22.10	-23.37	1.65	-23.91	1.61	15.15
2003	28.68	26.38	1.82	26.31	1.03	0.54
2004	10.88	8.99	1.73	7.38	1.43	4.59
2005	4.91	3.00	1.85	1.45	3.30	3.16
Average 2001-2005	2.10	0.39	1.67	-0.49	2.14	5.79

Source: Global Financial Data, Los Angeles. Averages added and prepared by the author from the data.

How do coins compare? What about other assets?

The coin portfolio charts back to at least 1928, so it is relatively simple to adjust for the 55-year period from 1950 to 2005. The average annual rate of return is 11.3 percent. During the same period, the Consumer Price Index increased an average of 3.91 percent annually. The Dow Jones average rate of change was 8.92 percent. And corporate bonds showed a 54.4-percent change in rates. Farmland prices changed 6.04 percent, and U.S. Treasury bills

1916 Standing Liberty
quarter.

1928 Hawaiian
commemorative half dollar.

of more than one month returned 4.97 percent. So with that data in hand, it is fair to conclude that rare coins do offer an attractive return.

If the coin marketbasket had been compiled in 1928, it would have cost about $128 to build a collection of its components. By 1947, the amount increased to about $430. Considering defense lawyers for Wall Street insurance companies were paid $31 a week at the time, the sum is significant.

By 1955, the marketbasket had nearly doubled in cost, to $781. Except for some brief inflation during the Korean War, the Consumer Price Index advanced only modestly in the intervening years. But rare coins increased almost 14 percent over the previous year, a trend that continued for at least the next two decades.

At the same time coins increased by nearly 14 percent, U.S. government long-term bonds (15 years and more) yielded 2.32 percent. High-grade municipal bonds, according to the *Statistical Abstract of the United States* and the *Economic Report of the President*, returned 1.98 percent. (The average stock in the Standard & Poor's 500 index had a dividend rate of about 6.3 percent.)

Coin collecting is fun, but it's also about numbers. When I worked full time as a *Numismatic News* assistant editor in 1973, we often surveyed our readers on why they collected coins. Many liked holding history in their hands; some liked that it was a way to collect military victories from the Caesars to the present. Still others said they enjoyed the political component of how coins were authorized and then made. But when our surveys asked what they read first in *Numismatic News* each week, the answer was always the same: Telequotes, the pricing guide in the center of each issue.

Numbers matter to collectors and investors. When I first started writing about coins professionally, in 1965, the Dow Jones industrial average topped out the year at 911 on its way back down to 792 the following year. Corporate bonds paid out an average of

4.49 percent, according to Moody's, which quoted the rate for corporate Aaa-rated bonds.

Coins had value, too. A 1794 half cent in grade extremely fine (XF-45) might have sold for around $220. A proof 1873 2-cent was $600. A proof 1866 Shield nickel would set you back about $1,000.

Other prices included about $30 for an 1862 silver 3-cent, $15 for an 1862 uncirculated Seated Liberty half dime, $450 for an 1807 uncirculated Draped Bust dime, and $50 for an 1866 Seated Liberty dime. An 1876 20-cent piece in uncirculated sold for about $90. The accompanying chart shows the quarters, half dollars, silver dollars, and commemoratives, all in uncirculated.

1886 Seated Liberty
Quarter

1965 coin prices (grade uncirculated)

1873 Seated Liberty quarter, with arrows	$40
1886 Seated Liberty quarter	$85
1916 Standing Liberty quarter	$1,000
1815 Liberty Cap half dollar	$500
1834 Liberty Cap half dollar	$18
1855-O Seated Liberty half dollar	$40
1921 Walking Liberty half dollar	$265
1795 Draped Bust dollar	$850
1847 Seated Liberty dollar	$60
1884-S Morgan dollar	$23
1881 Trade dollar	$125
1928 Hawaiian commemorative half dollar	$600

The analyses in this book use a number of starting points – 1928, 1935, and 1993. So 1965 is a midpoint.

Looking at the earliest date, in 1928 the XF half cent was offered in a Barney Bluestone ad in *The Numismatist* for $14.75. A John Zug advertisement around the same time lists it at $12.50. By 1933, in the midst of the Great Depression, the price had fallen to $9. By 1935, as the Depression deepened, the price fell to $6 before it started its upward march.

To properly compare apples to apples – not the kind

sold on Depression street corners – it is useful to list the economic and other criteria by which tangible assets will be measured. The precious metals in the component are gold, silver and platinum. The Consumer Price Index is measured. So are the Standard & Poor's 500 stock index, Moody's Aaa-rated corporate bonds, Treasury bills of more than one month, and Iowa farmland.

There is replication of some of the Salomon survey of the 1980s, but there are also omissions.

In 1935, Treasury bills paid 0.17 interest. The accompanying chart shows other measures.

1935 values

Gold	$35
Silver	$0.43
Consumer Price Index	14.20
Dow Jones industrial average	121.00
Platinum	$33
Standard & Poor's 500	13.43
Moody's Aaa-rated bonds	3.19 percent
Iowa farmland	$77.91 an acre
U.S. Treasury bills	0.17 percent

In 1965, Treasury bills of one month or more averaged about 3.93 percent on their way, thanks to the Vietnam buildup, to 4.76 percent the following year. The Standard & Poor's 500 was 92.43 on its way down to 80.33 in 1966. The Consumer Price Index had yet to explode; today's index is based on 1982 equaling 100. But in 1965, it was a modest 31.03. A year later, inflation brought it up to only 31.56, a 1.72-percent increase.

Gold was priced officially at $35 an ounce. It traded for $35.15 on a free market that barely existed because Uncle Sam would gladly exchange gold for dollars from anyone in the world except his own citizens, who had been prohibited from owning gold (except for rare and unusual coins) since 1933.

Silver was $1.29 an ounce, a Rubicon of sorts because at that price coins bought at face value and sent to the melting pot turned a profit for the holder.

Silver coins still circulated in 1965 but barely. By July, the Coinage Act of 1965 ended silver in the dime and quarter and moved toward a 40-percent-silver half dollar. In 1967, silver ended the year above $1.55, though gold stayed at $35.

Platinum was a mere $98 an ounce, up 10.8 percent from the previous year, and Iowa farmland, according to the U.S. Department of Agriculture and Iowa State University, sold for $318 an acre – up 9 percent from the year before. Over the succeeding 42 years, it averaged about 5.4 percent annually, though obviously with some ups and downs.

This review of the coin market, which I've followed for more than 40 years, is written from the perspective of a collector who also buys stocks and remembers when it made the front page of *The New York Times* when the Dow Jones industrial average lost a mere 15 points in a single day. As this book was written, the Dow moved over 14,000 and then retreated some.

My charting for the Dow today is based at 13,649, where it was in the summer of 2007. Iowa farmland today goes for $3,500 an acre "or more," according to an Iowa State University professor interviewed by e-mail in early July 2007.

Gold is figured at over $900 an ounce in many charts (it broke through to $1,000 in March, 2008) up consistently since 2004; silver figures in the mix at over $17 (it jumped to over $20 in March, 2008). Platinum is figured at around $1,900 an ounce having shattered the $2,200 barrier in February, 2008. The Consumer Price Index was catching a little bit of inflation, averaging about 3.43 percent annually. In 2008, it was at about 211 on the 1982-equals-100 scale.

Where do coins stand in all this? First, a word about the portfolio, which has averaged 13.5 percent annually since 1937 and about 9.8 percent since 1965. The Dow during the same period averaged about 7.5 percent, using year-end numbers as the basis. The Dow's components changed during the period; the coin index's components have been static because the index was ini-

The U.S. Mint sells precious metals in the form of gold, silver and platinum American Eagle bullion coins.

tially compiled by someone else and was discontinued after 1990. I have kept the original components because they are such a good representative mix and because, frankly, someone other than me picked them.

The Dow is calculated daily and based on components and prices published in many periodicals. Salomon Brothers calculated the coin index annually from 1978 through 1990. Because of the timing, that can lead to somewhat misleading results, but the index is still a useful benchmark for specific times.

For the analysis that follows, the Salomon Brothers raw data were not used. Instead, backward and forward pricing was examined independently. Coin-grading changes over the years are taken into account. The coins, except for a high-end circulated early American copper, are either choice uncirculated or proof (about MS-63 or proof-63 on the numerical grading scale). If higher grades were used, such as MS-65, the results would be substantially higher.

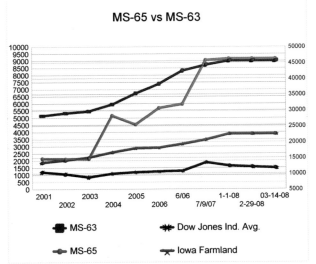

Marketbasket average
MS-65 vs MS-63

In fact, Dennis Baker, whose NumisMedia supplied me with data for the past six or seven years, also included MS-65 data so I can compare. It is so off the chart that it makes the comparisons ridiculous. Besides, broad-based market purchases of MS-63 coins are possible; MS-65 versions of many older rarities are either thinly traded or not widely available.

The analysis in this book does differ from Salomon in several ways. The Salomon analysis included Chinese porcelain, stamps, farmland, foreign exchange, various precious metals, the Consumer Price Index, and a variety of stocks and bonds. Some of the other collectible components are not replicated in my analysis because of the difficulty in creating a database that is reliable over an extended time or it covers areas with which I am unfamiliar.

For example, when my wife, Kathy, and I traveled abroad, we bought Chinese porcelain, but that hardly counts as a basis for price comparison. I was able to find a farmland index but no luck yet for stamps or foreign exchange in marketbasket form. The Federal Reserve Bank of St. Louis maintains a database, but I am uncomfortable integrating it for comparison purposes. Suffice to say that the U.S. dollar has gone up, down, and sideways during the period.

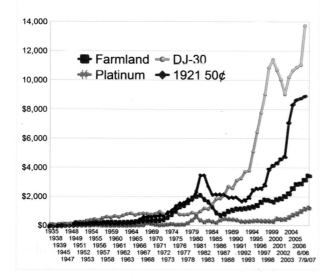

Farmland vs Other assets

Mike Duffy, an Iowa State University professor, provided me with good data on farmland value. I guessed originally a 5-percent increase from 2006 to 2007. He set me straight: "The bankers estimated that our values went up 7 percent in just the first quarter [of 2007]. I would think that we are probably about 10 percent up from the November estimate. That would mean about $3,500 [an acre]. It could even be higher. Things have slowed down a bit, but there is still a lot of strength in the market. At a meeting, I asked the increase for the year, and that group thought it would be about 20 percent."

Internet research developments – not widely available until the last couple of years – have made it possible to use government and other statistics for farmland value (based on average value per acre), corporate Aaa-rated bonds, and other items.

For this book, as it was in process, in January 2007, I retroactively changed my model for farmland to cover only Iowa land because the data seems more current and is reliable and accessible. U.S. government statistics are sporadic, and finalized numbers are still two to three years old. Those who compare this book to old "Under the Glass" columns will see minor differences.

Gold is omitted in this market examination – but is looked at carefully in the review of Harold Bareford's collection of gold coins – because Salomon felt generally gold coins would mirror the gold market (a measured component) and be influenced by non-numismatic events. Dealer and author Scott Travers advanced the same argument to me about 10 years ago. I spent a hundred hours or more trying to prove him wrong – only to discover the data does not lie. It might work with gold $1 or $3 pieces, but generic Saint-Gaudens $20 coins just parallel the gold market with a small numismatic profit margin.

Coins included in the marketbasket are each broadly representative of a class or type that is

1908 Saint-Gaudens $20

widely collected and hence easy to value, even if the individual dates and conditions are not easily replicated. For example, an 1876 20-cent in uncirculated condition is approximately the same as an 1875 20-cent piece and even an 1875-S. A 1795 Draped Bust dollar is similar to a 1796 or even a 1797 or 1798, though clearly not a 1794, which is in a class by itself, as a later chapter shows.

Mintages and scarcity vary, but overall trends can be followed with reasonable adjustments. The portfolio Stack's initially selected for Salomon Brothers was designed so that if, for example, a proof 1873 2-cent piece did not come up in auction or over-the-counter trading, then an 1871 or even an 1865 (with adjustments) could be substituted to check the appropriate price.

This marketbasket approach was initially designed in a largely pre-computer age, except in the most technologically advanced offices. That's the origin of the Dow, as well; 30 numbers and calculations are easier than 1,200. For coins, 20 is easier than 2,500.

Technology in 1978 precluded an examination of each of the thousands of coins in the marketplace. Personal computers at that time were virtually non-existent, except for the occasional Kaypro or Exxon 520, and they were designed to do only modest calculations.

I've tracked the coins on a computerized spreadsheet for many years. The sheet includes a total amount for the coin portfolio, its annual average rate of change, the average price of gold and silver, the Consumer Price Index and its rate of change, gold's rate of change, the Dow Jones industrial average and its rate of change, and the price of platinum. Also included now are the Standard & Poor's 500 index, the average annual rate of return for Moody's Aaa-rated bonds, Iowa farmland values, and the rate of return for Treasury bills.

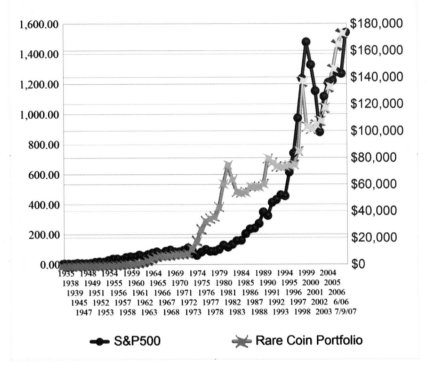

Rare Coins vs S&P500

When first soliciting data, I initially went back to 1947 and then, as I got more data, to 1938 (except for platinum, which I initially tracked back only to 1978 because of insufficient data). Later, I added 1935, 1933 and selectively 1928. I also eventually found good data (government mining sources) that allowed me to value platinum back to the late 1930s. I expanded coin prices back to 1935, when *The Numismatic Scrapbook Magazine* began and when reliable auction results made it possible to track prices. Then I found advertisements and auctions from the earlier period, which allowed some coins to have an 90-year track record and even beyond. But even with 75 years or so, the trends become clear.

For a variety of reasons, not the least of which is that some of the other coins charted and discussed have easily constructed longer histories, some of the charts use arbitrary but logical dates in the more distant past. For instance, in charting some of the pedigreed 1804 silver dollars, there are Chapman sales from 1913. Consumer Price Index data from that year were located, and for comparisons with other coins from the marketbasket, volumes of *The Numismatist* were combed for advertised prices.

In 2006, for my column "Under the Glass," I added the Iowa State University survey on Iowa farmland going back more than 25 years, replacing the U.S. Department of Agriculture statistics. It appeared in the old Salomon Brothers survey, too, using sporadic interpretive data. With Professor Duffy's help, I managed to get solid annual data back to 1951 and then sporadic data back to 1935 – again, fine for charting purposes.

The price per acre is an average of the federal statistics, which are provided for each of the 50 states and are available through the USDA Economic Research Service and National Agricultural Statistics Service. The current figures quoted are from Iowa State University's agricultural extension program.

Moody's Aaa-rated corporate bonds were added for comparison. Numbers were picked up from the *Statistical Abstract of the United States*, a Census Bureau-Department of Commerce publication. Updates were acquired online; the *Statistical Abstract* in print runs a little behind.

My current spreadsheet has more than 4,200 entries that analyze a variety of markets. For convenience, some of the charts cover only the last quarter century. The Standard & Poor's data, which originally started at 1957 in my column reports, now goes back to the 1930s.

Charting is highly arbitrary but important – as are how it is composed. For gold bullion, I have gener-

1857 Seated Liberty
Dollar

1794 Liberty Cap
Half Cent.

ally not used statistics prior to 1968. There wasn't a lot of movement between 1934 and 1968. The U.S. government enforced a rate of $35 an ounce through its purchase and sale program and the prohibition of domestic private gold ownership. The charts covering the past 25 years or so are more interesting when gold or platinum are included.

Regardless, my index uses the same coins that Salomon Brothers did from 1978 to 1990 and about which I wrote extensively during that time. It also uses the same chart and target points – though expanded – that I've utilized in more than 40 years of writing about the rare-coin market.

Prior to 1999, I used a wide variety of independent sources for the chart, checking my data against reliable price guides. Since then, Dennis Baker of NumisMedia has been kind enough to lend me his fair market values for each of the coins. Dennis was editor of the *Coin Dealer Newsletter* in the Ron Downey days. He struck out on his own, and NumisMedia offers a fine print pricing guide as well as a fine online version (www.NumisMedia.com).

Dennis provides me with pricing (I don't go to the Web site; we do this by e-mail) at great cost of time and effort, and he is truly my unsung hero. Without his help, I could never find the time to do my column even once a year much less twice – nor put forth the effort needed to produce this book.

The accompanying chart shows pricing for a particular coin, the 1794 half cent in grade extremely fine (XF-40). It shows that rare coins go up, down and sideways – that is, sometimes they don't change from year to year. Even with no change, the overall picture over 80 years shows an average annual return of 13.4 percent since 1928 – not bad for a circulated coin with a mintage of more than 81,000 pieces.

1794 half cent, grade extremely fine

Year	Coin price	Rate of change	Gold price	Rate of change	Consumer Price Index	Rate of change
1928	$13	x	$20.67	x	17.10	x
1933	$9	-32.00%	$35.00	69.33%	12.60	6.35%
1935	$6	-29.41%	$35.00	0.00%	13.40	5.97%
1938	$8	25.00%	$35.00	0.00%	14.20	-1.41%
1939	$7	-4.00%	$35.00	0.00%	14.00	27.14%
1945	$13	73.61%	$35.00	0.00%	17.80	35.29%
1948	$10	-20.00%	$35.00	0.00%	24.08	-0.97%
1949	$16	60.00%	$35.00	0.00%	23.85	0.98%
1951	$16	0.00%	$41.00	17.14%	24.08	7.91%
1952	$10	-37.50%	$35.12	-14.34%	25.99	2.96%
1954	$23	125.00%	$35.00	-0.34%	26.75	0.50%
1955	$25	11.11%	$34.95	-0.14%	26.89	-0.37%
1956	$25	0.00%	$35.00	0.14%	26.79	1.50%
1957	$28	10.00%	$35.01	0.03%	27.19	3.56%
1958	$30	9.09%	$35.00	-0.03%	28.16	3.56%
1960	$40	33.33%	$35.65	1.86%	29.16	1.60%
1961	$48	18.75%	$36.79	3.20%	29.63	1.01%
1962	$53	10.53%	$35.06	-4.70%	29.93	1.12%
1963	$90	71.43%	$35.00	-0.17%	30.26	1.21%
1964	$125	38.89%	$35.00	0.00%	30.63	1.31%
1965	$210	68.00%	$35.15	0.43%	31.03	1.72%
1966	$265	26.19%	$35.00	-0.43%	31.56	ERR
1968	$285	7.55%	$39.26	12.17%	33.40	9.88%
1969	$300	5.26%	$41.51	5.73%	36.70	5.72%
1970	$275	-8.33%	$36.41	-12.29%	38.80	4.38%
1971	$310	12.73%	$40.25	10.55%	40.50	3.21%
1972	$310	0.00%	$58.60	45.59%	41.80	6.22%
1973	$300	-3.23%	$97.81	66.91%	44.40	11.04%
1974	$320	6.67%	$161.08	64.69%	49.30	15.42%
1976	$350	9.38%	$124.77	-22.54%	56.90	6.50%
1977	$400	14.29%	$148.31	18.87%	60.60	7.59%
1978	$450	12.50%	$194.75	31.31%	65.20	11.35%
1979	$475	5.56%	$307.58	57.94%	72.60	13.50%
1980	$575	21.05%	$613.28	99.39%	82.40	10.32%
1981	$1,250	117.39%	$459.61	-25.06%	90.90	6.16%
1982	$1,700	36.00%	$376.01	-18.19%	96.50	3.21%
1983	$2,200	29.41%	$423.68	12.68%	99.60	4.32%
1984	$2,250	2.27%	$360.68	-14.87%	103.90	5.49%
1986	$2,250	0.00%	$368.00	2.03%	109.60	3.65%

Year	Coin price	Rate of change	Gold price	Rate of change	Consumer Price Index	Rate of change
1987	$2,000	-11.11%	$448.00	21.74%	113.60	4.14%
1988	$2,100	5.00%	$438.00	-2.23%	118.30	4.82%
1989	$2,200	4.76%	$381.53	-12.89%	124.00	5.40%
1990	$2,200	0.00%	$383.70	0.57%	130.70	4.21%
1991	$2,375	7.95%	$362.38	-5.56%	136.20	3.01%
1992	$2,375	0.00%	$361.00	-0.38%	140.30	2.99%
1993	$2,375	0.00%	$360.00	-0.28%	144.50	2.70%
1994	$2,500	5.26%	$384.00	6.67%	148.40	2.60%
1995	$2,200	-12.00%	$388.50	1.17%	152.26	4.16%
1996	$2,200	0.00%	$418.14	7.63%	158.60	0.82%
1997	$2,750	25.00%	$335.00	-19.88%	159.90	1.63%
1998	$3,250	18.18%	$301.00	-10.15%	162.50	2.28%
1999	$3,300	1.54%	$265.30	-11.86%	166.20	3.73%
2000	$3,600	9.09%	$325.00	22.50%	172.4	3.25%
2001	$3,740	3.89%	$271.19	-16.56%	178	1.07%
2002	$4,060	8.56%	$310.07	14.34%	179.9	2.17%
2003	$4,170	2.71%	$359.10	15.81%	183.8	2.88%
2004	$4,310	3.36%	$403.15	12.27%	189.1	2.80%
2005	$4,410	2.32%	$437.70	8.57%	194.4	1.65%
2006	$4,650	5.44%	$574.65	31.29%	197.6	2.68%
June 2006	$4,910	5.59%	$627.00	9.11%	202.9	2.66%
July 9, 2007	$5,060	3.05%	$661.50	5.50%	208.3	2.66%

A decade before the Salomon survey was created, a hypothetical acquisition of each of its coins identically described would have cost about $8,000. In 1978, the fair market value, double checked with the Red Book, was about $35,000. That is a 341-percent gain (or a simple rate of return of about 34 percent annually). Analysis of the portfolio components and the rate of change each year shows an overall positive trend. Not every year was a gain, but there are many more gains than losses. The same is not true of gold, silver, or most other assets in the survey.

The Consumer Price Index increased an average of 4 percent yearly. There were dramatic changes during the Depression and postwar years. The chart hints at the rate that left President Richard Nixon to institute wage and price controls and destroyed the

Jimmy Carter presidency. Gold, by contrast, averaged 6.5 percent annually during the same period. The change, however, was incremental and mostly during specific periods: 1933, 1974-1975, 1980, and later. The half dime, by contrast, could be called the little coin that could. It averaged 15 percent annually since 1928 (9.5 percent annually since 1965) to a price of about $300 (nothing earth shattering).

Over the last 75 years, the average annual rate of change for the Consumer Price Index is around 4.4 percent. The greatest increases came in 1945-1946, 1974, and 1980-1982, when rates averaged from 10.3 percent to 13.5 percent. Coins moved dramatically ahead of inflation during that period.

Over 75 years, the marketbasket of coins shows negative growth in only 10 of those years. The rate of change over that time averages around 12 percent. By contrast, high-grade municipal bonds averaged about 5.7 percent annually during this period, and U.S. government long-term bonds averaged 6.5 percent annually. There was minimal risk with those investments for the return; the 11.47 percent received for coins carried more risk.

The ups and downs of the Dow Jones industrial average played havoc with preparing a chart. I picked an arbitrary day (June 25, 2007), when the Dow had just jumped upward again. The surprise is that if stocks as investments are ahead of coins, it's only by a small margin. Gold, silver and many other tangible investments have fallen by the wayside.

The stock market is so volatile that it makes comparison and analysis difficult. By contrast, rare coins could almost be described as stable investments and storehouses of value.

This review suggests that Salomon Brothers was on to something. Namely, rare coins, as tangible assets, have proven good investments over time. Nothing is guaranteed; last year's performance is this year's fodder. But it's clear that rare coins are worth more than a quick look.

1793 Flowing Hair Cent with Wreath

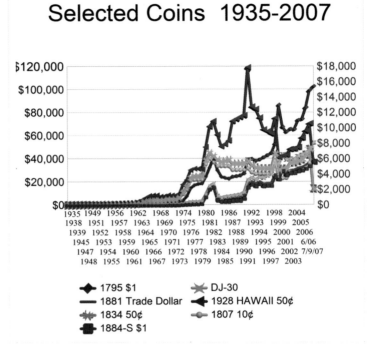

Selected Coins 1935-2007

Legend:
- 1795 $1
- 1881 Trade Dollar
- 1834 50¢
- 1884-S $1
- DJ-30
- 1928 HAWAII 50¢
- 1807 10¢

Comparing individual coins from the Salomon Brothers survey to the Dow Jones industrial average is an interesting exercise. The 1921 Walking Liberty half dollar, for example, substantially outperforms the Dow over time. So does a 1795 Draped Bust dollar, though not as well as the Walking Liberty.

Coins have also fared well against the Consumer Price Index (the new 1982 CPI base required all numbers to be re-classified). That makes them a decent hedge against that old bug-a-boo, inflation, which decreases the dollar's purchasing power.

As a precious metal, silver under-performs against the CPI, except in the mid to late 1970s and early 1980s and not a single year since 1987. Although their prices have been volatile, platinum and gold have easily out-performed silver.

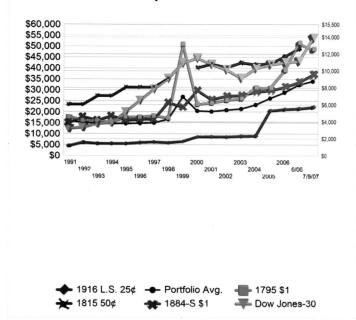

Selected coin prices 1991 to 2007

Legend:
- 1916 L.S. 25¢
- 1815 50¢
- Portfolio Avg.
- 1884-S $1
- 1795 $1
- Dow Jones-30

Though it is difficult to show and compare all of the coins in a single graph – even in color it's crowded – it is nonetheless impressive to look at a small portion of them. They have out-performed the Dow year in and year out for quite some time – though it is now more muddied and harder to read.

More than thirty years after the Salomon survey began and a generation after it was discontinued, critics still claim that the failure to include gold coins, the use of grade choice uncirculated (rather than MS-65) coins, the use of a mere 20 coins as a marketbasket, and the failure to account for grading changes make the study inaccurate, non-representative, or worthless.

They are wrong.

The Salomon Brothers Survey of Tangible Assets, and its inclusion of numismatic items, helped transform a hobby into a cottage industry and later into the dynamo that it is today.

Does it precisely parallel how thousands of different coins have gained or lost through the years? The answer, obviously, is no. Neither does the Dow Jones industrial average, the Standard & Poor's 500 index, or any other marketbasket approach to statistics.

The question today is whether a 1978 marketbasket, or for that matter any marketbasket, is an anachronism or a valuable tool. With today's computer programs, it takes nothing but expanded memory to load in the prices of tens of thousands of coins and then chart their growth based on sales and resales. There are commercial Web sites that do thus.

But if a model index were constructed anew today, it would probably have several different components.

First would be a generic coin index designed to show what has become of "cookie-cutter" coins, a term dealer Bill Nagle gives to coins that are popped out of slabs with the alacrity of a chocolate-chip cookie in a bakery oven.

How about a one-coin bellwether? Maybe the 1881-S Morgan dollar? By charting its gains and losses, it becomes possible almost at once to view how coins sold by telemarketers fare from time to time. It's an ideal coin to market in substantial quantities because more than 325,000 examples have been graded and encapsulated by the Professional Coin Grading Service and the Numismatic Guaranty Corporation combined.

For a two-coin index that includes gold, add a Saint-Gaudens $20 in grade MS-63. Yes, it will be affected by the price of gold, but recently, that effect has gone down a lot.

The Salomon Brothers index is gone but not forgotten. Its statistics will continue to be misquoted by those of the ilk to do so. New indices will be put forth to replace it and to also be misquoted. Such is the fragility of man and telemarketers.

A generic coin index today could include a common Morgan dollar (top) and a common Saint-Gaudens gold $20.

Harold Bareford: the man with the Midas touch

On December 1, 1978, Stack's Rare Coins sold at public auction the Harold S. Bareford collection of U.S. gold cons. Its size was not especially spectacular; the collection comprised 242 lots and had been assembled over a decade, along with other coins that the executors of the Bareford estate held back for another time.

The former general counsel to Warner Bros. Pictures, who died in early 1978, was known for his discerning eye and spent $13,832.15 purchasing the 242 lots, as Bareford's precise records show. He acquired the coins from 1941 to 1954 through auctions, private treaty with dealers, and over-the-counter sales. What makes the Bareford story so alluring and enduring is that more than 30 years after the collection's sale by Stack's, people are still talking about the results and the coins. The auction's total prices realized was an incredible $1,207,215.

Every coin in the catalog experienced substantial growth, some as much as 100 times what Bareford paid for them less than 30 years earlier. Most of the coins were in uncirculated condition, or nearly so, or were choice proofs. The 275 people who attended the auction as well as the many mail bidders were evidently impressed with quality. Almost two generations later, Bareford coins have been sold (and in some cases re-sold) for record prices.

All of the coins had pedigrees – that is, the catalog documents when and how they were acquired. Examination of the Bareford collection and its legacy shows the importance of pedigrees, which allow researchers, collectors and investors to track the values of specific coins over time. More than the Salomon Brothers report, which is a generic chart for generic coins, the Bareford examination charts real coins over time – before and after the sale.

1840-D gold $2.50.

Grading change

In looking at the Bareford legacy, it becomes immediately apparent that the discerning eye of a collector in 1955 and earlier periods differs from today's standards. Coins that were earlier graded adjectivally – numbered grading was reserved almost exclusively for old large coppers – were judged differently in 1978 and again on subsequent resale. By the time secondary sales were taking place in the 21st century, the Bareford coins were graded numerically (PCGS MS-65, NGC MS-66, and so forth). Sometimes both services examined the same coins and differed in their grades.

Two examples are 1840-D and 1849-D gold $2.50 pieces, both from the Dahlonega, Georgia, mint. In his classic study of a quarter century ago, David Akers thought the 1840-D was unknown in uncirculated; there were two auction records of the 1849-D in mint state. Dealer and author Paul Taglione likewise is unable to identify any brilliant-uncirculated 1840-D gold $2.50 pieces, specifically referring to the Bareford-Montgomery coin as part of the condition census group – all grade about uncirculated. (Arthur Montgomery obtained the Bareford specimen and kept it in his collection until Stack's sold it as part of Auction '84.)

Stack's termed the 1840-D just a "hair's breadth away from uncirculated" when the Bareford collection was cataloged, and it got no better for Auction '84, though the cataloger thought it to be the finest known. The grading services thought otherwise. PCGS assigned a mint-state grade (MS-61), and subsequently, so did NGC (MS-62), the grade used when Heritage re-sold it at the 2006 American Numismatic Association sale in Atlanta. The same held true for the 1840-D, which became PCGS MS-61 (finest known) and was sold in the 2006 Atlanta ANA sale as NGC MS-62. None of this made a difference in the prices realized (more about grading in chapter 2).

1840-D gold $2.50, NGC MS-62, PCGS MS-61

Sale date	Auctioneer	Sale	Lot No.	Price
November 1956	New Netherlands	48th sale	219	$65
December 1978	Stack's	Bareford collection	86	$6,750
August 1984	Stack's	Montgomery collection	1309	$8,500
April 2006	Heritage	Dukes Creek collection	1495	$74,750

1849-D gold $2.50, NGC MS-62, PCGS MS-61

Sale date	Auctioneer	Sale	Lot No.	Price
March 1948	Mehl	Renz collection	3581	$20
December 1978	Stack's	Bareford collection	97	$3,800
August 1984	Stack's	Montgomery collection	1318	$5,500
1April 2006	Heritage	Dukes Creek collection	1506	$24,150

1849-D gold $2.50.

Auction results

Bareford's remarkable success was no accident. He collected silver and copper coins, and great rarities. In October 1981, Stack's sold his silver coins – including the fabulous 1804 silver dollar Bareford had owned since 1950 – to impressive results. But what remained remarkable is that his gold coins – so few in number with not many eagles ($10) and double eagles ($20) – yielded such an overwhelming result.

Typical of the gains was an 1853 gold $1, which Bareford purchased for $8.50 at the February 1947 auction of the Frederick W. Geiss collection. In spirited bidding that began at $525, the 1978 price realized was $750, or 88 times Bareford's purchase price.

More dramatic was a proof 1855 gold $1, which was sold in the June 1, 1948, auction of the Memorable Collection for $75. At the 1978 Bareford sale, bidding started $28,000 and increased by $2,000 increments to a record price of $46,000. (A colorful account of its sale appears below.)

Equally impressive was the gain for an uncirculated 1933 gold $10. Purchased for $310 at the 1947 Mason Williams sale, it sold in 1978 for a whopping $92,500, or 298 times the original purchase price.

Bareford collected fine quality coins, but what is remarkable about his limited holding of gold is that it concentrated on low-denomination, modestly priced coins in spectacular condition. The 242 gold lots largely consisted of $1, $2.50, $3, and $5 pieces, with several $10 and $20 pieces included. Bareford's detailed records were made available to me by his son, William, in 1978 and have been in my files ever since.

The first two lots alone in the Bareford auction – a pattern 1836 gold $1 (Judd No. 67) and a pattern 1849 gold $1 (Judd No. 115) – nearly returned the collector's $13,832.15 investment. The two coins combined cost Bareford a mere $350 at the 1954 King Farouk auction in Egypt. In 1978, the 1836 brought $4,800 and the 1849 brought $9,000.

The remaining 240 lots over the next four hours were punctuated by audience gasps at high prices and astonished looks on the faces of major dealers in attendance as price record after price record was shattered.

Some present, such as Abner Kreisberg of Quality Coins in Beverly Hills, California, were among the dealers who had originally auctioned the material Bareford purchased. (Kreisberg was partners with Abe Kosoff in the 1940s and '50s, first in New York, then in Los Angeles.) These old-timers could merely shrug at the price gains, which were typically 100 times the price paid a quarter-century earlier.

Others, such as William Bareford, the collector's son, who was present at the sale, were more expressive. "We were very surprised at the results," he told me. "If it had the word 'gem' on it, the prices went out of sight." "Gem" at that time was equivalent to today's MS-65 or better; most of those adjectival designations held up over the years.

Prior to the sale, Stack's estimated the 242 lots would realize approximately $700,000 if the market held firm, slightly less if some of the rarities showed slippage. This was hardly the case, however. Harvey Stack told me at the start of the auction that his firm's "book," representing pre-sale mail bids, totaled $850,000.

In the end, prices realized totaled $1,207,215 for a per-lot average of almost $5,000, a record for Stack's as well as any other dealer at the time. Although there were moderately priced coins that sold for less than that, the super-sexy rarities jumped through the roof to carry the average upward.

Regular auctions then conducted by Stack's at the New York Sheraton Hotel typically sold 150 lots or more per hour. That rate would have meant a sale of about two hours for the Bareford lots. But so active was the floor bidding at this sale that nearly four hours were required to complete it, making it the "slowest auction in memory," according to Benjamin Stack. Bidders on the floor cagily watched their competitors, trying to see whom they were bidding against and trying to guess their opponents' outer limits.

1855 gold $1.

1933 gold $10.

A typical sale: the proof 1855 gold $1 (a latter-day PCGS proof-65)

Auctioneer Benjamin Stack introduced it as the "first specimen that I have ever sold." Bidding commenced at $28,000. For a time, there seemed to be no competition for the coin, which Bareford purchased at the 1948 Memorable Collection auction for $75. It had sold for even less at the 1946 World's Greatest Collection auction, conducted by Kosoff and Kreisberg.

Just as Stack cried "last call," a hand shot up, carrying the coin to $30,000, and then the competition began. From $30,000 it went to $32,000 and then, without a moment of respite, to $32,500 on a rare oral challenge to the auctioneer's bidding cadence. A bid of $33,000 was then heard; the next jump was to $35,000, as three or more bidders in the room began competing. Finally, a $46,000 bid was received, and when the auctioneer heard no more bidders, a new price record was set as the coin was awarded to a bidder with initials "JHB".

Not every coin advanced so dramatically or had its final ownership and disposition draped in mystery, but the audience could not help but be overwhelmed and impressed at the numbers that were flowing back and forth.

The 1933 gold $10 in grade choice brilliant uncirculated had appeared at auction only 17 times over the previous 34 years. (Akers' research for his six-volume opus was reported to be in manuscript form at the time.) Prior to the auction, the coin was estimated at $50,000, but there was a pre-sale mail bid of $60,000. That's were the bidding slowly opened to an audible gasp in the Skyline Suite, which accommodated 275 active floor bidders. Some present could still remember that Bareford paid $310 for the coin in 1947 at the Mason Williams collection auction.

When the 1978 bidding was over several minutes later and a $92,500 price was realized, the enormity of it all began to sink in. Harvey Stack commented that the price had gone up nearly 300 times in 31 years. The actual percentage gain was a mind-boggling 29,738.

And yet, this was not even the most dramatic of gains. That honor probably belonged to an 1853-D gold $5 in grade brilliant uncirculated (termed "finest known" by cataloger Norman Stack). It sold for just $25 at the Memorable Collection auction in March 1948. Its 1978 price at the Bareford auction was $17,000, representing a nearly 700-fold increase (67,900 percent).

It went next to Arthur Montgomery, whose collection was sold as part of Auction '84. (The "apostrophe auctions" were a consortium consisting originally of Stack's, Paramount, Superior, and Rarcoa, who held just one 2,000-lot sale a year – 500 lots for each firm – from 1979 to 1990.) Stack's did the selling, and bidder No. 131 did the buying. My notes in my catalog, from personal observation, showed that number assigned to Rarcoa, whose principal was Ed Milas. It turned out he was buying for his own account, for the next appearance of the 1853-D came when Stack's sold the Ed Milas collection in May 1995. By then, the coin was encapsulated (NGC MS-64), but the result – $55,000 – was downright startling.

1853-D gold $5

Sale date	Auctioneer	Sale	Grade	Lot No.	Price
March 1948	Kosoff	Memorable Collection	Unc	459	$25
December 1978	Stack's	Bareford collection	Gem BU	474	$17,000
August 84	Stack's	Montgomery collection	BU	1345	$18,000
May 1995	Stack's	Milas collection	NGC MS-64	400	$55,000

At that time, I wrote in the trade press that collectors and dealers at the Bareford auction bid competitively, receiving "what some actually consider to be bargains in coins which have not fully reached their maximum maturity," and all had an evening to remember.

1862 proof double eagle.

Selected gold $10 and $20 coins in the Bareford sale

Gold $10 (eagle) and $20 (double-eagle) coins comprised the smallest category of the Bareford holdings; just 25 lots of the two denominations were in the sale. Yet the price trends they produced are impressive and show major market growth. An 1862 eagle, for example, with a book value in proof of $7,000, jumped to $13,500. Bareford purchased the coin for just $210 at Stack's 1954 auction of the Davis-Graves collection. That means the coin increased 64 times (6,370 percent) in value over 24 years.

Another eagle, a proof 1900 specimen, which Bareford purchased from New Netherlands Coin Company in May 1948 for $57.50, jumped 100 times its purchase price when it realized $5,750.

A grade extremely fine 1850 double eagle, which cost Bareford $67.50 at Stack's George Ragee collection auction in 1950, went for $1,100. Also way over market trends was a brilliant-uncirculated 1861 double eagle, acquired in a Stack's January 1948 auction for $65, which brought a whopping $4,250.

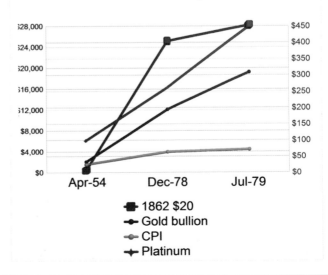

1862 $20 proof

Four proof double eagles were included: (1) An 1862, purchased at the Davis-Graves sale in 1954 for $575, brought $25,000. (2) An 1886 went for $26,000, up from a $310 purchase from New Netherlands in 1948. (3) The more common 1894, a Memorable Collection offering of March 2, 1948, went from $160 to $8,500. (4) A 1907, ex-Ragee sale in 1950 at $170, jumped to the $9,000 mark.

Bareford gold $5 coins

An extraordinary 68-piece set of gold $5 (half-eagle) coins was also included in the auction. The first, a 1795 with the small-eagle design in grade about uncirculated, traced its pedigree back to 1914, when it sold for $20 at the William Gabel collection auction. In 1946, it brought $150 when Kosoff-Kreisberg sold the F.C.C. Boyd collection, billed as the "World's Greatest Collection." It jumped to $9,500 at its 1978 resale.

Another rarity, the 1795 with the heraldic-eagle design, also AU, traces its pedigree to the King Farouk collection, sold by order of the Egyptian government in 1954 after the monarch was overthrown by Colonel Gamal Abdel Nasser. It cost about $500 for Bareford to acquire this and other coins at Cairo auction. At the 1978 auction, the coin opened at $18,000 and jumped to $23,000.

An 1803/2 overdate half eagle in brilliant uncirculated, which was sold at the 1941 American Numismatic Association auction by dealer Ira Reed for $17, brought $4,400 in 1978. An 1823, grade gem BU, acquired at the 1947 ANA auction for $200, jumped to $21,000 for a gain of 105 times its cost. Another half eagle, the 1844-C in BU, came from the H.R. Lee collection auction of October 1947 (when Stack's sold the Louis Eliasberg duplicates). It was acquired for $29 and sold for $4,750.

Less dramatic, but equally impressive, was the performance of two proof half eagles, the 1874 and 1875. The former brought $12,000; the latter went for $76,000. Bareford spent $700 combined for the specimens in 1954.

1874 proof gold $5

Sale date	Auctioneer	Sale	Grade	Lot No.	Price
February 1954	Sotheby's	Farouk collection	not individually graded	256	$100
December 1978	Stack's	Bareford collection	Brilliant proof	186	$12,000
October 1999	Bowers and Merena	Bass collection, part II	PCGS proof-65	1193	$21,850

An 1873-CC half eagle, grade about uncirculated, was another former Farouk collection coin. In 1952, Nasser led a coup d'état against Farouk. Nasser's provisional government seized all of Farouk's assets and ordered that they be sold for the benefit of the Egyptian people. When Sotheby's sold Farouk's coin collection on behalf of the provisional government, many Americans participated, including Bareford, John Jay Pittman, Kosoff, and Hans M.F. Schulman.

Although Farouk was notorious for cleaning and mishandling coins, non-proof gold generally fared well. A grade about uncirculated 1820 gold $5, large letters, caught Bareford's eye, and when his collection was sold in 1978, another connoisseur, Harry Bass, was the buyer.

1820 gold $5, large letters

Sale date	Auctioneer	Sale	Grade	Lot No.	Price
February 1954	Sotheby's	Farouk collection	not individually graded	251	$35
December 1978	Stack's	Bareford collection	AU	184	$1,600
May 2000	Bowers and Merena	Bass collection, part III	AU-55	511	$32,200

An even earlier half eagle, from 1820, also part of the Farouk sale, shows how a coin becomes a star. The coin was acquired by Schulman, who used Farouk's indebtedness to his firm as a buying tool. The story's short version is that Schulman, Kosoff, and others received credits to avoid protracted litigation over coins they had sold to Farouk but were not paid for. Schulman, in turn, sold his acquisitions at a profit, using new capital to retire the Farouk debt.

1820 gold $5, large letters

Sale date	Auctioneer	Sale	Grade	Price
February 1954	Sotheby's	Farouk collection	not individually graded	85 Egyptian pounds
October 54	Schulman			$250
December 1978	Stack's	Bareford collection	BU	$17,000
October 1999	Bowers and Merena	Bass collection, part II	PCGS MS-65	$71,300

The holding period prior to Bareford's sale was on the order of a generation, about 25 years. The reported secondary re-selling began almost immediately, but those that waited did pretty well. Some of the accompanying charts show how these half eagles made out against the Salomon marketbasket (using the same time frames) while others tracked against individual non-gold coins.

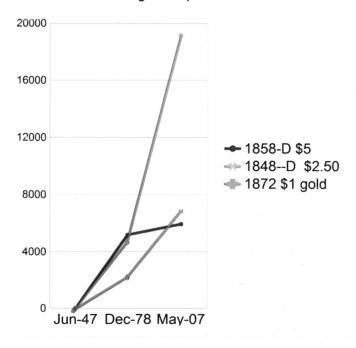

Gold coin eagle comparisons-1947-date

- 1858-D $5
- 1848--D $2.50
- 1872 $1 gold

Selected half eagles

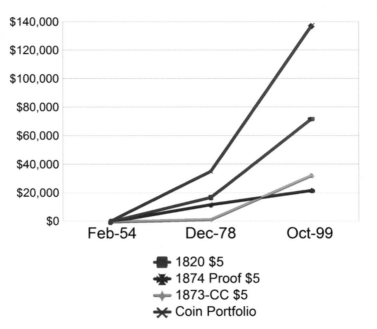

Legend:
- 1820 $5
- 1874 Proof $5
- 1873-CC $5
- Coin Portfolio

Gold $3

Price records were shattered in every category among the slightly more than two-dozen gold $3 coins in the Bareford sale. A gem 1854, acquired by Bareford in Stack's auction of December 6, 1949, for $20, went for $4,200 to a mail bidder. A brilliant-uncirculated 1855, ex-Kagin's sale of January 1948 at $27.50, went for $3,500. A BU 1855-S, one of the rarest of the mint-state gold $3 pieces, came from B. Max Mehl's November 1954 auction at $52.50 and re-sold in 1978 for $11,000.

Other important results showed a proof 1859, ex-Memorable Collection of 1948 at $90, selling to Paramount's David W. Akers for $14,000 in a spirited contest. A proof 1862, ex-Memorable at $72.50, went for $8,500. A BU 1869, sold by Hans Schulman in April 1951 for $28, opened in 1978 at $4,200 and jumped to $9,000.

1869 gold $3

Sale date	Auctioneer	Sale	Grade	Lot No.	Price
April 1951	Schulman	Private treaty	unknown		$28
December 1978	Stack's	Bareford collection	Gem BU	136	$9,000
November 1998	Bowers and Merena	Great Lakes sale	PCGS MS-65	684	$29,900

Several proof gold $3 coins from the Frederick W. Geiss collection, auctioned in February 1947, were included in the 1978 auction. The prices realized showed an astonishing gain over the 31 years. An 1886, acquired for $64.50, sold for $6,500. An 1888 went from $46.50 to $3,250, and an 1885 went from $74.50 to $8,000.

It is always useful to review a coin with a subsequent history or pedigree, such as the BU 1860 gold $3, referred to as "gem" in the Bareford catalog. Formerly an H.R. Lee (1947) Eliasberg duplicate (at $25 in October 1947), the coin opened at the Bareford sale at $4,200 and fell to the hammer at $12,000 to a bidder with the initial "X". It next appeared at the Harry Bass collection sale, part II, which Bowers and Merena sold in fall 1999. The coin bore a PCGS MS-66 (a real gem) grade, and the price realized was $27,600.

1860 gold $3.

1860 gold $3, gem MS-66

Sale date	Auctioneer	Sale	Lot No.	Price
October 1947	Stack's	Lee collection	1176	$25
December 1978	Stack's	Bareford collection	129	$12,000
October 1999	Bowers and Merena	Bass collection, part II	671	$27,600

Gold $2.50

There were many prizes in choice condition among the 53 lots of quarter eagles in the Bareford sale, and the prices realized reflected this quality. A brilliant-uncirculated 1836, from the 1941 American Numismatic Association convention auction (Ira Reed), jumped from $6.25 to $8,000. A BU 1841-C, purchased in 1947 for $25 (attributed as ex-H.R. Lee [Eliasberg duplicates]) went for $2,600. The BU 1846-O, which cost $18 at the 1951 Talmadge collection sale, brought $1,100. The AU 1847-C went for $950, an incredible gain from the $25 price at the 1947 Windau sale.

Lawrence Goldberg, then of Superior Stamp & Coin in Los Angeles, tendered a winning floor bid of $26,000 on the grade choice uncirculated 1848 "CAL." quarter eagle. He told me at the time that he was not aware that it had originally sold for $275 at the 1951 Hollinbeck-Kagin sale of December 1951. But he said the price was "worthwhile" even at the appreciated level.

A BU 1859-D, sold at the famous Atwater collection in 1946 for $41, jumped to $3,200. A proof 1862 quarter eagle, ex-Davis-Graves 1954 auction by Stack's at $110, opened at $4,000 and progressed upward until Don Kagin, then of Des Moines, Iowa, captured top honors with a $5,250 bid.

Among late-date proofs, the following prices were realized: 1893, ex-Will W. Neil collection (Mehl auction, 1947) at $26.50, $2,500; 1894, ex-Geiss (1947) at $26.50, $2,800; 1899, ex-Neil at $26, $2,400; and 1905, ex-Neil at $22.75, at $2,700.

An 1928 quarter eagle, which Bareford apparently kept from change, still BU, went for $400, itself a high appreciation of 160 times acquisition cost.

One of the most interesting pieces with a subsequent history is the 1840-D quarter eagle, alternatively graded MS-61 by PCGS and MS-62 by NGC. Its earliest known origin is New Netherlands' 48th sale in

November 1956 at $65. In the Bareford sale, it achieved $6,750 – a handsome return on investment. It next appeared publicly in the Arthur Montgomery collection, sold as part of Auction '84. It opened at $3,250 and sold to bidder No. 118 at $8,500. Its most recent appearance was in the Dukes Creek collection, auctioned at the 2006 ANA convention in Atlanta, where (as NGC MS-62) it brought a whopping $74,750.

1840-D gold $2.50, uncirculated

Sale date	Auctioneer	Sale	Lot No.	Price
November 1956	New Netherlands	48th sale	219	$65
December 1978	Stack's	Bareford collection	86	$6,750
August 1984	Stack's	Montgomery collection	1309	$8,500
April 2006	Heritage	Dukes Creek collection	1495	$74,750

Another example with a good subsequent history that clearly shows coin-market movements is the 1849-D quarter eagle, which Bareford acquired from the Russell Renz collection, sold by mail auction in 1948 by B. Max Mehl. The purchase price for lot No. 3581 was $20. Bareford's specimen (lot No. 97 in the 1978 auction) opened at $1,500 and was hammered down at $3,800 to bidder "HIIO," according to my notes. It went from Hancock & Harwell to the Arthur Montgomery collection and Auction '84 (lot No. 1318). It opened at $2,750 during the Stack's session and shot to $5,500, including the 10-percent buyer's fee.

The coin appeared again, graded MS-62 by NGC, at Heritage's Dukes Creek collection sale. It realized $24,150.

1849-D gold $2.50, NGC MS-62, PCGS MS-61

Sale date	Auctioneer	Sale	Lot No.	Opening bid	Price
March 1948	Mehl	Renz collection	3581	NA	$20
December 1978	Stack's	Bareford collection	97	$1,500	$3,800
August 1984	Stack's	Montgomery collection	1318	$275	$5,500
April 2006	Heritage	Dukes Creek collection	1506	NA	$24,150

1849-D $2.50 Gold

Title

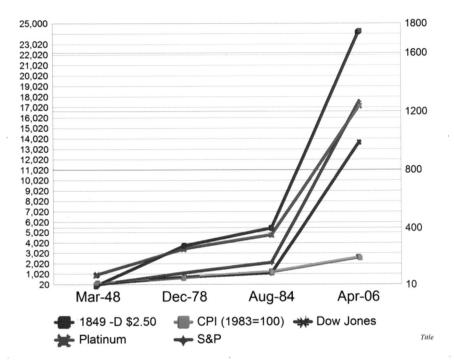

1849 -D $2.50	CPI (1983=100)	Dow Jones	
Platinum	S&P		*Title*

The accompanying graph compares the 1849-D quarter eagle with platinum, the Consumer Price Index, the Dow Jones industrial average, and Standard & Poor's 500 at four pivotal points: 1948, 1978 (the time of the Bareford sale), 1984, and 2006. Inflation's effect is vivid. The Consumer Price Index nearly doubled from 1984 (103.90) to summer 2006 (202.90). Platinum was around $48 an ounce in 1948 and $261 in 1978. It then took off to $357 in 1984 and about $1,233 in 2006.

Gold $1

Included in Bareford's 73 lots of gold $1 coins were many rarities and specimens in superior condition. An 1849 with open wreath, grade brilliant uncirculated and sold to Bareford by Numismatic Gallery in 1950 for $19.50, went for $650. An 1851-D, ex-Hollinbeck-Kagin sale of November 1947 at $31, brought $7,500, a whopping return of 241 times its acquisition cost. Its subsequent history was even more spectacular, making that $7,500 look downright inexpensive, as the accompanying chart shows.

1851-D gold $1

Sale date	Auctioneer	Sale	Grade	Lot No.	Price
November 1947	Hollinbeck-Kagin				$31
December 1978	Stack's	Bareford collection	BU Gem	15	$7,500
August 1984	Stack's	Montgomery collection	BU Gem	1297	$9,900
April 2006	Heritage	Dukes Creek collection	NGC MS-65	1483	$37,375

Bareford acquired an 1854-D gold $1, graded gem brilliant uncirculated, at the Memorable Collection auction of 1948 for $87.50. At the 1978 auction, it opened at $3,500 and was finally hammered down at $5,000. A representative of Manfra, Tordella & Brooks purchased the coin, which was estimated at $3,500. A market was being made.

A proof 1855 gold $1, the first such example Stack's ever sold at auction, had a pedigree dating to the World's Greatest Collection auction and, later, the Memorable Collection auction. A major gain was incurred when the coin went from $75 in 1948 to $46,000 in 1978. The consensus is that this coin is a proof-65. It is one of only 20 proofs struck, of which about 11 or 12 are known to survive today. In 1997, the sale of a similar, but not identical, coin exceeded all expectations; the John Jay Pitt-

1872 gold $1. Catalogers disagree as to MS68 or Proof.

man specimen, graded MS-65, sold for $121,000. In 2005, another example sold at the Florida United Numismatists convention auction for more than $280,000.

Other gold $1 price samplings include $1,000 for a BU 1861 (ex-Barney Bluestone, December 1948, $8) and $3,700 for a proof 1863 (ex-Memorable Collection, 1948, $125). Proofs of the 1870s saw some surprising prices realized: 1871, $2,900; 1872, $7,750; 1875, $11,500; 1876, $3,250; 1877, $3.750.

Typical of the gains was an 1853 gold $1, sold to Bareford at the February 1947 auction of the Frederick W. Geiss collection for $8.50. In spirited bidding that began at $525, the 1978 price realized was $750, or 88 times Bareford's purchase price 31 years earlier.

It took about a dozen years for Bareford to acquire his coins. The prices he paid were not extravagant. Proof gold $1 pieces for under $150 seem typical, and subsequent resales show Bareford knew quality.

1872 gold $1, uncirculated

Sale date	Auctioneer	Sale	Grade	Lot No.	Price
June 1947	Mehl	Neil collection	Perfect brilliant proof	2321	$53
December 1978	Stack's	Bareford collection	Brilliant proof	57	$4,750
May 2007	Heritage	CSNS convention	MS-68	2202	$18,975

Typical is an uncirculated 1872 gold $1, which Bareford acquired in a B. Max Mehl mail-bid sale of the Will W. Neil collection (1947) for $53. The 1978 price realized was $4,750 – a hefty return. The coin next surfaced at the Central States Numismatic Society convention auction in 2007. Heritage sold it for $18,975. The results are all the more impressive when compared to other assets that promise a storehouse of value. They show that although common-date gold follows the bullion market, gold rarities in superior grades do not.

The 1858-S gold $1's pedigree – two auction appearances before Bareford – opens an unusual window of more than 60 years of price history. The 1858-S has a reported mintage of 10,000 coins but is scarce as a gem. Some databases suggest that only the Bareford coin, graded PCGS MS-65, has sold as a gem in the last half century. (The highest NGC has graded an example is MS-62. PCGS has graded only one at MS-65, which was the Bareford specimen.)

The 1858-S's first auction appearance was the J.F. Bell sale by Stack's in 1944. It was lot No. 75 and realized $32.50. At the Memorable Collection auction by Kosoff in 1948, it rose to $41. That sounds like small potatoes but is a 26.1-percent change in value, or about a 6.5-percent annual average. At the time, Moody's Aaa-rated corporate bonds returned about 2.7 percent. Treasury bills were less than 1 percent.

Cataloged as a gem in the Bareford sale, the 1858-S opened at $2,200 and realized $4,750. It sold for $25,300 at part IV of the Harry Bass collection sale by Bowers and Merena in 2000.

1858-S gold $1

Sale date	Auctioneer	Sale	Grade	Lot No.	Price
December 1944	Stack's	Bell collection	BU Gem	75	$33
March 1948	Kosoff	Memorable Collection	Uncirculated	73	$41
December 1978	Stack's	Bareford collection	Gem BU	36	$4,750
November 2000	Bowers and Merena	Bass collection, part IV	MS-65	56	$25,300

1858-S gold dollar

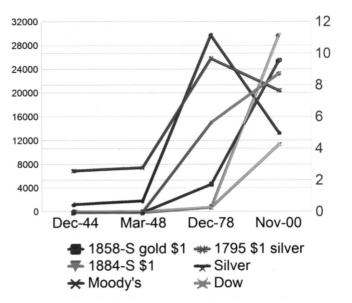

The gains expressed as percentages are impressive, but so are the gains in dollars.

It may seem that Bareford had a Midas touch, but he made his share of mistakes, as every collector does. An 1854-S gold $1 (about 14,000 mintage) with an impressive pedigree failed the test of time. Bareford bought an example as uncirculated, but it was later viewed with a more critical eye and determined to be about uncirculated. The price plummeted to the level of an AU-58 or MS-60 piece

1854-S gold $1

Sale date	Auctioneer	Sale	Grade	Lot No.	Price
March 1948	Kosoff	Memorable Collection	Unc	72	$36
December 1978	Stack's	Bareford collection	Unc	27	$2,400
Nov 2000	Bowers and Merena	Bass collection, part IV	AU-58	37	$1,840

The Bareford collection, painstakingly built over a dozen years, is a good barometer of the coin market. You can see from the actual prices that the theoretical prices of Salomon Brothers' survey are realistic and that the addition of gold rarities would not have diminished the result. In fact, it may have enhanced the findings.

Bareford-coin prices are well documented, and in coming years, as more are sold and re-sold, a window to the past will open for collectors and investors to see, review and analyze.

Chapter 2

Making the Grade

C oin grading is a necessary adjunct of coin collecting and investing. It is imprecise, though it claims to be exact. It is difficult to master, though it appears easy to learn the basics. Ultimately, it is both a description of a coin's physical condition and a synonym for its price or comparative value.

Grading is based on an examination of the metal's surface and focuses on eye appeal, strength of the strike, and the luster or sheen that time has given the piece. Graders evaluate coins and offer their opinions on the coins' state of preservation and relative condition, which ultimately affects value.

Unfortunately, coin grading lacks a single definitive standard. Generally, for starters, coins are either uncirculated or not (i.e., circulated), but even this is imprecise, shaded with nuance, and subject to degree.

About Good 6

Sometimes a new collector or investor asks about the fundamentals of coin grading, hoping for a panacea or a revelation. It's similar to buying a used car. The buyer tries to discern if the car is a "cream puff" – virtually uncirculated – or an average vehicle for its age and body-type – grade fine if it were a coin. A vehicle with mechanical difficulties is usually not desirable – grade good if it were a coin.

Coin grading is also similar to the rating systems for fine wines. Connoisseur periodicals typically grade wines on one of three scales: (1) 1 to 5 (similar to an A-to-F grading system in school), (2) 1 to 20 (similar to a quiz in school), and (3) 1 to 100 (a major school exam). The difference is that coins are graded either adjectivally, using one of about 12 common terms, or numerically on a 1-to-70 scale. The number 1 is the worst; 70 is the best.

To understand the numerical grading system, visualize a 12-inch ruler, with the numbers running from left to right. Generically, grade good is at the left end, perhaps at the 1-inch mark, and refers to well-worn coins that served as pocket change for a long time. The grade fine coin is in the middle, perhaps at the 6-inch mark. Its design elements are all quite clear, but it, too, has circulated. The typical uncirculated coin falls at the 10-inch mark. It still has its mint sheen, without a lot of contact marks on its surface. The other, better grades of uncirculated coins fall in the 10-inch to 12-inch range.

Very Good 8

In 1958, *A Guide to the Grading of United States Coins* by Martin R. Brown and John W. Dunn revolutionized coin grading. For the first time, it comprehensively systematized descriptions of all circulated grades. Another important grading book is *Photograde* by James F. Ruddy, first published in 1970. This book marked the first commercial attempt to photograph each type of coin in each circulating grade. It also demonstrated that photographs could reveal the differences among coins in various states of grading preservation.

Adjectives and even numbers alone cannot adequately convey what is unavoidably a subjective impression, although many collectors try to ignore this inherent limitation. If the best example of a piece known to a grader, cataloger, or collector changes, so do all comparisons based on it.

Given the subjective nature of coin grading, it is not surprising that many examples of the same coin have been graded differently over time. A good example is a rare 1870-CC gold $20 that was sold at auction three different times by three different firms. Each cataloger agreed the coin was the "finest known," but one graded it about uncirculated and the other two graded it extremely fine. Several of the same gold coins in the Har-

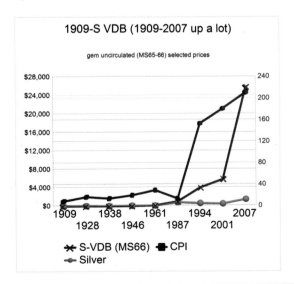

1909-S VDB (1909-2007 up a lot)

gem uncirculated (MS65-66) selected prices

old Bareford collection have been graded MS-61 by the Professional Coin Grading Service and MS-62 by the Numismatic Guaranty Corporation.

There are also numerous examples of coins that were identically graded but sold at widely disparate prices at the same auction, which is evidence that some buyers believed the coins were better or worse than the catalogers' descriptions.

Although rare coins and steaks may seem disparate, what happened with coin grading is similar to what transpired when the U.S. Department of Agriculture changed the standards for "prime" and "choice" meat. The quality grading system for beef includes quantitative and qualitative factors, which are combined to form a final grade. So, too, is it with grading coins.

Eight quality grade designations for beef – prime, choice, good, standard, commercial, utility, cutter, and canner – are applied to steer and heifer carcasses. They are the loose equivalents of coin grades uncirculated, extremely fine, fine, very good, and good.

The degree of marbling of intramuscular fat in meat and the physiological maturity of the slaughtered cattle (the five maturity groups are identified as A, B, C, D, and E in order of increasing maturity) are the palatability-indicating characteristics of beef. This is similar to the mint-state grades in coins.

The marbling requirements for this group of meat were set at the lowest level previously acceptable in the prime, choice and standard grades. For the more mature beef in these grades, increased marbling is still required to compensate for advancing age, but the minimum marbling required was lowered by one degree. To make the grade good more uniform and restrictive, the secretary limited this grade to carcasses in the A and B maturity groups and raised the minimum marbling required by one-half degree. The degrees of marbling in descending order are abundant, moderately abundant, slightly abundant, moderate, modest, small, slight, traces, and practically devoid.

Fine 12

Fine 15

Very Fine 30

Extremely Fine 40

Unlike coin grading, Congress stepped in and a government agency defined the standards for beef. Coin grading is an art, not a science. The 1-to-70 numerical scale gives the impression of precision and accuracy, but coin grading in reality is imprecise and inexact. The grade choice uncirculated may be identical to MS-63 or just merely seem so, but the numerical shorthand lacks the descriptive feeling of the adjectival grade.

I have a unique perspective on all this. First, I've collected coins for more than 45 years and remember when three letters visible in the word "Liberty" on the Indian bonnet meant you had a grade very good cent, as described in the Brown and Dunn book. Seven letters visible meant it was grade fine. I still prefer the words "very good" to VG-8 and "fine" to F-12.

Second, for nearly 30 years, I've practiced law and litigated a score of cases involving coin grading and pricing, and related disputes. I've seen how the lack of precision, but the appearance of it, can wreak havoc in a courtroom, not to mention the lives of the litigants. (Some of the cases are reported in official legal publications; many are not. But the results are always the same: The lawyer wins.)

Third, for a time, I served on the board of governors and later as president of the American Numismatic Association. The ANA is the largest educational, non-profit organization of coin collectors in the world. It started the first grading service, the American Numismatic Association Certification Service (ANACS), which began as an authentication and certification service and later, of necessity, expanded into grading.

As such, I was privy to the ins and outs of running a grading business for profit. As the ANA looked to expand its services, we looked at Compugrade, a computer-based grading service founded by James Diefenthal of New Orleans. Diefenthal almost got it right but was too early in showing that coins – or at least silver dollars – could be accurately and consistently grade to a tenth of a scale (i.e., MS-64.1, MS-64.2, and so on).

About uncirculated 58 - PL

Fourth, when you look at a dealer's or auction-eer's terms of sale, you see that they all disclaim their merchandise essentially the same way. (As a lawyer, I had more than a little to do with that.) So it's not hard to understand why hobby insiders recognize that grading is inexact but outsiders or novices eventually get stuck on the concept. Excellent books such as the *N.C.I. Grading Guide* by James Halperin and the *Official PCGS Grading Guide*, edited so well by Scott Travers, go a long way toward making the process scientific and teach reliable techniques.

About Uncirculated 55

But a 1-to-70 scale remains confusing to newcomers, who may identify better with the A-to-F or 1-to-100 scales used in schools. In 1970, my "Under the Glass" column in *Numismatic News* quoted veteran professional numismatist Abe Kosoff as saying grading issues were a "fear of the bogeyman." It hasn't changed much in the intervening years, even as grading has become more objective and refined.

Another respected numismatist, Steve Ivy, co-chairman and chief executive officer of Heritage Auction Galleries, once had some world-class graders examine a series of coins and place grades on them. At issue: their ability to grade to the marketplace. The prize: a job with Heritage, one of the world's largest and fastest growing coin companies. The result: Across the board, there were significant variations of one, two or even more points on the MS-60 to MS-70 uncirculated grading scale.

In 1989, the Federal Trade Commission brought a claim against Security Rare Coins of Minneapolis and its principal, William Ulrich. I participated in the defense of that claim, working with his then-counsel Barry Cutler, who later did a stint of government service and went on to become an FTC leader before returning to the private sector.

Mint State 60

One conclusion the U.S. District Court judge in Minneapolis came up with is significant: "There are a number of grading services. Today, the most accepted grading service is the Professional Coin Grading

Mint State 61

Service (PCGS), an independent grading service established in early 1986 and based in California. Before PCGS gained acceptance, the American Numismatic Association Certification Service (ANACS) was the most widely used service and was widely recognized during 1985 and 1986, even though some dealers raised questions about its reliability." (Today, the Numismatic Guaranty Corporation and several others would be added to the list of prominent grading services.)

"It is not uncommon," the judge continued, "for dealers to send certified coins back to PCGS for re-grading, and it is not uncommon for such returned coins to receive a different grade."

In other words, cracking coins out of their grading-service holders and re-submitting them can result in grades different from the ones originally assigned. That was not surprising, even then. In an in-court demonstration, two expert graders, Julian Leidman and Ken Goldman, disagreed with each other widely on the condition of various coins. (Both men are world-class graders whose opinions are widely sought and whose selling practices and grading abilities are highly regarded.)

"That experts can differ in assigning grades was illustrated by two FTC experts, Leidman and Goldman," the judge wrote, "who graded the same 31 U.S. gold and silver coins and disagreed as to 19 of them, in five cases by more than two points."

The judge also recited what happened when other experts reviewed a series of coins that are generally considered easy to grade – U.S. gold $20 pieces, which are large and show marks and scratches easily.

"One coin," the judge wrote, "a $20 gold piece, was assigned four different grades by five FTC experts, ranging from AU-58 to a 'very nice' MS-63. Another gold piece was graded MS-63 by one expert and MS-60 by another."

Thus, even the once-vaunted distinction between uncirculated and circulated can prove to be difficult.

Collectors of Carson City Mint gold coins are long aware of this. The finest known 1870-CC $20 was graded about uncirculated by Stack's, XF-40 by Superior, and XF-45 by Paramount. Most grading disputes, however, involve uncirculated coins because generally that's where the most value is.

A major court case involving grading was decided January 27, 1998, in a ruling by the U.S. Tax Court in Washington, D.C., on the estate of Ed Trompeter, a well-known collector of proof gold coinage and other rarities. Trompeter's estate became embroiled in a tax-fraud claim because of allegations that the gold coin collection, part of which was sold by Superior Galleries, was deliberately undervalued. A $14.8 million fraud penalty assessed by the Internal Revenue Service was the subject of the dispute.

Mint State 63

The court's decision recites that over 180 coins were submitted to PCGS for grading. The conclusion: A total of 69 were proof-63, 78 were proof-64, and 12 were proof-65. (There was just one found to be proof-66, one proof-67, and one proof-69.)

Trompeter's gold was then shipped to NGC, whose experts had a different view of the coins' grades. NGC's graders agreed that there was one proof-69, but after that they parted company. NGC's findings were five proof-67, 22 proof-66, 51 proof-65, 71 proof-64, and only 21 proof-63 coins. In contrast to the 15 pieces PCGS found to be 65 or better, NGC believed 78 to be in that state of preservation.

Other experts were provided by the two sides in the litigation – the IRS and the Trompeter estate. Maurice Rosen, a well-known writer and investment counselor, was one of those experts. "He graded 61 percent of the coins the same as PCGS, 26 percent of the coins lower than PCGS, and 13 percent of the coins higher than PCGS," the court reported.

There were other experts who focused on the coins' value, which is, after all, what grading really is – a short-hand term for a coin's value.

Mint State 65

In the final analysis, the court rejected all of the experts except one: the decedent himself, Ed Trompeter, who had placed a value on the coins that Superior sold at auction before his death. The court's reasoning: Trompeter predicted within 2 percent the selling prices received at auction.

In another court case – one I was involved in as an expert (but not a grader) – the government sued on what I call a grading and pricing case. The 2nd Circuit Court of Appeals summarized the issue: "This case involves the question of whether the presence of objective and subjective grading factors immunizes a seller of coins from a criminal charge of fraudulently misrepresenting the grade and value of coins to purchasers."

The facts were compelling. "[Rick] Montgomery [then president of PCGS] graded 702 coins that were admitted in evidence," U.S. District Court Judge Arthur D. Spatt wrote in his 2001 opinion. "Of the 702 coins he examined, Montgomery arrived at the same grade as the ... Defendants 67 times," or just less than 10 percent of the time.

"Montgomery graded 397 coins lower than did the Defendants and deemed another 200 coins ungradable because they were either cleaned, altered, or damaged. So that a total of 597 of the 702 coins [about 85 percent] were either graded lower or could not be graded because of detrimental conditions.

"Furthermore," Spatt wrote, and essentially the 2nd Circuit concurred, "a survey of the grades determined by Montgomery with respect to the 397 coins that he graded lower demonstrates that Montgomery graded 39 coins at 1 point lower than did the Defendants." That meant about 10 percent were off by a single point (mostly uncirculated degrees).

There were 67 coins at 2 points lower (17 percent), 45 coins at 3 points lower (11.3 percent), and 17 coins at 4 points lower (4.2 percent). There were also 17 coins at 5 points lower, 46 coins at 6 points lower,

59 coins at 7 points lower, 50 coins at 8 points lower, 20 coins at 9 points lower, and 37 coins were graded by Montgomery at 10 or more points lower than the defendants' grade.

Judge Spatt queried, "Why, if coin grading standards are as inconsistent and inherently subjective as the Defendants contend, not one of the 397 grades assigned by [the seller] was higher than the corresponding grade determined by Montgomery?

"The evidence clearly reflects that the customers also believed that the value of the coin was commensurate with the explicitly represented grades. This belief is reflected in the substantial sums of money customers paid for the coins they received."

Mint State 66

The MacMillan Encyclopedic Dictionary of Numismatics by Dr. Richard Doty (1982) refers to "MS-65s, sometimes called 'choice uncirculateds,' ... [which] will command much higher prices than MS-60s." In his book *Rare Coin Investment Strategy* (1986), Scott Travers terms "choice mint state-65," using American Numismatic Association grading standards, the "most frequently traded investor-quality coin." He goes on to say, "Although A.N.A. grading standards indicate that an MS-65 may be lightly fingermarked, the marketplace often dictates that MS-65 be virtually mark-free. ... Although A.N.A. standards indicate otherwise, an MS-65 is generally expected to exhibit all of the detail that the Mint intended it to display."

In his book *How to Make Money in Coins Right Now* (second edition, 2001), Travers says, "Coin grading is a process of subjective evaluation. However it becomes somewhat objective when groups of experts examine coins and achieve a consensus of subjectivity."

In Mort Reed's book *Coins: An Investor's & Collector's Guide* (1973), James F. Ruddy contributed a chapter on coin grading and noted, "Certain early coins are extremely difficult to find in Uncirculated condition without any bagmarks or handling. Such flawless pieces are sometimes designated as a Choice Uncirculated or Gem Uncirculated. Choice describes an above average Uncirculated specimen, well struck and with a minimum of minor bagmarks or minting defects. Gem Uncirculated is the finest available, a sharply struck coin that is free of the usual minor bagmarks or minting defects."

In the 1958 book *Penny Whimsy* (also known as *Early American Cents, 1793-1814*), Dr. William H. Sheldon, who invented the 1-to-70 scale, said something that differed from all of this: "The MS-65 is a coin that would be a perfect MS-70 except for some small minor blemish. It may lack full mint luster, or some microscopic or almost negligible blemish may be demonstrable. There may be a spot of discoloration, a fingermark or a barely discernible nick."

An approximation of grading numbers with their adjectival equivalents, as used in the revised version of the Sheldon grading guide, are as follows: uncirculated, 60 through 70; about uncirculated, 50, 53, 55, and 58; extremely fine, 40 and 45; very fine, 20, 25 and 30; fine, 12 through 15; very good, 7 through 10; good, 4 through 6; very fair, 3 through 5; fair, 2; and poor, 1.

Sheldon's grading system was originally intended to correlate with the value for U.S. large cents minted prior to 1815. For example, a coin in "fine-12" condition had one-fifth the value of an "uncirculated-60" coin. The numerical designations continue to be used and assigned to other types of coins, but there is no longer a direct mathematical relationship between coin grades and values.

Even though a coin is uncirculated, meaning it has no wear, there may still be other blemishes on it. In grading uncirculated coins, experts consider the number and placement of "bag marks." The term refers to contact marks – nicks and abrasions on coin surfaces – that occur when coins are shipped from the

Mint State 67

mint in bags and rub against each other. The number of bag marks and their location on a coin are important factors in grading.

As Abe Kosoff wrote in 1973, "Application of the numeral system is an attempt to apply an exact or mathematical standard to the process of grading coins." This attempt has partially succeeded, but it wrongly implies that there is a single standard. The numbers, are widely used in the marketplace, as are adjectival descriptions, but are subject to differing interpretations.

A variety of other factors are also considered in grading. These include "toning," whether a coin's original color has changed through oxidation or other factors; "strike," whether the figures and devices on the coin are particularly clear; and overall "eye appeal."

In his *N.C.I. Grading Guide*, Halperin notes that the ANA standards use "choice uncirculated" to denote coins that are MS-65 or proof-65. He also notes, however, that many dealers apply "choice uncirculated" to MS-63 and proof-63 coins and "gem uncirculated" to MS-65 and proof-65 coins. Thus, even the adjectives can have different meanings.

When the book *Official A.N.A. Grading Standards for United States Coins* was first published, in 1977, it divided uncirculated coins into three categories: MS-70, MS-65 and MS-60. By the time the second edition was published in 1981, two new grades were added: MS-63 and MS-67. This reflected grades commonly used in the late 1980s and early 1990s.

The book gave the following descriptions:
– MS-70 (perfect uncirculated). "… the finest quality available. Such a coin under 4X magnification will show no bag marks, lines or other evidence of handling or contact with other coins."
– MS-67 (gem uncirculated). A coin midway between MS-70 and MS-65. It may be either brilliant or toned, except for a toned copper coin, which should be described as MS-65.

Mint State 68

Extremely Fine 45

– MS-65 (choice uncirculated). An above average uncirculated coin. It may be brilliant or toned (and described accordingly). It must have fewer bag marks than usual but can have scattered occasional bag marks on the surface or perhaps one or two very light rim marks.

– MS-63 (select uncirculated). A coin midway between MS-65 and MS-60.

– MS-60 (uncirculated). A coin with a moderate number of bag marks. A few minor edge nicks and marks may also be present. Unusually deep bag marks, nicks and the like must be described separately. The coin may be either brilliant or toned.

The sixth edition (2005) of the ANA grading guide showed modest changes to the 1989 edition. In the following descriptions, underlined text represents additions to the earlier edition; strike-through text indicates deletions. Most changes are in higher grades.

– MS-60. Unattractive, dull or washed-out mint luster may mark this coin. There may be many ugly or large contact marks, or damage spots, but absolutely no trace of wear. There could be heavy concentrations of hairlines, or unattractive large areas of scuff marks. Rim nicks may be present, and eye appeal is very poor. Copper coins may be dark, dull and spotted.

– MS-61. Mint luster may be diminished or noticeably impaired, and the surface has clusters of large and small contact marks throughout. Hairlines could be very noticeable. Scuff marks may show as unattractive patches on large areas or major features. Small rim nicks may show, and the quality may be noticeably poor. Eye appeal is somewhat unattractive. Copper pieces will be generally dark and possibly spotted.

– MS-62. An impaired or dull luster may be evident. Clusters of small marks may be present throughout with a few large marks or nicks in prime focal areas. Hairlines may be very noticeable. Large unattractive scuff marks might be seen on major features. The strike, rim and planchet quality may be noticeably below average. Overall eye appeal is below average. If copper, the coins will show a diminished color and tone.

– MS-63. Mint luster may be slightly impaired. Numerous small contact marks, and a few scattered heavy marks may be seen. Small hairlines are visible without magnification. Several detracting scuff marks may be present throughout the design or in the fields. The general quality is about average, but overall the coin is rather attractive. Copper pieces may be darkened or dull. Color should be designated.

About uncirculated 50

– MS-64. Has at least average luster for the type is necessary. Several small contact marks in groups, as well as one or two heavy marks may be present. One or two small patches of hairlines may show. Noticeable scuff marks might be seen within the design or in the field. Overall quality is attractive with a pleasing eye appeal. If copper, the coins may be slightly dull. Color should be designated.

– MS-65. Shows attractive high quality of luster for the date and mint. May have a few small scattered contact marks or two larger marks may be present. One or two small patches of hairlines may show. Noticeable light scuff marks may be seen on the high points of the design. Overall quality is above average and eye appeal is very pleasing. If copper, the coin has some attractive luster with original or darkened color, as designated.

Mint State 62

– MS-66 Has above-average quality of surface and, mint luster, with no more than three or Four minor or noticeable contact marks. A few very light hairlines may show under magnification or there may be one or two light scuff marks showing. Eye appeal is above average and very pleasing for the date and mint. If copper, the coins displays original or lightly toned color (which must be designated).

Mint State 64

– MS-67. Has original luster and normal strike for date and mint. May have three or four very small contact marks and one more noticeable but not detracting mark. On comparable coins, one or two small single hairlines may show or one or two partially hidden scuff marks may be present. Eye appeal is above average. If copper, the coin has luster and original color.

– MS-68. Has attractive sharp strike and full original luster for date and mint, with no more than four light scattered contact marks. No hairlines or scuff marks show. Has exceptional eye appeal. If copper, the coin is lustrous and has original color.

– MS-69. Has very attractive sharp strike and full original luster for the date and mint, with no more than two small nondetracting contact marks or flaws. No hairlines or scuff marks can be seen. Has exceptional eye appeal. If Copper, the coin is bright with full original color and luster.

– MS-70. The perfect coin. Has very attractive sharp strike and original luster of the highest quality for the date and mint. No contact marks are visible under magnification. There are absolutely no hairlines, scuff marks or defects. Eye appeal is attractive and outstanding. If copper, the coin is bright with full original color and luster.

Whether the standards of the 1980s, '90s or the new century are used, the descriptions in the ANA guide and its successors are quite vague and leave room for interpretation. For example, previously an MS-65 would have "fewer bag marks than usual," but there is no definition of what is "usual." Now, it's OK to have "few small scattered contact marks or two larger marks may be present," not further defined. An MS-60 will have a "moderate number of bag marks." An MS-63 will be somewhere in-between. Where coins fall in the grading scale can vary from series to series, design to design, and, most important, grader to grader.

Walking Liberty Half Dollar
Mint State

Jeffrey J. Pritchard, in his book *Heads You Win, Tails You Win: The Inside Secrets of Rare Coin Investing* (1983), sums up prevailing opinion when he says grading uncirculated coins "remains somewhat arbitrary, even among so-called experts."

I always thought grading differences were summed up best by Q. David Bowers in his book *Adventures with Rare Coins* (1979): "Often five different sellers will assign five different grades to the same coin, perhaps differing just slightly but still differing, often with important financial consequences. ... As the evaluation of the grade or condition of a coin is a largely subjective matter, experts can legitimately differ."

Why do grade descriptions and opinions differ? Grading is inherently subjective and represents one person's view of a coin's state of preservation and, if the coin is uncirculated, the degree or extent of pleasure (eye appeal) it beholds to the purveyor.

Liberty $20 Gold Proof

As I wrote in my "Under the Glass" column in the September 20, 1975, *Numismatic News*, grading standards, "no matter how precisely defined, nonetheless remain subjective. Differences of opinion – not only between collectors and dealers, but even between dealers themselves – are bound to arise."

The original ANA grading guide said, "Grading is not that precise and using such finely split intermediate grades is imparting a degree of accuracy which probably will not be able to be verified by other numismatists."

From this, it should be clear that there is neither a unified grading standard nor some single subjective standard. There are, instead, multiple standards, each of which are somewhat inconsistent with the other.

Of course, there are some who believe that there should be a uniform standard. Collector C.E. Bunnell of Rochester, New York, advocated a uniform grading standard in the following letter: "It is very

$20 Carson City. This coin was struck circulated

important to members of the ANA that the Board of Governors take some stand with reference to issuing some kind of statement classifying coins so that all dealers that catalogue and sell coins ... must use the same classification."

He wrote that in a letter to *The Numismatist*, monthly journal of the American Numismatic Association, in February 1913. The issue has been with the coin business for a long time and will continue for the foreseeable future.

The dispute over grading took a dramatic turn in the late 1980s when there was a major shift in market grading. Coins graded MS-65 several years ago are now routinely graded MS-63 and even lower in the marketplace because of changing grading interpretations. Disputes over the grades of several Harold Bareford coins show up in the pedigrees when the coins are cataloged for resale.

On February 19, 1986, the ANA board passed the following resolution:

"Grading is an art and not an exact science. More precisely, grading is a matter of opinion. Differences of opinion may occur among graders as a to a particular coin, and any grader could conceivably change his interpretation of the grading standards over the years. When the *ANA Official Grading Standards for United States Coins* book was published in 1978, it represented a new grading system, previously untried. ... The grading standards as enumerated in the book were and are not precise, with the descriptions lending themselves to different interpretations. The marketplace composed of collectors and dealers has tightened its interpretation in recent years and ANACS [the ANA certification and grading service] has reflected those changes. Accordingly, the ANA Grading Service, endeavoring to keep in step with current market interpretations (rather than create interpretations of its own) has in recent times graded coins more conservatively than in the past, in many instances.

"Hence, it may be the situation that a coin which was graded MS-65 by the Grading Service in 1981 or 1982, for example, may, if regraded in 1985 or 1986, merit the current interpretation of MS-63 or less. Similarly, dealers and others in the commercial sector have found that coins that they graded MS-65 several years ago may merit MS-63 or lower interpretations today."

Environmental contaminants created colorful toning on this mint state coin.

Grading changes wreak havoc with price analysis during the periods they took place, especially in the year following changes. Fortunately, the Salomon Brothers price table and guide never used gem coins (either MS-65 or proof-65 at a minimum), preferring more common MS-63 (then called "choice" uncirculated) coins. Adjustment in an analysis is still required but less so.

It's not that different now. Several years ago, I traveled to New Orleans with then ANA executive director Bob Leuver to look at Compugrade and see what was possible in computerized coin grading. I admit that I am not a grading expert, but inside of a day working with a computer, I could grade silver dollars to industry standards within a tenth of a grade pretty consistently. (We did not try other coins.)

Coin-grading services

Acronym	Name	Web site	Location
ACCGS	American Coin Club Grading Service	www.accgs.org	Beverly Hills, Calif.
ACG	ASA Accugrade Inc.	www.asa-accugrade.com	Melbourne, Fla.
ANACS	ANACS Certification Service Inc.	www.anacs.com	Englewood, Colo.
ICG	Independent Coin Grading Company	www.icgcoin.com	Englewood, Colo.
NGC	Numismatic Guaranty Corporation	www.ngccoin.com	Sarasota, Fla.
NTC	Numistrust Corporation	www.numistrust.com	Boca Raton, Fla.
PCGS	Professional Coin Grading Service	www.pcgs.com	Newport Beach, Calif.
PCI	PCI Inc.	www.pcicoins.com	Rossville, Ga.
SEGS	Sovereign Entities Grading Service	www.segsgrading.com	Chattanooga, Tenn.
SGS	Star Grading Service	www.stargrading.org	Bellville, Ohio

In fall 2007, a major disruption to traditional market forces occurred when the online auction giant eBay announced that listings for coins that were either "raw" (not professionally graded and encapsulated) or graded by services other than ANACS, ICG, NGC, or PCGS would not be permitted to include the coins' relative prices or grades. Some believe this is in anticipation of a renewed attempt to get Congress to allow coins in retirement accounts again and to weed out all but the strongest of grading companies. How it ultimately affects the coin market remains to be seen.

The professional coin-grading services and much of the coin market focus on gem coins (MS-65 and

ANACS

better). But there are at least 10 circulated grades that are investment quality. They are not only worth collecting but worth including in a million-dollar portfolio.

Dr. William Sheldon's original numerical grading system for large cents started with 1, which he called "basal state." He described it as "identifiable and unmutilated," a coin "so badly worn that only a portion of the legend or inscription is legible. ... Enough must remain for positive identification of the variety."

Not precisely the type of coin that you would want to have in your collection, right? Surely not a coin that could have even a modicum of value, right? Given your choice between a basal-1 coin and an MS-65 1881-S silver dollar, there's not even an issue, right?

Well, if the coin is a 1793 Sheldon NC-2 basal state-1 cent, the answer is probably not what you would expect, even though its description says there are a "number of minor nicks, digs and scratches consistent with the grade, but only two serious rim dents."

The coin, however, is unique. It was acquired by Richard Winsor right after the Civil War and sold by dealer Henry Chapman on December 16, 1895, for $21. The buyer was none other than Sylvester Crosby, another famous name in American numismatics.

Crosby knew the coin for what it was, and the following year, he doubled his money by selling it to Dr. Thomas Hall for $42.50 (about six times the average weekly wage at the time).

From there, it went to the ubiquitous Virgil Brand, the Chicago brewing baron, and then to Charles Williams, a Cincinnati insurance executive. Abe Kosoff sold Williams' collection in November 1950, and the well-worn piece brought an astonishing $1,025.

Floyd Starr was the purchaser, and in June 1984,

PCGS

NGC

Stack's sold his collection as part of a mega-sale that attracted enthusiasts from across the country. This lowly cent, at the lowest end of the grading scale, sold as lot 6 for $50,600, including the buyer's fee. (Its subsequent history has no public auction records, but the 1996 American Numismatic Society Coinage of the Americas Conference listed six subsequent owners.)

After basal state-1, Sheldon's next grade is fair-2 followed by very fair-3, in which the date is actually "clear and practically all of the detail of the coin can be made out." That's quite a contrast to an encapsulated MS-65 coin, where a single ding or contact mark seems almost enough to change its caliber.

Floyd Starr's collection had another good example, also a 1793 cent, grade very fair-3, strawberry-leaf variety (Sheldon NC-3, lot 7). This coin was described in the auction catalog as having a "heavily flaking and corroded obverse," not necessarily a desirable characteristic. "Despite the rather battle-scarred appearance of the obverse," the catalog said, "its detail is fairly distinct. ... The reverse, though porous and with a sizable rim dent over ST, is relatively clean."

Three examples of the Sheldon NC-3 are known, and Sheldon himself termed this coin (the William Rabin example) as "rough and blackened but perhaps can be rated condition 3." It was not even the best of the known pieces. The 1984 price realized: $51,700.

Old large coppers hold their share of great rarities and even seem to make condition of little importance. They almost shame those who strive for the mythical perfection of an MS-70.

When Superior Galleries sold the Robinson S. Brown Jr. collection of large cents, an 1800 Sheldon NC-4 in grade about good-3 came up. The coin had "heavy rim breaks on the obverse" with reverse legends "obscured due to honest wear" and "minute signs of handling."

Only nine examples are known to exist. The price: $6,050 – for a coin that doesn't even make grade good.

Good is perhaps the first grade most collectors learn of when they start and is common to coins found in pocket change. Yet, it can also be a major rarity for some coins.

Favorite among grade good specimens in my book is the G-4 1894-S dime. The coin was found in pocket change in 1957. Robert Friedberg purchased it from the coin department of the old Gimbels department store.

Author Walter Breen traced its history to dealer Art Kagin, a New Netherlands sale, Harmer Rooke's 1969 sale, Jim Johnson, and then to the 1980 ANA convention auction, where Steve Ivy cataloged it as good-4 with ANACS certification No. 5468.

Imagine describing with virtue a coin as having "full rims on each side" and "no abnormal marks for a coin of this grade, but the scratch above 'One' should be mentioned on a coin of this magnitude." It is then compared to the 1804 dollar, the 1913 nickel, and the 1838-O half dollar.

The coin brought $31,000 in spirited bidding. It might be the most ever paid for a dime in grade good, and it was well worth the price.

Two very good grades – VG-8 and VG-10 – are worth mentioning. A VG-8 of one particular coin type is described in the ANA grading guide as "entire head is weak and most hair details are worn smooth. Date and Liberty are weak but clear. Parts of the eye and ear are visible. Stars are outlined." For the reverse, the eagle is boldly outlined, and only a few details are showing on the wings and tail. Some of the letters are very weak.

Imagine a Franklin half dollar with partial bell lines or a slabbed Morgan dollar being collectible in that condition. But this is a Flowing Hair dollar, dated 1794. The coin is scarce, but not as scarce as its mintage of 1,758 suggests. An example crops up at auction every now and again.

Two specimens were included Superior's section of Auction '88. One was described as having a "slightly erratic strike" and stars at left that were "extremely faint" and a date that was "half visible." Still, the cataloger correctly noted that it was a "beautiful example of our first silver dollar." The coin opened at $7,500 and sold to a California dealer for $9,500.

A second, slightly better example (VG-10) of the same coin was in the Mid-America auction at the 1989 Midwinter American Numismatic Association Convention in Colorado Springs, Colorado. Lot 1196 was described as "evenly worn" and "quite attractive" with "most details clearly visible," meaning that some details weren't.

Minor adjustment marks were present on this coin as well, and the borders were weak. Nonetheless, this coin was deemed highly desirable, and an $11,000 price was achieved.

Nowhere is the change that has enveloped grading over the past four decades more evident (at least among circulated coins) than it is in grade fine. An example can be seen in Abe Kosoff's Lahrman collection auction in February 1963. It is another large cent – Sheldon 11a, vine-with-bars variety, which came out of the Pearl collection and was sold by Kosoff in 1944 as F-12. By 1963 he had a definite opinion: "It is Fine-15." The coin had a pre-sale estimate of $325 and sold for $335. It is worth considerably more today.

Moving up the scale, grade very fine is already a less-worn coin. A VF-25 is a pleasing specimen, as a 1796 gold $2.50 with stars on the obverse proves convincingly. Numismatic Gallery's Adolphe Menjou collection auction of 1950 saw a specimen called "about very fine" bring $300. In 1978, Kagin's sold it at the Great Eastern Numismatic Association convention auction as VF-25 with "light file marks in central portion" of the reverse. It realized $11,000.

Many would consider such a coin a premier piece in their collection – even though it is a long way from mint state. (Akers' standard reference work analyzing auction records shows 33 sales in the 20th century, with very fine the average grade.) Paul Taglione's major opus on federal gold coinage says the average grade encountered is VF-35.

Extremely fine, even for a gold $3, is a nice grade, though few who would consider it investment quality. But there are exceptions for a coin that would have "light wear on tops of feathers, on hair at high points, and above eye" on the obverse, with bow knots showing wear on the reverse together with the cotton bolls.

This would probably be the case even if the coin had not been polished and lacked pin scratches at the top of the wreath with the numerals "893" etched into its surface. This coin: the 1870-S gold $3 from the Louis Eliasberg collection, sold by Bowers & Ruddy in October 1982.

No encapsulation is necessary to appreciate the value of a coin like this; it is unique. No other specimen is known. And when it sold, Jane Bryant Quinn of CBS News was in attendance. Bill Hawfield, the auctioneer, began by saying, "Thirty seconds on TV is worth $70,000. So, dealers, raise your hands accordingly."

It opened at $100,000 and jumped to $325,000 on a bid from dealer Harvey Stack. It then went to $375,000, $425,000, $475,000, $500,000, and $525,000, when Lester Merkin jumped in. It finally settled at $625,000 to bidder No. 138, who was Stack, bidding on behalf of a client. It was a record price for a gold $3.

There simply aren't many 1881-S silver dollars in any grade that meet the excitement or history of this abused gold $3.

Second choice for grade extremely fine might be the Bebee 1804 silver dollar, now on view at the American Numismatic Association museum in Colo-

$3 Gold Choice Uncirculated

rado Springs, Colorado, through the generosity of Aubrey and Adeline Bebee. Author Walter Breen described the coin as "EF, rubbed, and scratched" with "rust on the eagle's head."

Its illustrious owners start with William Idler, Captain John Haseltine, H.O. Granberg, Treasury Secretary William Woodin, W.C. Atwater, Will Neil, and Edwin Hydeman, and proceed through World Wide Coin Investments and Bowers & Ruddy to Dr. Jerry Buss. Superior's sale of his specimen in 1979 saw Bebee as a buyer. No one would turn down this specimen for his cabinet.

Nor would they with my third choice EF piece, also vintage Bebee and also residing in the ANA museum as a result of the Bebees' extraordinary gift to the association. It is the 1913 Liberty nickel, which Breen described as "nicked, scratched, cleaned, exhibited at hundreds of conventions, reportedly used by [former owner J.V.] McDermott for barroom betting," and, incidentally, priceless.

With the 1913 nickel and the 1804 silver dollar, the ANA museum displays a million dollars' worth of coins, compliments of the Bebees. Neither is encapsulated; neither is pristine. And neither has to be. They are eminently desirable and highly collectible.

It is time to touch on some encapsulated pieces – this one an AU-53, a grade with some light friction at the highest points. The piece in question: a scarce 1799 gold $10 sold by Mid-America at the 1989 Midwinter ANA Convention for $5,000.

Even though the coin had a small rim cud from natural die deterioration visible on the obverse, the catalogers noted that most early gold doesn't come this nice. And as they also allude to, it is quite collectible.

Another example is an 1886 gold $20 in AU-55. The coin in question was purchased in January 1977 for $14,450 for New England Rare Coin Fund I. In April 1980, at a New York auction, the coin opened at $7,000 and sold for $37,000.

Dealer and researcher David Akers says EF is the typical grade for this coin, so perhaps that was what was on collectors' minds when they ignored the wear on the high points of a coin that was nice enough, the catalog says, to fool an expert into thinking it was actually uncirculated.

Another favorite AU is another 1794 dollar, this one Bolender No. 1 from Akers' section of Auction '88. The pedigree includes a Bowers and Merena sale from the Connecticut Historical Society (as grade extremely fine). Akers notes, "That grade was overly conservative," even with the adjustment marks, since the coin has "very little real wear."

There is nothing magical about mint state. A variety of collectible coins – some rare, some not – can be found n various lesser grades, from basal state-1 to AU-50 and even higher (but beneath uncirculated).

Today's passion is for quality. Dr. Sheldon showed that 40 years ago, condition meant little if the coin itself was scarce. That means more than mintage; it means availability and desirability to collectors. And to determine that, a collector needs to do more than read a grade on a slab. He needs to know coins, the coin market, and the very stuff that makes coin collecting tick.

Chapter 3

Investment Strategies for the 21st Century

❧

I f you're like many people, you want to start investing in coins right now. You also want to know which coins are easiest to buy and sell, and recognizing that past performance is no guarantee of future results, you want to know which coins have been the top performers over the last half-century.

The Midas Touch

In March 2008, gold topped $1,000 an ounce, an all time high. A few month earlier, the dollar sank to a new low against the euro and Japanese yen. Iran refused to eliminate its nuclear program, the king of Saudi Arabia lowered his subjects' gasoline price to 65 cents a gallon – while the price of a barrel of crude oil topped $100 – and U.S. pump prices topped $3 a gallon.

About 2 years earlier, in April 2006, gold was at a 25-year high (more than $660 an ounce), and oil and gasoline prices jumped. Gold had risen $100 an ounce in a year and almost $50 an ounce in just 30 days.

In early 2008, the Canadian dollar was worth $1.02 U.S., and the U.S. dollar was worth 70 percent of the euro. The record high for gold on the New York Mercantile Exchange prior to 2008 was $875, set January 21, 1980. The record settling price is $825.50, set on the same date.

In the 21st century, gold is on a march that should take it through $1,000 an ounce and perhaps beyond. Hard-asset groups, who predicted $1,000-an-ounce gold for many years, are now hawking $2,000-an-ounce gold.

All of these events are related and, more than ever, show just how important the global economy is to everyday economic matters and how the rare-coin prices respond by also rising.

It's no accident that also in April 2006, a 1792 half disme from the Floyd Starr collection sold at the Central States Numismatic Society convention auction for a record $1,322,500. When Stack's Rare Coins sold the same coin at auction in October 1992 – just 14 years earlier – it realized a mere $87,500.

In mid-2007, the Eliasberg specimen of the 1913 nickel, graded proof-66 by the Professional Coin Grading Service, sold by private treaty for $5 million, another record. Just 14 years earlier, the Reed

1792 Half Disme
(Actual Size About 17mm)

Hawn-Dr. Jerry Buss 1913 Liberty nickel (PCGS proof-64) sold at auction for $962,500 in another Stack's sale.

As gold goes up, so does the rare-coin market, even for non-gold items.

There's a numismatic economy all right. Collectors see it every time they want to buy a new issue that has sold out and have to acquire it at a higher price on the secondary market. Investors become aware of the numismatic economy when they see gold or silver prices jump and expect all of their coins to do the same, only to find that the two markets, however parallel, don't always follow the same track. Even dealers find out that changing grading standards and traditional supply-and-demand factors affect their business.

Anyone involved in the buying, selling and trading of coins learns the numismatic economy quickly or gets a rude awakening when, relying on what might otherwise be common sense, they do something that contradicts the rules of the game.

Some of the stakes seem hardball. Perhaps for that reason, it is important for those involved in coins to like what they're doing, instead of just being a glutton for potential profits. Some of the aspects almost resemble Monopoly, the Parker Brothers classic board game that cheered America through a depression and later gave several generations a roll of the dice for their money.

For more than 40 years, over five decades & two centuries, I have been writing about the economics of numismatics and how the events of our everyday lives impact our hobby and the coin business in general. That includes the ups and downs of the stock market, changes in the Consumer Price Index, and announcements of a revised figure for the gross national product of Pakistan.

In the backwater years, economic news was located in the financial sections of daily newspapers, usually at the back of the paper and often incorporated in the stock tables. In October 1965, Vantanig G. Vartan, respected financial reporter for *The New York Times*, wrote, "'It's bullish.' That sentiment expressed by the vice president in charge of research for E.F. Hutton & Co., Inc., summed up Wall Street's view as the Dow-Jones industrials boomed to a new closing high of 942.65, up an impressive 4.33 points."

Yes, 4.3 points were significant back in 1965; the Dow Jones index was under 1,000. The change is equivalent to more than 60 points today, which would get only a routine mention in the news.

In 1965, the price of gold was immutably held at $35 an ounce by force of government regulation. In 1933, the Hoover administration pegged it at $20.67 an ounce, where it had been irregularly since 1837. (At that rate, a gold $20 coin contained $19.99 worth of precious metal.)

The stability of gold – it rose briefly during the Civil War and a bit later when Jay Gould tried to corner the market – was important to American economic development but also the cause of economic depressions when the federal government, lacking the precious metal to back an increase, was unable to inflate the currency.

1882-CC gold $5

By the time of Franklin Roosevelt's administration, there was a solid Keynesian belief that the dollar's value relative to gold was seriously understated. It is said the Great Depression began when the U.S. economy sneezed and the world caught pneumonia. Government problems adding currency to the marketplace hampered efforts to combat it.

Another problem was the way debt was financed in those days. People had home mortgages, as they do today, but with an important difference: Nearly all were balloon mortgages. During the first two or three years of the loan, only interest or a small amount of principal and interest were paid.

1890 gold $2.50.

1890-CC Morgan silver dollar.

As bank after bank threatened to fail, their first recourse was to seek capital from balloon loans that came due. Borrowers, who typically counted on continuous refinancing of short-term mortgage debt, went into default.

The government's ability to find financing was limited to several sources: customs and excise taxes (imports fell dramatically, and so did this source), taxes (incomes fell dramatically), taxes on exports (the world wasn't buying as much either), and investments (stock and bond markets were in the tank).

During the last quarter of the 19th century, the free coinage of silver was the dominant political issue – much as pro- or anti-Vietnam War sentiments characterized the 1960s. As government authority to purchase silver expired, silver-dollar production fell precipitously, from more than 6 million pieces in 1892 to a mere 1.4 million in 1893.

Professor Milton Friedman wrote in his book *Monetary History of the United States 1867-1960* that by 1894, $153 million in 1890 Treasury notes, which were backed by precious metal, were in circulation. More than $540 million in gold coins were also in circulation that year along with some $390 million in silver coinage. (The bulk of this was not in government hands.)

Flash forward to the Roosevelt administration and the Depression that started in 1929. The government believed that if it could pump up the economy, it could cure the economic cold. To do that, however, it felt it needed to control gold, which was a storehouse of value. (Lacking the controls today, gold jumped to more than $800 an ounce in part because of economic uncertainty.)

Gold clauses were frequently written into contracts in the 1930s. For example, they called for rents to be paid in gold coin. Actress Sarah Bernhardt's Broadway show contracts required payment in gold coin after each performance.

In 1933, Roosevelt issued an executive order recalling gold coins, abrogating the gold clauses in contracts, and, shortly thereafter, re-valuing gold from $20.67 to $35 an ounce – effectively devaluing the dollar by 59 percent. All gold coins that were not "rare and unusual" – numismatic values were paramount – were declared forfeited to the government at face value. You didn't lose anything – you got your face value – but you missed the upside of the new free-market price of gold.

Gold coins were required to be turned in for melting, thereby increasing the government's control over the money supply. The government's gold stock in 1933 consisted of $2.3 billion in bullion and $806.4 million in coins of various denominations. The Federal Reserve held $743 million in gold coins and a fraction of that amount ($66.5 million) in bullion.

1883-CC Morgan silver dollar.

The nation's national banks had $141,000 in gold coins, and public, state and private banks (other than national banks) had $310 million. From 1934 to 1950 (mostly from 1934 to 1937), the U.S. Mint melted $1.59 billion in gold coins. Of that amount, $1.3 billion were $20 coins.

When it was over, only $226 million in gold coins remained.

It is useful to consider the melt statistics, never fully explored by most books and researchers, as shown on the accompanying chart. The data were gathered from annual Mint director reports.

Gold coins melted by the U.S. Mint

	$1	$2.50	$3	$5	$10	$20	$50
Mintage	19,874,754	20,426,833	539,792	78,911,869	57,683,485	174,105,606	3,019
Number melted	31,373	3,193,733	58,267	26,474,887	27,149,715	67,880,757	1,921
Number remaining	19,843,382	17,233,100	481,525	52,436,982	30,533,770	106,224,849	1,098
Percent melted	0.16	15.63	10.79	33.55	47.07	38.99	63.63
Percent remaining	99.84	84.37	89.21	66.45	52.93	61.01	36.37

The $226 million treasure trove that survived the melting pot was all the domestic gold coin and bullion that could legally be owned by U.S. citizens from 1933 until December 31, 1974, when private gold ownership was legalized again. By that time, gold's international convertibility into the dollar had been suspended, a two-tiered market emerged, and profits in gold began to march.

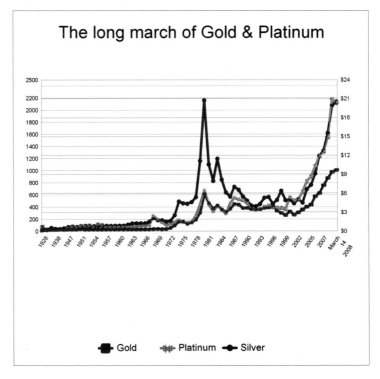

The long march of Gold & Platinum

Gold   Platinum   Silver

Gold's tie to various international events continued in ensuing years. Price spikes occurred during times of crisis. Inflation, started in the 1960s by the Vietnam War and later by other causes, resulted in substantial runs on the precious metal. The free market governed from 1968 onward, however, and at one point, on January 16, 1970, the price dipped slightly below $35 an ounce. Since then, it has never looked back. After breaking $700 an ounce in non-inflationary times, there probably is no top. It topped $900 in February 2008 and is poised to go higher.

There's talk of even higher prices, with a pillar of stability as stock-market indexes see daily swings of 2 percent or 3 percent. Gold's change has been more moderate.

In 1999, IBM lost $23 a share in a single day's trading. Because 1.8 billion shares are held publicly, the loss for that single day was about $35 billion, which was then about half of Pakistan's annual gross national product.

But gold – and for that matter platinum and silver, too – didn't react. Nor did gold react when there was a suspected coup d'état in the Soviet Union in the 1980s. Instead of going through the roof, it notched down more than a peg. The same thing happened when Saddam Hussein sent chemical rockets toward Tel Aviv. Gold simply took to the tank and dropped another $50 an ounce.

Economics, from my perspective, is different now than it was 40 years ago, when I first started writing my "Under the Glass" column in *Numismatic News*. As economic numbers are announced, they still affect coin prices and the coin business, but not necessarily as they did in the past. That makes periodic market reviews and commentary essential, and makes price guides published in *Numismatic News* and its related products useful tools in understanding market happenings.

If the coins are marketed properly, new-millennium economics may move the market for rare gold coins – those left from the major melts of the 1930s and modern issues that are perhaps even more scarce than the melted-down remnants of a century ago. Look at any value guide and compare the mintages. Economics 101 tells you that supply and demand will set the price. There's an increasingly smaller supply and higher demand. Now is the time to consider adding some gold coins to your portfolio.

For hundreds of years, gold has been an asset of last resort. In times of desperation, it has sometimes made the difference between life and death. It has outpaced inflation and frequently outstripped other investments. Yet at other times, it has been a stick in the mud, going nowhere.

From 1837 to 1933, for example, with some narrow wartime exceptions, gold had a fixed international value of $20.67 an ounce. That guaranteed rate was forcibly retained until the late 1960s, when gold was freed from a fixed rate and allowed to float on the open market. In August 1971, the dollar was again devalued and gold's price was raised to $38 an ounce. A subsequent devaluation to $42.22 an ounce for gold followed during the Nixon administration. Today, more than 35 years after Nixon devalued the dollar by raising the price of gold, the official price remains $42.22 an ounce.

That's right; the government's books show the asset at a diminished value. With gold leaping above $800 an ounce on the open market, official U.S. gold reserves are valued at $42.22. That means that as of September 30, 2007, the Federal Reserve and Treasury have 261 million ounces of gold with a book value of $11 billion. Each time gold goes up a dollar an ounce on the open market, the actual value of the government's gold increases by more than a quarter of a billion dollar.

U.S. gold reserves and values

	Gold bullion	Gold coin, blanks	Total
Ounces	258,641,851.49	2,856,047.83	261,498,899.32
at $42.22	$10,920,427,976.14	$120,630,844.95	$11,041,058,821.09
at $500	$129,320,925,743	$1,428,523,915	$130,749,449,658
at $700	$181,049,296,040	$1,999,933,482	$183,049,229,521
at $800	$206,913,481,188	$2,285,638,265	$209,199,119,453
at $900	$232,777,666,337	$2,571,343,048	$235,349,009,384

For all the talk of American economic collapse internationally, U.S. gold reserves still far outstrip those of any other country (see accompanying chart).

1 oz. $50 Gold Eagle Bullion Coin

South Africa "Ounce"
Gold Bullion Coin

Saint-Gaudens
$20 Gold Coin

World gold reserves

One metric ton equals 32,150.7 troy ounces.
Source: World Gold Council, International Monetary Fund records.

	Metric tons	Troy ounces
United States	8,135.10	261,549,160
Germany	3,427.80	110,206,169
France	2,825.80	90,851,448
Italy	2,451.80	78,827,086
Switzerland	1,290.10	41,477,618
Japan	765.20	24,601,716
European Central Bank	719.90	23,145,289
Netherlands	694.90	22,341,521
China,	600.00	19,290,420
Spain	457.70	14,715,375
Taiwan	423.30	13,609,391
Portugal	417.50	13,422,917
Russia	386.90	12,439,106
India	357.70	11,500,305
Venezuela.	357.10	11,481,015
United Kingdom	310.80	9,992,438
Austria	302.50	9,725,587
Lebanon	286.80	9,220,821
Belgium	227.70	7,320,714
Total	24,438.60	785,718,097

The price of gold has been less stable since it was uncoupled from the dollar in 1968, but it has had some stability – if upward mobility – perhaps in part because the United States has about a third of the gold held by the top 20 gold-owning nations. That doesn't include the holdings of the International Monetary Fund, which has 3,217 tons of gold, or a little more than 100 million ounces of the metal. Since 1980 and its high of $800 an ounce, gold has generally traded at $300 to $450 an ounce, until 2006-08 when it doubled and continues to climb.

So which is the better investment – collectible gold coins or gold bullion?

I analyzed, not scientifically, several coins with more bullion value than numismatic value. That meant grades ran from about uncirculated to MS-63, but most were plain old MS-60.

The coins were an 1850-O gold $1, 1880-CC $5, 1932 $10 in MS-60, 1880-S $5 in MS-63, 1890 $2.50 in MS-60, 1925-D $2.50 in MS-60, 1880 $20 in MS-60, 1909-D $20 in AU-50, and a 1916-S $20 in MS-60.

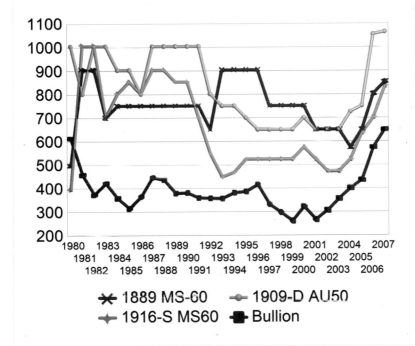

Double eagles vs Bullion

The accompanying graph shows bullion's average price from 1980 to 2007. (It's the lowest line on the chart.) There is no comparison with the trend line for the $20 coins; the small numismatic premium yields greater rewards. The bullion value is the floor, but the numismatic differential provides a greater rate of return. There are certainly other ups and downs and bumps on the coin prices, but even the 1909-D double eagle in grade about uncirculated charts its own course.

I also charted gold bullion, the Dow Jones industrial average, an MS-63 1921 Walking Liberty half dollar, an MS-60 1850-O gold $1, and an about-uncirculated 1880-CC gold $5. The Dow topping 14,000 in fall 2007 is a hard train for other investments to catch, but the coin results are far from shabby.

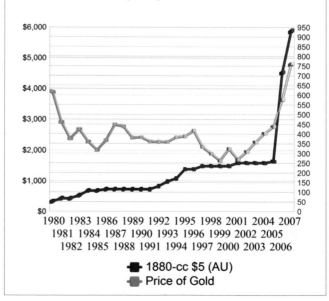

It's also interesting to look at proof gold American Eagle bullion coins, especially those with mintages below 10,000. They seem to afford a strong upside.

Proof gold American Eagle bullion coins

Date	Size	Total mintage limit	Proof mintage limit	Proof sales	Selling price
1998	Half ounce	32,000	7,000	5,806	$285
1998	One ounce	25,000	10,000	6,318	$570
1997	One ounce	38,000	8,000	6,339	$299
2001	Half ounce	32,000	7,000	6,676	$285
1999	Half ounce	32,000	7,000	6,956	$285
2002	Half ounce	32,000	7,000	6,967	$285
2000	Half ounce	32,000	7,000	6,979	$285
2003	Half ounce	29,000	8,000	7,758	$315
2002	Onc ounce	33,000	8,000	7,820	$570
2003	One ounce	29,000	8,000	7,832	$630
2004	Half ounce	33,000	8,000	7,835	$335
1999	One ounce	33,000	8,000	7,956	$570
2000	One ounce	33,000	8,000	7,958	$570
2001	One ounce	33,000	8,000	7,991	$570
1997	One ounce	45,000	10,000	8,029	$589
2004	One ounce	34,000	9,000	8,720	$675
2005	Half ounce	35,000	9,000	8,850	$360
2001	Quarter ounce	36,000	11,000	9,049	$150
2004	Quarter ounce	36,000	11,000	9,344	$175
2002	Quarter ounce	36,000	11,000	9,563	$150
2003	Quarter ounce	31,000	10,000	9,780	$165
2005	One ounce	36,000	10,000	9,785	$720
1997	Quarter ounce	45,000	15,000	9,800	$159
1998	Quarter ounce	36,000	11,000	9,935	$150

Those who thought gold's role in the monetary system or even the coin market was dead and buried need to re-think their position. A new era for gold may have begun.

The platinum touch

Platinum, the noble metal, remains on the move. It topped $1,400 an ounce in late 2007 and $2175 in early 2008 – up from $980 in January 2006 – and was relentless in its surge forward. More exotic and lesser known than gold, platinum has coinage, bullion and jewelry components, which drive its prices and profits. Even as gold hits 30-year highs, platinum seems to be on a different trajectory.

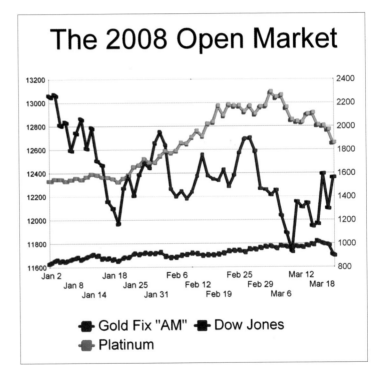

The 2008 Open Market

The dominant uses of platinum are in automotive catalytic converters and jewelry. Coins are a small but important component, affording fungibility and easy ownership in small quantities. Both are historically important to those seeking precious-metal holdings as a hedge against the unknown.

Singapore's *Business Times* says platinum prices are being buoyed because demand has exceeded supply for seven straight years. Most of the added demand came from the auto industry, which used almost 3.9 million ounces of platinum in 2006, up from about 1.9 million ounces in 2000. Several other business reporters suggest the Chinese jewelry market has also fueled the increase – as it well could have given the number of potential consumers in that expanding marketplace. Having recently visited China, I find credence in this report.

Platinum's price has allowed the mining industry to look at possible areas that previously would have been too expensive to mine.

One of the heaviest substances known (about 21 times the weight of water of the same volume), platinum, like gold and silver, is easy to shape, does not tarnish, and has been used for coinage for more than two centuries. It is No. 78 on the periodic table of elements. It has a high density of 21.5 grams per cubic centimeter and a melting point of 1,772 degrees centigrade (3,224 degrees Fahrenheit). Discovered by Italian scientist Julius Scaliger in 1557, platinum is also the most valuable "impurity" of most nickel deposits. The platinum group of metals, all derived from nickel mining, consists of ruthenium, palladium, osmium, and iridium.

Large quantities of platinum were not available until about 1750, when the Spaniards found it in Peru. They named it "platinum" from their word "plata," which is Spanish for silver. Miners frequently refer to it as "white gold" because it can be found in beds of gold-bearing sand.

Like gold, platinum can be found in nugget form. In 1843, a 21-pound lump was found in Russia, which issued platinum coinage from 1828 to 1845 in denominations of 3, 6 and 12 roubles.

1814 Platinum
Half Dollar "Judd 44"

Just 64 years after platinum's major commercial availability began, the U.S. Mint produced its first pattern coin from the metal – an 1814 half dollar (Judd No. 44). In his book *United States Pattern, Experi-*

mental & Trial Pieces, Dr. J. Hewitt Judd describes the coin as an experimental piece from regular dies.

Only three specimens are known. One is "defaced with 33 P's punched in the field on the obverse and the word 'Platina' is engraved on the reverse," Judd wrote. Earlier, Edgar H. Adams and William H. Woodin's book on patterns, *United States Pattern, Trial and Experimental Pieces* (1913), called this coin (AW No. 29) a unique specimen residing in the collection of Chicago beer baron Virgil Brand.

There was also an example without the punched letters (AW No. 30) in the Philadelphia Mint collection (now part of the Smithsonian Institution's national coin collection). Interestingly, Adams and Woodin wrote, "So far as is known ... there has never been any consideration of the use of the metal for coinage by the United States government." That changed, of course, with the advent of bullion coinage in 1997.

Judd, whose 1959 classic work mined previously ignored government records, located a reference to platinum in a letter dated March 19, 1836, to Treasury Secretary Levi Woodbury. The letter writer proposed platina coins, "like those issued by Russia."

In response to the letter, Mint Director Robert M. Patterson wrote, "This is no novelty to us. It would, indeed, require a change in the Constitution." Patterson incorrectly believed that the Constitution limited coinage metals to gold and silver.

It remained for researcher Andrew Pollack a generation later to nail down the contemporary nature of the platinum coin. He quoted a later Mint director, James Snowden, as being "familiar with the variety" and noted that Snowden "considered it an authentic experimental issue of the U.S. Mint."

Snowden's classic 1859 work, "A Description of Ancient and Modern Coins in the Cabinet of the United States," notes, "A platina piece struck from the dies for the legal half dollar of that year. It was an experiment, platina being then a new metal."

By comparing the die varieties used with A.C. Overton's classic reference *Early Half Dollar Die Varieties, 1794-1836*, Pollock concluded that Overton No. 107 is the die variety that was used, the same dies that were used for 1814 circulating coinage.

Although Russia is generally credited with producing the first modern platinum, a search through the archives of *The Numismatist*, monthly publication of the American Numismatic Association, found a reference in May 1917 to 2-real pieces of Peru dated 1729, struck in platinum on irregular planchets. The writer, William J. Hayes of the Anglo-Columbian Development Company, located the metal in Quibdo, capital of the Choco district, where it appears the coin was made casually from regular dies.

Whether other American coins were struck in platinum is questionable. The consensus is no, but in October 1939, ANA member M. Joe Murphy wrote that he purchased a platinum $5 pattern "possibly struck at the Mint by some employees for their own or other personal use around the date of 1869."

Since then, a review of literature and auction catalogs reveals a number of platinum coins available to collectors. One major source for information is the holdings of Edwards H. Metcalf, a California collector who acquired a penchant for platinum coinage in the 1940s. When his collection was sold by Superior Galleries in October 1987, it was probably the largest auction of platinum coinage ever held. The catalog is an invaluable resource for researchers.

"Continuing into the 1950s through the 1970s, he was very active as a buyer," the catalog says. "He added more platinum to his already impressive collection."

Among the Metcalf coins not generally known in platinum was a 25 dinars of Andorra dated 1960 (Krause-Mishler No. 1). Comparable issues are dated 1963, 1964 and 1965. Despite the rarity – just two 1960 examples are known in platinum – the prices re-

Russian 1828 platinum 3-rouble coin.

2006 proof platinum
American Eagle bullion coin.

alized were reasonable: $484 to $577.50. They would be much higher today, responding to the higher price of the metal.

Other platinum coins represented in the auction were from Bhutan (1966 set, one of 72 produced), Bolivia (8 escudos, 1782, Potosi mint), Colombia (8 escudos, 1801), Denmark, France, Germany-Prussia, Britain, Haiti, Hawaii, India, Iran, Isle of Man, Italy, Japan, Lesotho, Liechtenstein, Macao, Madagascar, Mexico, Monaco, Panama, Poland, Russia, Spain (4 and 8 escudos), Switzerland, Tonga, and Venezuela.

There are others that Metcalf missed, including Bhutan (5 sertums, 1979), Dominican Republic (a 1991 issue celebrating the 50th anniversary of the Columbian voyages), Turks and Caicos Islands (a commemorative honoring the 25th anniversary of the lunar landing and coin collecting, struck in collaboration with the ANA), and Portugal.

Today, many countries strike platinum commemorative coins and bullion coins. Among the latter are Canada, China, Mexico, Australia, and Isle of Man. The former Soviet Union also struck platinum bullion coins. Investment in platinum bullion coins is modest. The U.S. Mint sold about 19,000 ounces of platinum in 2004 and about 10,000 ounces in 2005. Preliminary 2006 sales surpassed those of 2005, no doubt because of the white-hot platinum market.

South Africa accounts for about two-thirds of the world's annual platinum production, about 3 million ounces annually. Significant amounts are also recovered in Russia (1 million ounces annually) and Canada as a byproduct of nickel mining. Other notable platinum producers are the United States, Finland, Australia, and the Philippines, according to the CPM Group, whose publications cover the field. U.S. production was about 6.5 percent of the world's newly mined platinum in 2005.

About 6.2 million ounces of platinum are used each year, according to Johnson Matthey, one of the oldest and largest dealers in the metal. In the early 1980s, about 17 percent of that use came from individual investment demand in the form of coins and bars. Johnson Matthey says the rate now is less than 2 percent, or under 120,000 ounces annually.

Canadian nickel ore principally comes from the International Nickel Company (Inco). Recently, the company was pulling 2,650 tons of nickel ore a day from its mine, which yielded about 200,000 ounces of platinum and 410,000 ounces of palladium.

Two percent of the world's newly mined platinum-group metals are derived mainly from Inco's Ontario ores, making Canada the world's the third largest producer, after South Africa and Russia. Inco produced about 380,000 ounces of platinum-group metals in one recent year.

The mathematics of all this is mind-boggling. A total of 967,250 tons (1.9 billion pounds) of ore (rock and metal) had to be moved to recover 16,666 pounds of platinum and about double that amount of palladium.

U.S. production of platinum and palladium is presently limited to the Stillwater and East Boulder mines in south-central Montana. Both are owned by Stillwater Mining Company. The two mines combined mined more than 1.2 million metric tons of ore and recovered more than 18,400 kilograms of palladium and platinum in 2005. Virtually all of its product is shipped to Europe for refining.

Small quantities of platinum-group metals were also recovered as byproducts of copper refining by companies in Texas and Utah. A total of 4,200 kilograms of platinum were mined in 2005.

Supplementing American needs last year were 89,000 kilograms of imported platinum. The U.S. Geological Survey says the imported metal came from South Africa (45 percent), United Kingdom (16 percent), Germany (12 percent), Canada (6 percent), and others (21 percent). Palladium imports came

2007 proof platinum American Eagle bullion coin.

2007 platinum American Eagle bullion coin.

from Russia (33 percent), South Africa (22 percent), United Kingdom (15 percent), Belgium (8 percent), and others (22 percent).

Bringing the metal to the surface is difficult; it is hardly alluvial. At Stillwater, a new shaft was sunk a third of a mile into the earth with the hope of doubling production.

If platinum is your investment vehicle, the platinum American Eagle bullion coins, struck since 1997, are attractive options, principally because mintages are so low. In 2007, mintage limit for the one-ounce platinum Eagle was only 6,000. As of September, only 1,356 had been sold. Imagine a U.S. coin with a mintage under 2,000.

The fractional platinum Eagles also had low numbers: half ounce, 606 sold of 5,000 authorized; quarter ounce, 719 of 5,000; and tenth ounce, 1,263 of 10,000 authorized. Even the uncirculated versions, struck at West Point with a "W" mint mark, have low mintages: 420 one-ounce coins, 358 half ounce, 487 quarter ounce, and 2,164 tenth ounce. Just 1,610 four-coin sets were produced as of September 2007.

The historic first striking of proof platinum Eagles took place May 1, 1997, at the West Point Mint. The first issue was a $100 coin containing just a tad over one troy ounce of 0.9995-fine metal. Philip N. Diehl, the 35th director of the U.S. Mint, used the large Grabener hydraulic press a few minutes after 11 a.m. to commence the striking, using 120 metric tons of pressure to strike a hand-fed blank platinum planchet.

Each proof one-ounce platinum Eagle is struck nine times – the most per-coin strikes ever for a large-issue program. Only one other coin in Mint history, which dates back to 1792, has taken a total of nine strikes to bring up the design – the famed ultrahigh-relief 1907 Saint-Gaudens gold $20, struck with 172 tons of pressure. That was for a circulation strike, and the demands of volume production precluded using so many blows on a hydraulic press intended for low-production medals. Thus the gold $20's relief was lowered for subsequent issues.

Double striking of proof coins is not unusual. The second strike typically fleshes out the metal flow and produces a razor-sharp rim and extraordinary design detail that collectors have come to prize. But platinum is not as dense and ductile as other coinage metals. To obtain the proof relief collectors value, at least six strikes are required when working with platinum. The seventh through ninth strikes bring out the intricate design details in John Mercanti's "Portrait of Liberty" on the obverse and Thomas Rogers Sr.'s "Soaring Bald Eagle" on the reverse.

Holding aloft the newly struck first coin, Diehl proclaimed, "The eagle soars!"

Limited space and time necessitated a small first-strike ceremony. Besides Diehl, attendees included Jacques Luben, executive director of Platinum Guild International, a key ally and sponsor of the platinum Eagle initiative; Kimberly Day, a PGI vice president for marketing; Christy Bidstrup, U.S. Mint program manager for the platinum Eagle program; Lynn Parish, the Mint's director of public affairs; and Harry "Jim" Edwards, Mint plant manager and a 40-year employee. My wife, Kathy, and I were also there and were privileged to strike one of the first coins.

The one-ounce platinum Eagle is 32.7 millimeters in diameter – about 2 millimeters larger than a half dollar – and about a tenth of an inch thick.

All of the metal presently comes from three sources: Johnson-Matthey, Englehard Corporation, and Tanaka (Tokyo). The Mint purchases pre-made blanks that are already "upset," which means they are rimmed and ready for striking.

After every 18 proof strikes, or two coins, the press operator took out a special cloth and poured lubrication fluid to clean the die. Estimated proof die life is 550 to 600 coins, about 5,000 strikes.

The author at West Point Mint undertaking a ceremonial "First Strike" of Platinum Eagles (1997). *Photo by Kathy Ganz*

Mintage

A maximum of 21,000 of the proof one-ounce pieces were slated for the first year of issue. Also scheduled for proof production were the half ounce (18,000 maximum mintage), quarter ounce (23,000 maximum mintage), and tenth ounce (38,000 maximum). By the end of the 10th year, the initially successful program was a shadow of its former self.

A total of 8,000 of the proof platinum one-ounce coins were reserved for four-coin sets priced at $1,350. Another 5,000 pieces were reserved for a set of gold, silver and platinum one-ounce Eagle bullion coins priced at $1,499.

That means only 8,000 of the one ounce pieces were available for sale individually at a price of $695. The proof half ounce was priced at $395, the quarter ounce at $199, and the tenth ounce at $99. (The combined price was a $28 savings over individual prices.)

The proof tenth ounce required two strikes from the Grabener press working at 50 tons of pressure; the quarter ounce took three swipes at 70 tons of pressure. The half ounce also takes as many as nine strikes at 100 tons to bring the 27-millimeter-diameter coin up to snuff.

The regular platinum Eagle bullion coins were struck twice to achieve an attractive design for the Statue of Liberty on the obverse and the soaring eagle on the reverse.

With this program, the United States joined a number of other countries that produce platinum, gold and silver bullion coins, as well as proof versions intended for collectors. They are all highly collectible.

The uncirculated platinum American Eagle bullion coins are also highly collectible. Of the 39 issues (tenth ounce, quarter ounce, half ounce, and one ounce) struck from 1997 to 2006, an impressive 19 of them have mintages below 20,000 pieces — an important mark – and six are below 10,000. Clearly, these are good representative numismatic coins sold under the guise of bullion.

Proof platinum American Eagle bullion coins require multiple strikes from the coining press.

Platinum American Eagle bullion coins with mintages under 20,000

2006	One ounce	6,000
2005	One ounce	6,310
2004	One ounce	7,009
2003	One ounce	8,007
2005	Half ounce	9,013
2006	Half ounce	9,602
2000	One ounce	10,003
2006	Tenth ounce	11,001
2002	One ounce	11,502
2006	Quarter ounce	12,001
2005	Quarter ounce	12,013
2001	Half ounce	12,815
2004	Half ounce	13,236
2005	Tenth ounce	14,013
2001	One ounce	14,070
2004	Tenth ounce	15,010
2003	Half ounce	17,409
2004	Quarter ounce	18,010
2000	Half ounce	18,892

1992 gold American Eagle bullion coin.

1/10 oz. ($10) Platinum Bullion Coin

1 oz. ($100) Platinum Bullion Coin

The platinum one-ounce American Eagle bullion coin has a $100 face value, is 1.287 inches in diameter, and weighs 1.0005 troy ounces. The half ounce has a $50 face value, is 1.063 inches in diameter, and weighs 0.5003 troy ounces. The quarter ounce has a face value of $25, is 0.866 inches in diameter, and weighs 0.2501 troy ounces. The tenth ounce has a $10 face value, is 0.650 inches in diameter, and weighs 0.10005 troy ounces. All are 0.9995 fine.

Except for the 1997 tenth ounce, all proof platinum Eagles have mintages under 20,000. The accompanying chart shows the best numismatic bets among those with mintages of about 10,000 or less.

Best bets: proof platinum American Eagle bullion coins

Date	Size	Total mintage limit	Proof mintage limit	Proof sales	Selling price
2004	Half ounce	13,000	3,000	1,073	$735
2004	Quarter ounce	15,000	5,000	1,203	$410
2005	Half ounce	13,000	3,000	1,572	$735
2003	Quarter ounce	15,000	5,000	1,748	$329
2003	Half ounce	13,000	3,000	1,835	$587
2001	Half ounce	13,000	3,000	1,910	$405
2002	Half ounce	13,000	3,000	2,010	$405
2004	One ounce	14,000	4,000	2,017	$1,345
2005	Quarter ounce	15,000	5,000	2,222	$410
2005	One ounce	14,000	4,000	2,232	$1,345
2001	Quarter ounce	15,000	5,000	2,503	$227
2000	Half ounce	13,000	3,000	2,514	$405
2002	Quarter ounce	15,000	5,000	2,520	$227
1999	Half ounce	14,000	4,000	2,525	$395
2001	One ounce	14,000	4,000	2,625	$740
2003	One ounce	14,000	4,000	2,950	$1,073
2002	One ounce	14,000	4,000	3,072	$740
2004	Tenth ounce	20,000	10,000	3,171	$210
2000	Quarter ounce	15,000	5,000	3,460	$227
2005	Tenth ounce	20,000	10,000	3,734	$210
1999	One ounce	15,000	5,000	3,785	$695
1998	Half ounce	14,000	4,000	3,910	$395
2000	One ounce	14,000	4,000	3,918	$740
2004	Four-coin set		10,000	3,990	$2,495
2003	Tenth ounce	20,000	10,000	4,238	$170
2005	Four-coin set		10,000	4,370	$2,495
1999	Quarter ounce	15,000	5,000	4,929	$199
1998	One ounce	15,000	5,000	4,947	$199
1998	One ounce	15,000	5,000	4,986	$695
2003	Four-coin set		10,000	5,296	$1,995
2002	Tenth ounce	20,000	10,000	5,603	$118
2001	Tenth ounce	25,000	15,000	5,830	$118
2001	Four-coin set		10,000	6,344	$1,375
2002	Four-coin set		10,000	6,762	$1,375
2000	Tenth ounce	25,000	15,000	7,116	$118
1997	Half ounce	18,000	10,000	7,460	$395
1997	One ounce	21,000	8,000	7,915	$695
1997	Four-coin set		8,000	7,971	$1,350
2000	Four-coin set		10,000	8,535	$1,375
1999	Four-coin set		10,000	8,578	$1,350
1998	Tenth ounce	20,000	10,000	9,921	$99
1998	Four-coin set		10,000	9,926	$1,350

The silver spoon

Silver, the backwater of precious metals, is in the spotlight. It more than doubled in price from January 2005 ($6.39 an ounce) to October 2007 ($13.66), and February 2008 ($20.00). It crossed the $12-an-ounce Rubicon in mid-April 2006 and then retreated slightly, but it began its upward march with a price of $13.01 an ounce at the start of 2007.

In 1986, gold was $368 an ounce, platinum was $466, and silver was $5.40. In the ensuing 20 years, gold rose more than 60 percent, platinum tripled in value, and silver weighed in with an impressive 152 percent gain – not bad for a historic also-ran.

Platinum's excuse for popularity – the Chinese market – isn't applicable to silver. Gold's gains as a historic asset of last resort also don't apply, since silver is an everyman's metal that is relatively precious but not scarce.

Instead, old-fashioned economics appear to be driving the metal's price: modest supply, fixed reserves, and the knowledge that some hot-shot investors have taken a gander at the metal. Their names are Warren Buffett, and his Berkshire-Hathaway group, and Microsoft's Bill Gates.

Two of America's wealthiest men evidently became players in the silver market a decade ago, and it is apparent with hindsight that investors and collectors may never look at the grayish precious metal the same way again. In 1998, Buffett, whose net worth Forbes has estimated in the billions of dollars, took a 130-million-ounce position, according to documents filed with the Securities and Exchange Commission. He was joined by Gates, who on September 28, 1999, bought a 10.3-percent position in Pan American Silver Corporation.

Buffett's position amounted to about a fifth of the world's supply and constituted an investment of about $900 million. Gates' share of the tiny silver-mining company based in Vancouver, British Columbia, cost him an estimated $15 million. That is a frac-

tion of Gates' fortune, which also has been estimated to be in the billions of dollars.

Silver consumption for industrial use has outstripped supply in recent years. In 2005, the Silver Institute reported that demand for the metal had grown by more than 5 percent and that more than 1.5 billion ounces were consumed but not replaced. A small but not insignificant portion went to produce commemorative coinage.

The U.S. Mint has contributed significantly to the distribution of silver into the marketplace. Since 1986, it has sold more than 136 million ounces in the form of its silver one-ounce American Eagle bullion coin. Most went to investors purchasing several ounces at a time. Several million more ounces in the form of proof silver Eagles can be added.

Buffett's announcement in 2005 that he had taken a position in silver was electrifying and caused the metal's price to rise nearly 20 percent before falling back. The Gates announcement caused silver to jump from $5.35 an ounce to $5.76 an ounce, with nearly 50,000 contracts for December 1999 delivery exchanged on the COMEX in New York.

One of the reasons silver has had such intense activity over the last several years – after a hiatus in the early 1980s – is that industrial demand has outstripped supply in virtually every year since 1990. Mine production hovers at 300 million to 400 million ounces a year, but a little-known fact is that except for the company Gates bought into, nearly all silver production is ancillary to other mining. It is a byproduct from mining some other metal that incidentally yields silver.

With this as a supply factor, demand has exceeded 500 million ounces annually since 1990 and in several years has gone over 600 million troy ounces to fuel the industrial economy. Silver is used in jewelry, silverware, electronics, batteries, and as a brazing alloy for mirrors.

Photography remains a key element in silver's overall demand. According to the CPM Group, a widely respected industry analyst, there are "no economical substitutes for silver-halide technology." The higher a film's quality and the faster its speed, the more silver is required. Digital photography has reduced demand for silver in this sector, but in recent years, the photographic industry still consumed more than 90 million ounces annually.

Silver and gold as coinage metals were rooted in the federal Constitution, which required that coinage be composed of both metals. Alexander Hamilton suggested a gold-to-silver value ratio of 15-to-1. (Today, it is about 54-to-1.) The debate over coinage was considerable, and the *Annals of Congress* – the *Congressional Record* of the Federalist period – recites it movingly.

Hamilton may have been correct in his economic analysis, but by the time legislation was enacted, the ratio on the world market had slipped to about 15.5-to-1. As a result, silver was too inexpensive. Coins that were produced promptly left circulation. The imbalance was not corrected until the early 1830s, which accounts for the modest availability of gold coinage from that era.

Neil Carothers, whose book *Fractional Money* remains a classic more than 75 years after it was published, calls the original U.S. coinage system (1792-1828) a "discreditable failure." The Spanish pillar dollar remained the principal unit of value in the country until the late 1850s. As Carothers succinctly put it, "Spanish coin could not be driven out until the mint provided domestic coins in abundance."

Numerous bills were introduced to abolish the U.S. Mint outright. The Mint's presence in Philadelphia was extended every two years, long after the capital moved to Washington. Out of caution, Congress refused to eliminate the Mint, but it didn't outlaw foreign coinage either.

Significantly, the ability to deposit gold and silver at the Mint and receive coinage in return remained – a problem that would come back to haunt the Mint

A CC mint mark (just above the letters "DO" in "Dollar") denote coinage produced at the Carson City Mint.

decades later. The bullion was deposited, and the Mint refined it for a modest charge and turned it into coin.

The Coinage Act of 1837 attempted to re-balanced the appropriate ratio. It priced gold at $20.67 an ounce and silver at $1.29 an ounce. Gold remained at the fixed number for nearly a century (it was re-valued in 1933 by President Roosevelt). Silver was less lucky.

By the late 1860s, a mint had already been authorized for Carson City, Nevada. Its first coinage came in 1870. The original intent may have been to exploit the Comstock Lode, discovered in 1859, and to produce gold coins from metal mined in the region. But by the early 1860s, Carothers claims, the Mint was functioning for the benefit of bullion dealers. The Mint's coinage simply disappeared as soon as it was released.

For two years prior to the Civil War (1859-1860), silver was priced at $1.21 an ounce, and the Mint freely accepted silver, which it turned into coin, at that rate. A decade later, a bullion dealer testified before Congress that, in 1863, he sold $2 million in U.S. coins abroad and made a profit of more than $100,000.

The Coinage Act of 1873 eliminated the ability to deposit silver at the Mint and receive coin in return. (It also removed the 0.5-percent seigniorage charge to convert gold bullion into coin.) As a practical matter, it demonetized silver and created a de facto gold standard.

Also resulting was a political crisis of significant proportion, principally because silver now began to slip in value as the Comstock Lode and other Western silver mines began to fully exploit their significant contents. The price of silver moved toward free-fall.

There have been spikes through the years. The Silver Purchase Act of 1890 (Sherman Act), the post-World War I silver melts and sales to India, the 1980 Hunt Brothers' attempt to corner the market, and even the 1998 Buffett move and 1999 Gates purchase are part of the legend of silver prices.

If Buffett's entry raised the market significantly, so did Gates' relatively minor purchase. In each case, the market reacted because it believed both men could be significant players in the long-term market.

Silver is still a long way from the $48 an ounce it achieved when the Hunt Brothers attempted to squeeze the market in 1980. At the time, silver coins of every description were being melted.

One intervening factor has been the U.S. Mint's silver American Eagle bullion coin program. Demand for the coins was so substantial that it drained America's once great silver reserves – the legislative source for the silver Eagle program. By early 2002, it was apparent that demand would drain the supply by mid-year. In a concentrated study of brinkmanship, the Senate and House of Representatives acted quickly during the last week of June 2002 to assure that supplies of the world's most popular silver bullion coin would continue. Congress agreed to allow the Treasury secretary to buy silver on the commodities market.

Congress has made it clear that it favors continuation of the silver Eagle program, which has generated more than $260 million in profits since 2000 and even more since its initiation in 1986.

Results of the recent price run can be seen in coin advertisements in hobby periodicals. Silver quarters (1964 and earlier), for example, weigh 6.25 grams and contain at least 0.180847 troy ounces of precious metal. With silver at $12 an ounce, that gives even a common 1964 quarter a base bullion value of $2.17.

A common-date Franklin half dollar has double the silver of a quarter – 0.36 troy ounces – making its bullion value alone worth $5. That means the days of buying Franklin halves in grade about uncirculated for under $5 a coin are probably a thing of the past.

Silver has a fascinating history of being a second-class metal. In 2008, it seems like a first-class investment.

Having fun collecting and investing

Coin collecting is fun.

Coin investing is lucrative.

Coin collections can be fun investments.

That, in substance, expresses the viewpoint of dozens of dealers and collectors surveyed by me though the years.

Dealer Harvey G. Stack, a former president of the Professional Numismatists Guild Inc., an industry trade group, remarked that although "not every investment in coins is a collection, every collection of coins is an investment." That remark is echoed by nearly everyone surveyed.

Happiness without investing in coins is still possible, and perhaps part of this gets back to the basics that attracted people to collecting a generation or more ago: the ability to search through pocket change and find something worth more than face value.

Silver has been gone from coins for more than 40 years, but there is still a wealth of material that can be found in pocket change, ranging from the 1989 quarter without the Philadelphia mint mark (estimated at $2 to $3 by error-coin collector Bill Fivaz) to a 1972 doubled-die cent – still findable and worth several hundred dollars.

Serious collectors should also consider modern commemorative coins. They shouldn't necessarily buy them from the U.S. Mint upon issue. They are frequently available on the aftermarket for less than the issue price, but that doesn't mean they can't be topical, fun and eventually lucrative.

The uncirculated versions almost always cost less than the proofs and usually have much lower mintages. That means they have considerable investment potential for the person willing to buy now and not sell in the foreseeable future.

Coin buyers who can afford to put away their purchases – to just enjoy them – will inevitably be the most rewarded, but that sometimes requires a strong pocketbook and, of course, a desire to be a collector, not a vest-pocket dealer.

Most of my coin purchases were paid for over time using current discretionary income. Until 1988, when I bought my last silver pattern, rare was the time I was not making monthly payments to a dealer for another Hawaiian commemorative half dollar. My approach was not unique. Famed collector John Jay Pittman built a world-class collection on a chemical engineer's salary from Eastman Kodak.

I liked to collect Hawaiian coins, but there are clearly other areas that be collected relatively inexpensively. Among them are rare-date coinage, low-mintage pieces, and (in the case of encapsulated coins) coins with low slab populations.

Low-mintage gold $5 and $10 coins seem worthwhile. The key to profitability is choosing well-circulated specimens. (That has the added incentive of removing from consideration 11-point uncirculated grading.)

Many pieces in grades fine, very fine and extremely fine – with mintages under 20,000 – are available at relatively modest prices. With gold hovering at $800 an ounce, a gold $10 contains 0.48 troy ounces of precious metal (about $400 worth).

1873-CC gold $10.

A Carson City Mint gold $10 can be purchased for about $150 to $300 more, with little downside and a high potential upside. The series is affordable and can be acquired over time at shows, shops, or through advertisements in *Numismatic News*.

It's surprising how modest prices are. In fact, if someone tried to put together more than one set, it would be difficult to acquire duplicates of some dates in circulated grades. The reason for this is the high melt rate for many gold coins. And in any event, low mintages to start guarantee that there cannot be many complete sets, no matter how diligent the search for the low-mintage pieces.

Modern proof sets, those since 1950, also offer finite supplies. Current-year sales supply the top end, but the finite supply at the bottom end dictates that there can never be as many as 100,000 complete sets.

Coin collecting is what you make of it. If the collector instinct is prominent, the investor aspect may come along without even considering whether an item will increase in value.

What seems clear, though, is that creative collecting will ultimately lead to a solid investment in coins, even if it is not the collector's intent. That is a lesson generations of coin collectors have learned, often to their amazement and surprise when either they or their heirs offer up a collection for sale.

The production of modern proof sets results in finite supplies of certain collectible coins.

Clad coinage

With more than 125 billion clad coins produced by the U.S. Mint since 1965, the Coinage Act of 1965 has gone on, to the surprise of almost everyone, to become one of the grandest and most successful experiments ever to result from a failure. The downside: an end to silver dimes, quarters, half dollars, and dollars produced for circulation.

The origins of clad coinage date back to a coin shortage of massive proportions. Congress initially responded by freezing the 1964 date on coins and eliminating mint marks in 1965. The reason for these moves is that coin collectors were blamed for the national coin shortage, and the Treasury Department sold Congress a bill of goods that if the coins weren't collectible, the shortage would go away of its own accord.

Shortages of dimes and quarters (which were always produced in much larger quantities than half dollars, a near orphan denomination) occurred for entirely different reasons. Principally, the coins' previous precious-metal content approached and then exceeded face value. The Rubicon, so to speak, was $1.29-an-ounce silver, which had not been much of a problem since the 1870s and the discovery of the Comstock Lode.

That took the wind out of silver's sales and prices, and increased seigniorage – the profit between a coin's face value and its precious-metal content – substantially. (From roughly 1874 until 1963, with a few exceptions right after World War I, silver stayed way below $1.29 an ounce.)

Speculators figured out what was happening and began to withdraw silver coinage from circulation, thus precipitating a shortage of small change. In 1960, for example, 90 million silver quarters were produced at the Philadelphia and Denver mints. The following year, 123 million coins were produced. By 1962, the Denver mint alone produced 127 million quarters and by 1964 1.2 billion quarters.

Originally, President Lyndon B. Johnson's proposal called for a 40-percent-silver clad half dollar.

Until 1965, a Washington quarter contained 0.1809 ounces of silver. Today the coin is struck in clad layers of 75-percent copper and 25-percent nickel bonded to a pure-copper core.

An artist's conception of what a 1964 Peace dollar would have looked like.

This proposal was rejected by the House Banking and Currency Committee, which called for identical clad composition of all subsidiary coinage. This in turn was rejected by the full House of Representatives, though not before at least one member called for the elimination of the half dollar. "The quarters and dimes are sufficient," he said. Eventually, silver-clad coinage for the half was accepted and used for the half dollar from 1965 to 1970.

On July 23, 1965, Congress passed Public Law 89-81, popularly known as the Coinage Act of 1965. The law achieved multiple purposes. First, it removed silver from circulating dimes and quarters. Second, it authorized the 40-percent-silver clad half dollar.

There was also a strong prohibition against issuance of a silver dollar, or any dollar coin, for the succeeding five years. This was in response to Johnson's having ordered the striking of 1964-dated Peace dollars at the Denver Mint in 1965 (a result of the date freeze then in effect).

By 1967, the coin shortage ended, and Congress directed that mint marks be restored. By 1968, the focus had moved from silver to gold, and the nation's 25-percent gold cover (backing Federal Reserve notes) was quietly removed, almost without a whimper.

As the 1960s ended, Congress passed the Coinage Act of 1970 on December 31. It authorized the Eisenhower dollar as a copper-nickel circulating coin and a silver-clad collectible. It also authorized the government's General Services Administration to sell 2.9 million Carson City silver dollars that had been gathering dust in Treasury vaults in Washington for almost a century.

The House Government Operations Committee offered a comprehensive overview of the coin crisis of the mid-1960s. It first studied Treasury Department efforts prior to its "crash coin production program." It then examined the program itself and finally reviewed the entire coin situation. It is a classic view of the ad-hoc problem-solving approach to the nation's coinage laws in recent times.

Although the Mint initially focused on $1.29-an-ounce silver, a more serious Rubicon would have been reached if silver had risen above $1.38 per ounce. That is the level at which the bullion value of subsidiary coins – dimes, quarters and half dollars – would be worth more than their face values.

Despite the Treasury Department's crash program, which included greatly expanded production and conservation, it became clear that even if the silver situation was minimized, the dime and quarter, in particular, would remain hostage to future silver price increases.

The first solution proposed was a reduction in the silver content of the subsidiary coinage and the dollar, later modified in part and adopted as the Coinage Act of 1965. A wiser overall approach, total elimination of silver from the dime and quarter, was subsequently adopted. Anticipating Gresham's law, the Mint then began withdrawing silver dimes and quarters from circulation.

Today, 40 years after the inflationary trend began to be of concern, the clad dimes and quarters circulate freely, and silver has been removed almost entirely from circulating coinage. The Bicentennial quarters, issued in 1975 and 1976, were originally expected to cause production problems, but efficient manufacturing and distribution minimized potential shortages of the denomination. It set the stage for the successful 50 State Quarters program, which began in 1999. The state quarters created a whole new generation of coin collectors.

There are some rarities among clad issues. Among them are the 1982 no-mint-mark dime, errors in the state-quarters series, a 1974-D doubled-die half dollar, some low-mintage proof pieces (such as the 1981-S Anthony dollar with a clear mint mark), and others. Some of these coins sell for thousands of dollars and potentially can be acquired in pocket change for face value.

Collecting clad coins is now a substantial undertaking, in part because of the state quarters, which include Philadelphia, Denver and San Francisco mint marks. But it is still an affordable and fun way to collect coins of the modern era.

1994-W World Cup Soccer commemorative gold $5.

Modern commemoratives

The era of modern commemorative coins has now passed the quarter-century mark, and it has had a remarkable ride. More than 58 million coins have been minted. More than 68 percent – 46.5 million pieces – of them are proofs; the remaining 12.2 million are uncirculated issues.

Approximately $8,200 worth of proof issues and $7,500 worth of uncirculated issues would have been required to buy complete sets as issued from the Mint (1982-2007), with total surcharges of about $1,550 going to worthy causes. More than $449 million in gross surcharges were raised from the numerous programs, and sales are estimated at more than $1.9 billion over the period – impressive statistics by any standard.

Now for the bad news.

A total of 252 million coins were authorized, so only 37.8 percent of the authorized mintages sold. There were sellouts for some, like the 2001 silver dollar with the old Buffalo nickel design. The World Cup soccer gold $5 coins provided the low end; only 2.24 percent of the maximum authorized mintage sold.

When I served on the Citizens Commemorative Coin Advisory Committee, I made a chart showing all of these statistics and regularly took it to meetings. It showed the more than 94 thematic issues, dates and designs, providing more than 180 different coins in uncirculated and proof versions. (My chart didn't account for mint marks.)

When the charting started, in 1993, computers were not that common and spreadsheets were a novelty on PCs. I used Quattro Pro for Windows to do the calculations and data manipulation because Michael Haynes, then the chief financial officer for Heritage Auction Galleries, used that program as chair of the ANA Finance Committee and convinced me to learn it.

More than a dozen years later, the chart has been added to, but the original data is still there with totaling formulas, averaging and other datum that can be extracted. The conclusions derived, not surprisingly, are not very different.

Uncirculated coins are not that popular; collectors prefer proofs by a 3-to-1 ratio. But the uncirculated versions still sell and actually have a better aftermarket. (The law of supply and demand still works in numismatics; namely, if there are fewer coins available in a particular type or condition, the price goes up.)

Despite their low sales, more than $88 million in surcharges have come from uncirculated coins. Evidence suggests that buyers of uncirculated versions are souvenir hunters rather than real collectors, though I myself prefer to collect the uncirculated versions because the designs are the same and the mintages are lower. There's a better upside.

Statistics also show that the high point in sales occurred more than 20 years ago with the copper-nickel Statue of Liberty half dollars. A total of 7.8 million was minted (88 percent of which were proofs) with a modest surcharge of $2 a coin (bringing in about $15.7 million in surcharges).

I was a consultant to the Statue of Liberty program and suggested that a copper-nickel half be added to the mix of a silver dollar and gold coin. I bet Dr. Stephen Brigandi, executive director of the Statue of Liberty Foundation, that it would be worthwhile for two reasons: first, to spread the message of freedom, and second, to raise funds.

It did both, and it remains the best-selling commemorative coin in American history, dating back to the 1892 Columbian Exposition series (4.9 million minted, 2.5 million pieces melted; but still impressive since the coins sold for double face value more than a century ago).

1992-W Columbus Quincentenary commemorative gold $5.

1996-W Smithsonian
Institution 150th Anniversary
commemorative gold $5.

1997-W Franklin Roosevelt
commemorative gold $5.

Only eight modern commemorative coins have sold as many as a million pieces, even though Congress routinely used to authorize more than that, if demand warranted. The eight coins are two Statue of Liberty issues (clad half dollar and silver dollar), the 1982 silver half dollar commemorating the 250th anniversary of George Washington's birth, the 1987 Constitution silver dollar, the 1983 and 1984 Olympic silver dollars, the 1988 Olympic silver dollar, and the 1990 Eisenhower Centennial silver dollar.

There are also eight coins whose total mintage, proof and uncirculated, are less than 50,000 each. These clinkers, in terms of demand, are not so bad on the secondary market. They include the 1997 Jackie Robinson gold $5, 1996 Smithsonian gold $5, 2003 First Flight gold $10, 2000 Library of Congress platinum-gold $10, 1997 Franklin D. Roosevelt gold $5, 1996 Olympics gold $5 with flag-bearers design, 2002 Salt Lake City Olympics gold $5, and the 1996 Olympics gold $5 with the cauldron-flame design.

Others are just in-between. More than 15 pieces have mintages under 100,000 (proof and uncirculated combined) and more than 30 are under 150,000. There 21 designs whose total mintage runs from 150,000 to 300,000, and 80 whose mintages are 500,000 or under. (There are at least 25 whose mintage is 500,000 or more.)

Recently, the Citizens Coin Advisory Committee came to the same conclusion as the old Commemorative Coin Advisory Committee: Less is more. Lower mintages that sell out are better than higher mintages that come up short.

It's hard to explain, but when I was on the CCAC, we haggled with Jefferson Monticello Foundation representatives over the total mintage for the 1993 Jefferson silver dollar. They wanted 750,000 pieces and were certain they would sell. I, on the other hand, was certain from looking at the charts, statistics and trend line that such sales were improbable. What I finally suggested, and what flew with the committee and ultimately Congress, was a 600,000 total.

For a long time, I've advocated that the U.S. Mint set up a fund to sop up the market excess and then periodically sell at wholesale (not individually) what it acquires. Because this market is thin, a modest annual expenditure in the $5 million range would easily sop up the excess at lower-than-issue price while serving as an exchange stabilization fund.

The Mint's profit would be $5 million less than the billions being made on seigniorage and coin sales, but it would prevent rapid declines in issue prices because there would be a buyer of last resort up to pre-set or pre-established levels.

A common complaint among collectors is that the Mint's products are available a year after issue at a fraction of the price. My good friend John Pittman used to buy one set from the Mint ("as a courtesy," as he put it), but he purchased more sets in the aftermarket at lower prices.

I recommend acquiring any U.S. Mint modern commemorative gold coin with a mintage under 30,000 or thereabouts. Uncirculated versions that meet the criterion are listed on the accompanying chart. Some proof versions also qualify. A second chart lists recommended silver dollars and silver and copper-nickel half dollars with mintages of about 55,000 or less. Again, the sorting is based on uncirculated versions, but proofs are also provided as a reference point.

2003-W First Flight Centennial commemorative gold $10.

1995-W Civil War commemorative gold $5.

1999-W George Washington Death Bicentennial
commemorative gold $5.

2006-S San Francisco Earthquake and Fire Centennial
commemorative gold $5.

U.S. Mint modern commemorative gold coins
with mintages under 30,000

Coin	Denomination	Total mintage	Proof	% proof	Uncirculated	% unc.
1997 Jackie Robinson	$5	29,748	24,546	82.51	5,202	17.49
2000 Library of Congress	$10	33,850	27,167	80.26	6,683	19.74
1996 Smithsonian	$5	30,840	21,772	70.60	9,068	29.40
1996 Olympics (flag bearers)	$5	42,060	32,886	78.19	9,174	21.81
1996 Olympics (cauldron flame)	$5	47,765	38,555	80.72	9,210	19.28
2003 First Flight	$10	31,975	21,846	68.32	10,129	31.68
2002 Olympics	$5	42,523	32,351	76.08	10,172	23.92
1995 Olympics (stadium)	$5	53,703	43,124	80.30	10,579	19.70
1997 Roosevelt	$5	41,368	29,474	71.25	11,894	28.75
1995 Civil War Battle	$5	67,981	55,246	81.27	12,735	18.73
1995 Olympics (torch runner)	$5	72,117	57,442	79.65	14,675	20.35
2006 San Francisco Old Mint	$5	51,200	35,841	70.00	15,359	30.00
2007 Jamestown	$5	60,805	43,609	71.72	17,196	28.28
1999 George Washington	$5	55,038	35,656	64.78	19,382	35.22
1994 World Cup	$5	112,066	89,614	79.97	22,447	20.03
1993 James Madison	$5	101,928	78,654	77.17	23,274	22.83
1994 World War II	$5	90,434	66,837	73.91	23,597	26.09
1992 Columbus	$5	104,065	79,734	76.62	24,331	23.38
1992 Olympics	$5	104,214	76,499	73.41	27,715	26.59

1994-P National Prisoner of War Museum commemorative silver dollar.

1994-P Vietnam Veterans Memorial commemorative silver dollar.

1994-P Women in Military Service Memorial commemorative silver dollar.

1995-S Civil War commemorative silver dollar.

U.S. Mint modern commemorative silver dollars and half dollars with mintages under 55,000

Coin	Denomination	Total mintage	Proof	% proof	Unc.	% unc.	% sold
1996 Olympics, Paralympics	$1	98,777	84,280	85.32	14,497	14.68	19.76
1996 Olympics (high jumper)	$1	140,199	124,502	88.80	15,697	11.20	14.02
1996 Olympics (tennis player)	$1	107,999	92,016	85.20	15,983	14.80	10.80
1996 Olympics (rowers)	$1	168,148	151,890	90.33	16,258	9.67	16.81
1995 Olympics (cyclists)	$1	138,457	118,795	85.80	19,662	14.20	18.46
1999 Dolley Madison	$1	181,195	158,247	87.34	22,948	12.66	36.24
1996 National Community Service	$1	125,043	101,543	81.21	23,500	18.79	25.01
1999 Yellowstone	$1	152,260	128,646	84.49	23,614	15.51	30.45
1995 Olympics (runners)	$1	161,731	136,935	84.67	24,796	15.33	21.56
2000 Leif Ericson	$1	86,762	58,612	67.55	28,150	32.45	17.35
1997 National Law Enforcement	$1	139,003	110,428	79.44	28,575	20.56	27.80
1995 Olympics, Paralympics	$1	166,986	138,337	82.84	28,649	17.16	22.26
1997 Jackie Robinson	$1	140,502	110,495	78.64	30,007	21.36	70.25
1996 Smithsonian	$1	160,382	129,152	80.53	31,230	19.47	24.67
2001 U.S. Capitol	$1	179,173	143,793	80.25	35,380	19.75	35.83
1998 Black Patriots	$1	112,280	75,070	66.86	37,210	33.14	22.46

1998-S Black Revolutionary War Patriots commemorative silver dollar.

1999-P Yellowstone commemorative silver dollar.

2003-P First Flight Centennial commemorative silver dollar.

2006-P Benjamin Franklin 300th Anniversary of Birth commemorative silver dollar, continental dollar reverse.

Coin	Denomination	Total mintage	Proof	% proof	Unc.	% unc.	% sold
2007 Little Rock	$1	127,698	89,742	70.28	37,956	29.72	25.54
2002 Olympics	$1	$1	202,986	163,773	80.68	39,213	19.32
1995 Olympics (gymnasts)	$1	225,173	182,676	81.13	42,497	18.87	30.02
2006 Ben Franklin (flying kite)	$1	130,000	85,000	65.38	45,000	34.62	32.50
2006 Ben Franklin (bust)	$1	130,000	85,000	65.38	45,000	34.62	32.50
1995 Civil War	$1	101,112	55,246	54.64	45,866	45.36	10.11
2005 John Marshall	$1	180,407	133,368	73.93	47,039	26.07	45.10
1996 Olympics (swimmer)	$0.50	163,848	114,315	69.77	49,533	30.23	5.46
1994 Women in Military	$1	259,100	207,200	79.97	51,900	20.03	51.82
2000 Library of Congress	$1	249,671	196,900	78.86	52,771	21.14	49.93
1996 Olympics (soccer players)	$0.50	175,248	122,412	69.85	52,836	30.15	8.76
2003 First Flight	$1	246,847	193,086	78.22	53,761	21.78	49.37
1994 Prisoner of War	$1	267,800	213,900	79.87	53,900	20.13	53.56
1994 Vietnam Veterans	$1	275,800	219,300	79.51	56,500	20.49	55.16

2006-P Benjamin Franklin 300th Anniversary of Birth commemorative silver dollar, "Join, or Die" reverse.

1999-P Dolley Madison commemorative silver dollar.

1997-P National Law Enforcement Officers Memorial commemorative silver dollar.

2000-P Leif Ericson commemorative silver dollar.

2001-P U.S. Capitol commemorative silver dollar.

Early proof sets

U.S. proof sets from 1858 to 1916, when coin collecting was in its infancy, offer the surest way to value the coin market over a long period and a solid collection that at once affords the ability to reap substantial financial rewards.

Measuring them objectively is difficult, for until recently, they were typically graded as a set, adjectively rather than numerically, and the runs of sets offered at auction are not uniform. The number of instances when complete early proof sets are offered are few and far between.

In 1961, Stack's offered the Howard Egolf collection of early proof sets (complete from 1859 to 1911 plus 1913 and 1915). The auction grossed $24,335. The median price of a set was $340, and the average price was $435.

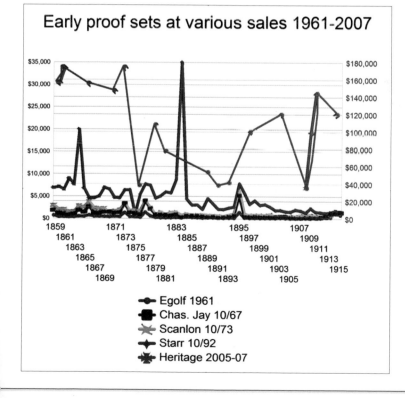

Early proof sets at various sales 1961-2007

- Egolf 1961
- Chas. Jay 10/67
- Scanlon 10/73
- Starr 10/92
- Heritage 2005-07

From 2005 to 2007, Heritage Auction Galleries sold (in several different sales) 17 old-time proof sets for a total of $324,230. The average price per set, $20,131, was almost equal to what Egolf's entire collection brought in 1961.

Virtually all early proof sets were assembled from individual coins by collectors, in contrast to the sealed, encapsulated sets produced by the Mint today. A century and a half ago, the Mint marketed individual coins and sets.

Individual proof coins are commonly available. Auctions often offer assembled subsidiary and minor coinage, together with the silver dollar, as a proof set. But major offerings of many old-time proof sets are rare today.

Coin collecting began in earnest in the United States in the late 1850s. One step that significantly helped foster the nascent hobby and bring it into its own was the 1858 recommendation of Mint melter and refiner James Booth to sell specimen coins irregularly produced by the Philadelphia Mint at a small premium. He called them "proofs," the term still used today.

Mint Director James Ross Snowden decided to sell minor and subsidiary specimen coinage as a set to collectors. The earliest of the sets consisted of seven coins – the cent, silver 3-cent, half dime, dime, quarter, half dollar, and dollar – bearing a face value of $1.94.

The set's selling price was $5.02. Of the $3.08 surcharge, just 8 cents went toward the cost of producing the coins. The remaining sum went toward the box that held them and a small profit for the Mint.

Originally, gold coins were omitted from the sets but were added later. They could be ordered individually or as a set consisting of the $1, $2.50, $3, $5, $10, and $20. Total face value was $41.50, and the sets sold for $43.

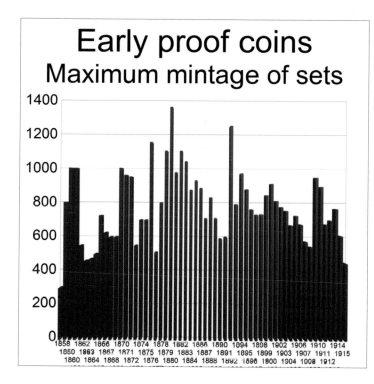

Early proof coins
Maximum mintage of sets

Mint production records for specimen or proof coins are spotty. By 1888, the procedure had been regularized sufficiently for Mint Superintendent Daniel Fox to state, "Silver sets are not separated. Proof sets are furnished of the current year only. The Mint has no Coins or Sets of back dates for sale."

By that same year, Mason & Company of Boston was already offering proof coins for sale on the after-market at modest price gains. For example, the 1865 2-cent was selling at 40 cents, the same price as the 1870 tuppence. The 1877 nickel 3-cent sold for $2, but all of the other nickel 3-cent coins from 1879 to 1888 sold for 25 cents.

The 1867 Shield nickel with rays – which brought $44,000 at Stack's 60th anniversary sale – sold for $2.50. More common coins, such as the proof 1879 nickel (estimated mintage, 3,200), sold for 12 cents.

Rare 1856 Flying Eagle Cent

Proof coinage has been part of our nation's numismatic history almost from the Mint's founding. The 1792 disme pattern coin, with some claim to come from Martha Washington's silver plate, may well have been the Mint's first specimen coin.

All proof coinage is struck on specially prepared planchets using highly polished dies of regular coinage design. The die is employed on a coining press; old-fashioned screw presses can be used as well as modern hydraulic presses. Proof coins are struck under far greater pressure than circulation strikes.

Few U.S. proof or specimen coins were produced prior to 1817. The Mint's screw presses at the time made proof production difficult. A fire at the Philadelphia Mint in 1816 resulted in a need for new equipment, which was capable of proof-coin production.

By the 1850s, proof coins were produced regularly. The 1856 Flying Eagle cent pattern was produced exclusively as a proof – though worn specimens that found their way into circulation are well known today. All are actually impaired proofs.

The Mint offered early sets to customers who frequently ordered by mail. Extensive correspondence from N.M. Kaufman, in which he requested the Mint send him proof sets via Adams Express, was discovered in the National Archives.

For some customers, such as T. Harrison Garrett, the Mint sent extended explanations. In 1880, Garrison transmitted two drafts totaling $51 to the Philadelphia Mint. On February 10, 1880, Superintendent A. Loudon Snowdon wrote that the Mint was sending by Adams Express an 1880 gold proof set (cost $43) and two silver sets (cost $4 each). (In the same letter, which Q. David Bowers published in his extensive book on the collection, Snowden revealed that the gold proof sets "were delivered to us just one hour ago.")

At that time, as now, Mint regulations required that the director approve prices for proof sets. The proof set of silver and minor coins cost $3, and a "minor coins proof set" was available at 12 cents.

The 1880 silver set (actually minor coins and silver) that John Work Garrett purchased was sold by Bowers & Ruddy in October 1980 during the dispersal of the fabulous collection that later resided at Johns Hopkins University. Bidding on the lot opened at $7,000 and immediately jumped to $15,000 on a floor bid. It was finally hammered down after nine other bids at $24,000 – a record that stood until October 1992, when the Floyd Starr set, also an original from the Mint, brought $26,100.

Many so-called "original" sets are typically repackaged from their original Mint shipping holdings. Determining their originality is based on a uniformity of color and toning. Trade dollars were always available as an extra piece.

Over the years, sets were broken up by collectors and dealers anxious for a particular date or denomination; other pieces were also added. Some coins are struck better than others, and some have hairlines resulting from bad cleaning of the dies or cleaning of the coins after striking. Thus, it is difficult to objectively compare sets that are not specifically pedigreed.

Despite this, it is instructive and useful to look at various significant sales of old-time proof sets to ascertain how the market overall has viewed them. The sets can be compared by date, and significantly, the average price per lot is a useful measure.

In 1961, the Howard Egolf sale was virtually complete in its issues from 1859 to 1915. Representative prices included $250 each for the 1892, 1894, 1897, 1900, 1901, 1904, and 1911 sets.

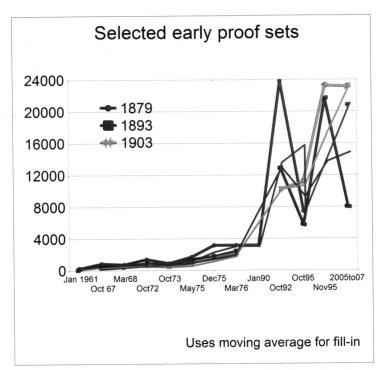

Selected early proof sets

- 1879
- 1893
- 1903

Uses moving average for fill-in

When Charles Jay's complete collection of early proof sets was sold by Stack's in October 1967, there was a significant change in the market. The average price per set was $1,205, and median price was $920. Nearly all of the sets had doubled in price in the intervening six years.

A half year later, Lester Merkin auctioned a significant offering of proof sets from 1877 to 1913. The results suggested a firming market and continued growth. And so it went through the years.

In October 1972, Stack's sold the S.S. Forrest collection of proof sets, which was also complete. George Scanlon's collection, also complete, was sold in October 1973. Prices in the Scanlon sale declined from those at the Forrest sale, but compared with 1967 or 1961, there were whopping gains.

Other sales were significant in 1975 and 1976. Bowers & Ruddy's Kensington collection, in 1975, was especially important because the sets were first auctioned individually and then re-sold as a single lot for more than $100,000. (The individual pieces and lots were re-offered at a 5-percent premium above the highest bids.)

The possible number of complete proof-set collections is quite low. Only 380 proof quarters and half dollars were produced in 1914, for example. Many otherwise complete collections lack this date. Egolf, for example, didn't have a complete 1914 set.

Floyd Starr's fabulous collection came to the auction block in 1992. It was truly an old-time proof-set collection from an old-time collector. Starr died almost 20 years earlier and had acquired these gems in a bygone era.

His proofs alone garnered $1.5 million – the most ever achieved for a complete run. They included an 1884 set, complete with the rare Trade dollar. The set brought a record price of $177,600.

Many of Starr's sets were original pieces with strong pedigrees, and the prices realized reflected that. Many of the proof coins and sets offered in Stack's 60th anniversary sale and at the Numisma '95 sale had pedigrees all their own.

To provide some measurement in recent times, Heritage Auction Galleries sales of 2005, 2006 and 2007 were added and analyzed. Although the Starr prices (based on condition) were significant, the Heritage coins were typically graded by the Professional Coin Grading Service or the Numismatic Guaranty Corporation and sold as sets or single coins combined. Individual coins in the 1860 set averaged proof-64, the 1897s averaged proof-65, and the 1910s averaged proof-66.

Setting a parameter for availability of these coins is difficult because Mint records are spotty. The late Walter Breen estimated that many existing coins are far below announced mintages because of subsequent meltings by the Mint. The 1859 set,

Proof Trade dollars are rare and seldom seen in year sets.

for example, has an official mintage of 800, but Stack's and Breen estimate that fewer than 100 sets exist.

A pedigreed 1859 set was offered at the 1976 American Numismatic Association convention auction, where it realized $4,250. In October 1995, the same set of seven coins brought $15,890, a threefold gain.

Another pedigreed set – an 1866 lacking the silver 3-cent – was offered at the same auction. It had previously sold in February 1966 at the C. Ramsey Bartlett collection auction for $2,700. In 1995, it fetched $11,426.50.

Not every set always goes up. An 1883 proof set, including the Trade dollar (a proof-only issue), traced its origins to the Century collection, which Superior Galleries sold in February 1992 for $52,800. The 1995 resale price was a respectable $30,222.50.

Another pedigreed piece was an 1885 proof set (lacking the elusive Trade dollar, of course), which brought $825 at a Stack's auction conducted in December 1964. In 1995, it jumped to $3,074.50, a 9-percent average annual rate of return.

The final pedigreed set in the 1995 offering was a 1901 consisting of six coins, cent through dollar, which traced its last sale back to the 1976 ANA convention. It sold for $1,900 then; in 1995, it crossed the block at $17,600, a hefty gain indeed.

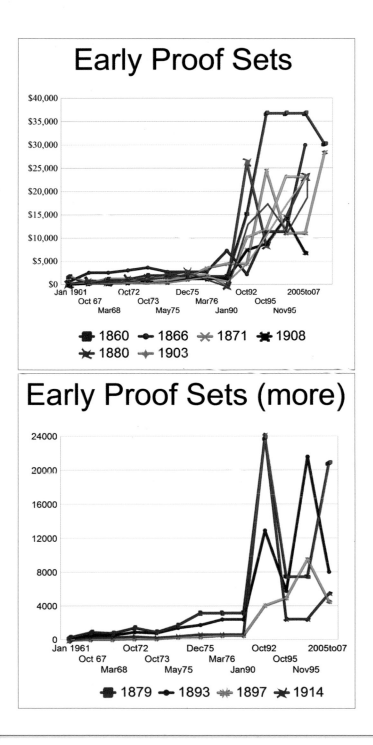

Early Proof Sets

| | 1860 | | 1866 | | 1871 | | 1908 |
| | 1880 | | 1903 |

Early Proof Sets (more)

| | 1879 | | 1893 | | 1897 | | 1914 |

Old Proof Set

The accompanying charts offer a glimpse of proof-set prices from a variety of sales since 1961. The coins, unless otherwise noted, have no particular provenance. Where there is a provenance, it is often startling. In 1976, for example, Johns Hopkins University sold off duplicates of the Garrett collection through Stack's. An 1862 proof set was included and brought $2,800. In March 2006, the identical set came back up at $13,225.

The accompanying charts also show mintages for early proof sets. They rarely max out as high as 1,500 pieces. In some cases, they are so low that assembly of sets is improbable. In some cases, fewer than 100 sets survive.

You can put together the sets coin by coin – a long-term but fun project. Or, you can watch for the infrequent postings of proof sets by major auction houses and compete for the coins you desire.

Old-time proof sets offer a unique view of the marketplace and the rare opportunity to compare prices of yesterday with those of today. That comparison has been favorable, making substantial profits for buyers and sellers.

Coins in pension funds

Coins in public pension funds, or for that matter private pension funds, are legal provided the applicable state law follows a "prudent man" rule. That is, any investment is legal provided a reasonably prudent person with knowledge of all the facts would comfortably make such an investment.

Recently, it was disclosed the Ohio Worker's Compensation Fund invested more than $50 million in rare coins as an alternative investment starting in 1998. This is not particularly surprising, since the Salomon Brothers surveys showed rare coins consistently outperformed many other investments and offered the possibility of high rates of return.

In the June 7, 2004, *Congressional Record*, Representative Marcy Kaptur of Ohio took to the House floor to denounce the fund's use of rare coins. "In Ohio," Kaptur said, "what is happening is that the Governor of our State has permitted millions and millions of dollars of workers' money from the Ohio Workers Compensation Fund to be invested in high-risk instruments, coins and we think perhaps what is called collectibles, although we are not sure yet. And these investments are ones that no other State in the Union has allowed."

With all due respect, the investment turned out to be sound. The numbers still make sense.

Since 1981 and the passage of Section 408(m) of the Internal Revenue Code, rare-coin investments in individual retirement accounts have been prohibited by legislatively declaring that the investments are taxable distributions, causing the holder all kinds of financial penalties.

But as long as a trustee for a private pension is satisfied that rare coins are prudent investments, not only has their use been appropriate, it has never been expressly disapproved. Ohio's theory evidently was that coins were a prudent diversification of assets – less than 1 percent of the worker's compensation

A Keogh favorite, pre-1991.

fund. Other individuals have done likewise – just not with their IRAs since 1981.

None of this guarantees that rare coins will go up in value or not lose their value; the same is true of stocks and bonds. The trustee's responsibility is to assure that the investments chosen have the opportunity for growth and that the choices have been carefully considered.

On August 15, 1981, Americans lost an important investment option – right to put rare coins and some other collectibles in self-directed IRAs and Keogh accounts (the 401(k) plans that are so popular among the self-employed and some businesses). Those involved in the coin market at the time remember the consequence: a precipitous decline in coin prices as a once fertile ground for placement of assets dried up.

For a number of years since, a coalition of interested parties, led by the Industry Council for Tangible Assets, has led the battle to overturn the 1981 legislation, which makes it useful to examine what brought about the prohibition and why the right should be restored.

Named for Representative Eugene Keogh of New York, Keogh accounts were intended to provide small businesses with the equivalent of a pension but without the heavy regulation that accompanies plans run by much larger companies. At one time, a proprietor could contribute up to $30,000 each year to such a plan and defer the tax due on the income until retirement or when funds were withdrawn from the account. The plans were designed to supplement pensions and Social Security, and severe penalties were imposed to make certain they were used as intended.

Still later, those who were not self-employed or were working for small companies that lacked pension plans were allowed to set up their own plans, known universally under the IRA acronym. Qualified individuals could set aside up to $2,000 a year, also as deferred income. (The limit is now $4,000 a year for individuals and $8,000 for a married couple filing jointly, whether or not both spouses work.) Under the Economic Growth and Tax Relief Reconciliation Act of 2001, these limits rise to $5,000 per person in 2008. For those over age 50, additional catch-up contributions of $1,000 are allowed.

Deferred compensation means the income isn't taxed until it is withdrawn, typically as part of an actuarially sound plan after a person reaches retirement age. The amount withdrawn is then taxed at current rates. Those who withdraw money prior to age 59 1/2 are subject to a tax penalty, in addition to regular income tax on the withdrawal, and are prohibited from making further contributions for five years.

Virtually all of the plans that were set up were self-directed, meaning the owner had the right to designate how the funds were invested. The choices were a simple bankbook, the equities (stock) market, corporate bonds, real-estate mortgages, real estate, collectibles, or virtually any other asset legal to own.

Wall Street's dirty little secret is that billions of dollars in self-directed plans went into the equities market. Buy-ins were cheap – the government was in essence a partner for the marginal tax rate –and there was no capital gains tax (because it is collected based only on distributions).

Now here's a novel result: The government sets up a system that allows investment virtually without regulation or taxation, and the equities market grows from a Dow Jones industrial average of 1,000 in 1972 to more than 13,000 in 2007.

The Tax Reform Economic Fiscal Responsibility Act of 1981 was genuine tax reform by the Reagan administration and substantially reduced the taxes that most Americans paid. It also placed coins on a list of prohibited assets for self-directed plans.

The following reasons were cited for the prohibition: The assets weren't productive and did not help the economy. The rationales were that the assets were risky and people shouldn't be able to keep a retirement asset in their homes, display it on their walls, or even enjoy it before they were taxed on it – the ultimate Puritan work ethic.

Who would have advocated the prohibition of collectibles – such as Oriental rugs, rare coins, and Scotch whisky – in retirement plans? Probably not rug manufacturers or antiques dealers. The distilled-spirits industry mostly likely didn't propose it either. Hmmm.

Penny stocks, which were highly volatile, were permitted in retirement accounts, even if it was likely that a pensioner would lose his shirt – and his underwear – before he saw a profit. Junk bonds, which promised high returns but had little collateral behind them and frequently could (and did) go into default, were eligible, too. And they were hyped to the max by securities salesmen.

Intelligent people can draw their own conclusions from the facts and arguments. Who sponsored the proposal probably doesn't matter anyway; they left no fingerprints, just a lot of circumstantial evidence.

The ban disrupted the coin market immediately, just as it would affect the real-estate market if the government said you could no longer buy and sell real estate in your own name, only corporately. Coin prices plummeted because major buyers – those with IRA and Keogh assets – were removed from the marketplace without warning and without replacement plans on the drawing board. (Non-self-directed plans can and still do include rare coins in their portfolios, but that requires an independent trustee to determine that it is prudent to do so and to assume liability if it is not. Some, but not many, are willing to make that choice; the State of Ohio, in the public sector, was one of them.)

About the only fortuitous result of this is that the National Association of Coin & Precious Metals Dealers was founded to help fight future assaults on the hobby, and later the Industry Council for Tangible Assets was born to have a permanent Washington presence. The NACPMD folded into ICTA a few years later, and since then, the Washington lobbying organization has saved the hobby's proverbial cookies on more than one occasion, including an IRS attack on broker reporting, which threatened the sale of even a simple Roosevelt dime.

The American Eagles still allowed in self-directed accounts.

In 1986, the U.S. Mint started selling gold and silver American Eagle bullion coins, and it occurred to the best and the brightest that the Mint's product line had a serious problem in the bullion-coin investment community: If a vendor sold 500 ounces of silver as a bar, it could be kept in an IRA or Keogh account. But the inclusion of 500 silver Eagle coins triggered all of the negative provisions of Section 408(m) of the Internal Revenue Code. These included considering the purchase a distribution – making it taxable, with penalties – and prohibiting future deposits for five years. As a result, there was pressure to change the law prohibiting coins in IRAs.

On October 11, 1986, the Tax Reform Act was passed, replete with an obscure provision that allowed American Eagle bullion coins to be placed in self-directed plans. The race was on to sell gold and silver Eagles, and sales soared to record highs. In 1986, the Mint sold 5.3 million ounces of silver in the form of Eagle bullion coins. The IRA addition came late in the fourth quarter of 1986. By 1987, sales soared to 11.4 million ounces.

In 1996, a platinum Eagle was authorized, but for obscure legal reasons, a tax bill had to be prepared to allow its inclusion in self-directed retirement plans. That happened, and as Goldline's Internet site remarks, "The United States government allows both proof and bullion American Eagles to be utilized in

The Silver Eagle inititally lost money. Today silver has gone over $20/oz. (3/08).

Individual Retirement Accounts (IRAs). Whether you prefer gold, silver, platinum, or a combination, these official U.S. coins can be added to your retirement savings by opening a new IRA account or transferring funds through an IRA rollover."

By the early 1990s, ICTA began to form a coalition designed to achieve equity and fairness in the treatment of the rare-coin industry, and it appears to have finally beaten back the non-productive-asset argument. Small wonder. What stock is ever productive? What stock purchase ever created a job, except in the same way that the sale of a rare coin creates one?

Yet in 2005 and thereafter, even as legislation has again been introduced annually to allow these self-directed plans to include rare coins, there remains a specter of prohibition. There are those who argue that rare coins have no business in a retirement account, that silver has proven to be a bad investment, that gold is speculative, and that rare coins can't be accurately valued and are prone to abuse.

The same can be said about stocks and bonds. Take a real blue chip, like IBM. I bought some shares in the 1980s when the stock was trading at about $89 a share. It promptly dropped to $67 a share (at which I bought still more).

That reminded me of the time I decided to add silver American Eagles to my retirement account as a hedge against inflation, as a strong affirmative statement that coins can be investment tools, and to practice what I preach. IBM went down still more, to $43 a share. The silver Eagles I bought declined less, but I still lost more than a dollar an ounce on several thousand ounces. IBM eventually began a profitable march toward $200 a share. (Fortunately for me, I sold my interest in IBM before its subsequent decline.)

Congress has asked what type of revenue is involved in the rare-coin field, and what was the total dollar volume of coins held in IRAs when they were permitted, from 1974 to 1981. Congress has also asked for a reasonable estimate of the ratio between coins and bullion, and other assets that were in IRAs and pension accounts during the same time.

The answers are elusive, but there are some guideposts. According to the *Mutual Fund Fact Book* and the Investment Company Institute of Washington, of $1.169 trillion in IRAs in 1995, 6 percent was in savings institutions (compared with 28 percent in 1985 and 54 percent in 1981). In 2005, the amount changed severalfold.

It is reasonable to conclude that 2008 will show another increase. Total assets in IRAs, according to the 2005 *Statistical Abstract of the United States*, exceeded $3 billion. Of this, most ($1.11 billion) is in securities, and $1.3 billion is in mutual funds. Banks and thrifts have $268 billion, or about 8.9 percent of the total.

As savings banks held fewer assets, commercial bank holdings have also declined, perhaps because some commercial institutions permit self-directed plans to make riskier investments, such as brokerage transactions, mortgages, and similar items.

Today, about 9 percent of IRA money is in commercial banks, compared with 12 percent in 1995 and 22.2 percent in 1981. The equities market has risen from a 1981 low of 9.9 percent to a 1995 high of about 35 percent, with 37 percent of that total in individual stocks and 43 percent in mutual funds.

Life insurance and credit unions took up 11 percent in 1995 (compared with 13.4 percent in 1981 and 10.4 percent in 2005). That means the remainder constitutes self-directed plans that can – even now – be in coins under narrow circumstances.

The 1997 *Statistical Abstract of the United States* estimates that in 1995, 36 percent of IRA assets were in self-directed plans, compared with no estimate in 1981, 14 percent in 1985, and 22 percent in 1990.

The 401(k) plans (which had $105 billion in assets in 1985, $300 billion in 1990, an estimated $675 billion in 1995, and $923 trillion in 2003) by contrast have only about 6 percent in assets other than equities, money markets, balanced accounts, bond funds, and stocks.

Although no one knows what volume of business the coin industry does, in the banner year of 1980, one of the largest coin and bullion houses apparently had about $800 million in sales. Another major house had $400 million in overall sales. The 10 largest firms probably had about $2 billion in sales, with the next 100 largest firms having another $1 billion in sales. That means, likely as not, numismatics in 1980 was a $3.5 billion business.

Of that gross, my best guess is that no more than a third, or about $1 billion, of 1980 sales was driven by the IRA benefits for bullion and gold. Some of that is still hidden in accounts (as it may lawfully be, so long as it was put in before August 1981). Rare coins and bullion "trapped" in IRAs are probably worth about $3 billion – a powerful sum considering that a buyer with even $1 million in fresh cash can substantially move an auction.

If purchasers in 1981 were 40 years old, they are about to turn 70, when the law requires that they start to dispose of IRA assets. That would be a second disruption to the market that could well be more dangerous than the original prohibition.

Although some members of Congress and some newspapers criticize coins as an investments, they are just as valid and prudent as stocks and bonds, including speculative issues. They have certainly brought impressive rates of return.

Investment choices are a conundrum. What's clear, however, is that rare coins are prudent choices but without the guarantee of a fixed rate of return. Good for some people, not so good for others.

GSA Silver Dollars

Over 2.9 million rare Carson City Silver Dollars were found in Treasury vaults and sold by the government in the 1970's.

Chapter 4

The 1794 Silver Dollar

Mintage: 1,758
Designer: Robert Scot
Diameter: 39-40 millimeters
Weight: About 26.96 grams
Composition: 89.24-percent silver, 10.76-percent copper
Total silver weight: 0.7737 ounces.

R are coins selling at rarified prices is a relatively new phenomenon. We speak of million-dollar coins today, but it was fall 1973 when Larry Goldberg, then of Superior Galleries, called me in the newsroom of *Numismatic News*, in Iola, Wisconsin, to announce with pride, and some measure of awe, "We just sold the first $100,000 coin."

That coin was an uncirculated 1794 silver dollar. (They weren't graded numerically for the most part back then. More about its contemporary grade later.). The coin actually brought $110,000 and was the first coin to officially sell at auction for six figures. It was purchased by television producer Ralph Andrews for his collection. The coin's pedigree was itself historic: Lord St. Oswald acquired it at the Philadelphia Mint on a visit shortly after its striking, on October 15, 1794.

In September 1973, Abner Kreisberg and Jerry Cohen (Quality Coins) sold a nice uncirculated specimen of the 1794 dollar for $51,000 – a record price – but that was no match for the pedigree of this coin.

Its earlier history did not portend its historic status. At Christie's sale of October 13, 1967, lot 138 was simply cataloged as "USA, dollar, 1794, a similar coin in mint state" to the preceding lot. Yes, two uncirculated 1794 dollars were offered, back to back, one a better class of uncirculated than the other.

"Light scratches on obverse" (planchet adjustment marks) and "some rim damage on the reverse" were noted, together with the opinion that it was "very well struck." It realized $11,500 at that sale. (The price was actually £4,000 British pounds for each of the coins.)

At the time of the 1967 sale, the coin commanded interest on both sides of the Atlantic. Dealer Norman Stack of Stack's Rare Coins flew from New York to London to bid on the coin. (This was before long-distance travel was commonplace. A business trip abroad was more likely to last several weeks rather than mere hours.)

1794 silver dollar.

Goldberg's announcement was a watershed, for it marked the beginning of consideration of numismatic items as investments worthy of attention from Wall Street types and others. Barely five years later, the Federal Reserve Bank of Boston used its prestigious *New England Economic Review* to quote the Salomon Brothers Survey of Tangible Assets to show that coins were indeed more than collectibles.

Of course, that's not the final story for 1794 dollars, a rare coin with a mintage of only 1,758. Perhaps as few as 150 pieces survive today.

Q. David Bowers, in his definitive *Complete Encyclopedia of U.S. Dollars* (1993) traces some of the subsequent history. In 1975, one example appeared in Bowers & Ruddy's Newport Collection sale (lot 371), where it realized $75,000. From there, it went to the block in heated competition.

By 1984, the Amon Carter specimen (originally purchased at the 1947 Will W. Neil collection sale conducted by B. Max Mehl for $1,250) hit the block in uncirculated condition (described as prooflike by cataloger Norman Stack). It was s significant event for the numismatic community.

Ed Milas of Rarcoa was in attendance and told me at the time that he had "$150,000 to bid and I thought that would take it." His presale estimate was $120,000, and he seemed confident. Bidder 187, Hugh Sconyers, instead took top honors at $240,000 ($264,000 with the buyer's premium).

The coin next showed up in the collection of Jimmy Hayes, who sold it through Stack's in October 1985 as Hayes prepared to run for Congress. Hayes was known for his eye for high-quality, better-graded material, and in this coin, he found a true mark.

David W. Akers attended that sale and spoke with me prior to the auction. He graded the coin MS-63+ and said that he came to the sale expecting to buy it. It opened at a respectable $75,000 from a mail bidder and moved rapidly in $5,000 increments to $80,000,

1794 Silver Dollar

A 125 year auction history

1794 Dollar (x-Adams, 1876)	
1876-1941 (same coin)	

$85,000 and then $90,000. Dealer Kevin Lipton jumped in with a bid of $100,000, and it was off to the races. When the smoke cleared minutes later, Akers had the winning bid at $200,000 ($220,000 with the buyer's premium). The coin's market was stabilizing but not moving steadily upward.

Another MS-63 specimen was the Amon Carter piece that showed up in Superior's sale of the Hoagie Carmichael collection in January 1986. It brought $209,000.

The companion Lord St. Oswald piece, sold to A.H. Baldwin and Lester Merkin on behalf of Ambassador and Mrs. R. Henry Norweb, was sold by Bowers and Merena in 1988. The price: $242,000. Bowers said it was a "toss-up" as to which of the two coins was better (at MS-63).

In 1995, Stack's sold another 1794 dollar (described as gem brilliant uncirculated) in its Numisma '95 venture with Akers and Rarcoa. The final bid: $577,500. Since 1995, a number of 1794 silver dollars have hit the market. Most have been in grades about uncirculated, extremely fine, or even fine. An uncirculated example, is rare in that superior state of preservation.

1794 Copper Pattern Dollar

If the 1794 silver dollar was a surprising coin to break the $100,000 mark, there were lots of guesses as to which coin would be the first to reach $1 million – either by private treaty or through auction. It almost made no difference what the coin was; it was the concept of getting there. There was plenty of speculation about when it would occur, what the coin would be, and whether the sale would be public or private.

By 1978, more than 15 coins had broached the $100,000 benchmark, and the race to $1 million was on. As the 20th century ended, the million-dollar barrier had been breached three times, once for a 1913 Liberty nickel ($1.485 million) and twice by different 1804 silver dollars ($1.815 million and $4.14 million).

Of considerable significance, beyond the one-shots, is that the overall market has risen. High-priced singular items, like a tide, have lifted the ocean of coin rarities. Thus, coin prices of $30,000 or higher are no longer the novelty that they were more than a quarter century ago.

Evidence indicates that all 1794 dollars were coined on October 15, 1794, from silver bullion deposited by David Rittenhouse, then U.S. Mint director and a prominent Philadelphia scientist. All of the 1794 silver dollars were delivered to Rittenhouse. Thus, all 1794 silver dollars can trace their pedigree to him. Rittenhouse passed them out to friends, many of whom kept them. Others were spent and circulated.

The silver bullion Rittenhouse deposited varied greatly in quality. There were many gas bubbles in the ingots. The bubbles caused laminations and planchet cracks, which plague approximately 30 percent of the 1794 dollar population. (A faint planchet crack through the 1 in the date can be seen on the 1794 dollar illustrated here.)

The 1794 silver dollar is an American classic. It was produced in our monetary system's first year of issue in extremely limited quantities. The total known population today is between 130 and 140 in all grades.

Selected 1794 silver-dollar sales

Provenance is designated by the letters A through N. For example, coin K starts its history with the Philip Straus auction, conducted by Stack's in 1959; continues with Bowers and Merena's McFarlane sale (1981); and, in several intermediate sales, was last sold by Stack's in 2007.

Sale date	Auctioneer, sale	Price
1876	Henry Adams, Cogan (A)	$80
1903	Spink, Murdoch (E)	$230
1906	Chapman, Major Wetmore (A)	$110
1910	Thomas Elder, Mougey (I)	$150
1912	Chapman, Earlc (E)	$620
1941	Mehl, Dunham (VF-30, Heritage, September 2002) (A)	$218
1945	Kosoff, Boyd (D)	$2,000
1945	Stack's, Hall (B)	$1,200
1946	Mehl, Atwater (E)	$1,575
1947	Mehl, Neil (L)	$1,250
1949	Kosoff-Kreisberg, ANA convention (D)	$1,800
1950	Stack's, fixcd-price list No. 47 (to B.M. Eubanks) (D)	$1,595
1956	Kelly, ANA convention	$8,000
1957	Stack's, Empire Collection (E)	$6,500
1958	Kosoff, ANA convention	$7,750
1959	Stack's, Straus (PCGS VF-30) (K)	$1,350
1963	Stack's, Walton collection (B)	$4,000
1967	Christie's (ex-St. Oswald) (M)	$11,500
1973	Bowers & Ruddy, Quality (D)	$51,000
1973	Superior (to Ralph Andrews)	$110,000
1974	Stack's, Groves (E)	$32,500
1974	Superior, Ruby (N)	$18,500
1975	Bowers and Merena (M)	$75,000
1975	Superior, ANA convention (C)	$11,000
1977	Superior, Davenport (C)	$9,750
1981	Bowers and Merena, McFarland (VF-30) (K)	$30,500
1981	Superior (C)	$29,500
1983	Heritage, Charlmont (D)	$121,000
1984	Stack's, Carter (PCGS specimen-66) (L)	$264,000
1985	Stack's, Hayes (PCGS-66)	$220,000

Sale date	Auctioneer, sale	Price
1986	Superior, Carmichael (L)	$209,000
1988	Superior, Auction '88 (VF-30) (K)	$27,500
1988	Bowers and Merena, Norweb (PCGS MS-63) (M)	$242,000
1989	Bowers and Merena, Albany (A)	$26,950
1992	Bowers and Merena, Somerset (D)	$115,500
1994	Heritage (ANACS XF-40) (C)	$31,900
1994	Heritage (PCGS VF-35) (N)	$33,550
1995	Stack's, Numisma '95 (D)	$577,500
1997	Superior, Gainsborough (VF-30) (K)	$39,600
1999	Bowers and Merena, Bass, (NGC MS-62) (E)	$241,500
2000	Bowers and Merena, Schwann (VG-8)	$34,500
2000	Superior, (cleaned and burnished XF-40)	$29,900
2001	Bowers and Merena, LaRiviere, (NGC AU-55) (F)	$132,500
2002	Bowers and Merena (ex-Quality Sale, 1978) (VF-20)	$66,700
2002	Heritage (PCGS VF-30) (B)	$92,000
2004	Heritage (SEGS AU-58) (B)	$115,000
2004	Heritage (VF-35) (N)	$33,550
2005	American Numismatic Rarities, Cardinal (NGC MS-64) (D)	$1,150,000
2005	Heritage (NGC MS-61) (E)	$747,500
2005	Heritage (NGC AU-55) (F)	$431,250
2005	Heritage (NCS VF-20, repaired)	$43,125
2006	Heritage, Long Beach (XF-45) (G)	$264,500
2006	Heritage (VG-10) (H)	$109,250
2006	Heritage (ex-Reiver), (NGC VF-25) (J)	$126,500
2006	Heritage (ANACS XF-40, damaged rim)	$69,000
2007	Heritage, Signature (VF-25)	$126,500
2007	Heritage, FUN, (NGC VF-35) (D)	$207,000
2007	Heritage, FUN (VF-25) (ex-Kelly, February 1964, lot 1028, Stack's; Robinson sale, February 1982, lot 1852; A & B Coins, Bob Cathcart; H.W. Blevins sale, June 1988, lot 3574, Superior; Jules Reiver, lot 23464, Heritage, January 2006; Luebke)	$126,500
2007	Stack's (VF-30) (K)	$207,000

1794 silver-dollar price history and comparative data

Sale date	Auctioneer, Sale	Price realized	Dow Jones*	Gold	CPI	Farmland	Platinum	Portfolio
1959	Stack's, Straus (PCGS VF-30)	$1,350	67	$35.00	28.92	$277	$80	1709
1981	Bowers and Merena, McFarland (VF-30)	$30,500	88	$459.61	90.9	$2,147	$446	60800
1988	Superior, Auction '88 (VF-30)	$27,500	217	$438.00	118.30	$1,254	$525	58800
1997	Superior, Gainsborough (VF-30)	$39,600	775	$335.00	159.9	$1,837	$388	80725
2007	Stack's (VF-30)	$207,500	1346	$664.00	202.8	$3,500	$1,307	170842
*One-tenth scale.								

This 1794 Silver Dollar, MS 61, sold for over $700,000 in a Heritage sale in 2005.

Chapter 5

1909-S "V.D.B." cent

Mintage: 484,000
Designer: Victor D. Brenner
Diameter: 19 millimeters
Weight: about 3.11 grams
Composition: 95-percent copper, 5-percent tin and zinc

From the day in August 1909 when the Old Granite Lady in San Francisco's financial district churned out its first Lincoln cent, the coin has been a leader in collections and as an investment. The initial investment – face value – was almost immediately returned. On August 10, 1909, *The New York Times* reported, "Small boys and other vendors, in Washington and other cities of the country are still making irregular sales of the coins at fancy prices. … It is estimated that the new issue has sold so far on the street at an average profit of 150 per cent, the coins going ordinarily two for 5 cents."

The Numismatist, the American Numismatic Association's monthly journal, reported prices as high as 25 cents.

Victor David Brenner's portrait of the martyred 16th U.S. president, Abraham Lincoln, was introduced into circulation in 1909. Its story began when President Theodore Roosevelt admired a bronze plaque with the Lincoln portrait by Brenner. This matured into a friendship between Roosevelt and Brenner, and a presidential invitation to redesign the cent, which could be done without congressional approval. Under an act of September 26, 1890, designs on coinage were required to remain stable for 25 years. In 1908, the cent, nickel, and silver dollar (which was not being coined at the time) were eligible to change.

Brenner submitted his first models to the Mint in early January 1909. He wrote Mint Director Frank A. Leach, "If it please you and the President as it is, or with some changes it would be ready for the 22nd of February. … I am working on the other models and improving them." Roosevelt left office on March 4, 1909.

Brenner thought the half dollar was more suitable for the design than the cent. He sent Leach by express four plaster casts, but noted, "I should consider it a privilege to have the cent … adopted during the president's administration whose time expires too soon."

Just days later, there was a changing of the guard as the Taft administration assumed office. William

1909-S "V.D.B." cent.

Howard Taft had already made clear, *The Numismatist* said, that the motto "In God We Trust" would appear on coinage, even though his mentor, Roosevelt, removed it from the 1907 Saint-Gaudens gold coinage, only to have Congress restore it.

Brenner's early design mimicked the French 2-franc coin, and Leach wrote to Treasury Secretary Franklin MacVeigh that to use the figure of Liberty on the reverse, "it seems to me, would destroy our license to use the Lincoln head, so desired, on the obverse side. The law does not provide for two impressions or figures emblematic of Liberty."

In February 1909, chief engraver Charles Barber weighed in by informing Brenner that the coin's field needed a fixed radius to accommodate the 120-coins-per-minute production rate. Although Barber had a reputation for being prickly with outside artists, a March 25, 1909, letter to acting Mint Director Robert Patterson asked that Brenner be allowed to look over reductions and "sharpen up some points that he may think have lost distinctness" in the reduction process. (He was looking to avoid assertions that the Mint "would not execute St. Gaudens' work as he desired.")

On August 4, 1909, *The New York Times* announced the arrival of the new "Lincoln pennies" with a description of the design elements, including the reverse: "Two conventional wheat stalks extend around the lettering and close to the base of the coin are the artist's initials 'V.D.B.' in minute type."

Referring overall to the design as "noteworthy for its simplicity of line," the *Times* was augmented by Cornelius Vermeule in *Numismatic Art in America* (1971), who refers to Brenner as having "succeeded in conveying the feeling that a photograph has been turned into a three-dimensional experience in metal."

The exquisitely bold portraiture and the simplistic reverse are representative of the coinage of that generation, which also yielded the Saint-Gaudens gold $20, Standing Liberty quarter, Walking Liberty half dollar, and Buffalo nickel.

The initials "V.D.B." on the reverse of a 1909 Lincoln cent represent the coin's designer, Victor David Brenner.

The prominence of the designer's initials caused consternation in a number of quarters. Within days of the coin's issue, Treasury Secretary Franklin MacVeigh ordered that they be changed to simple "B". Barber disingenuously suggested that this could lead people to conclude that the coin was his handiwork – adding that it would take two weeks to change the dies. So MacVeigh said the initials should be ground off and the spot left bare. Not until a year after Barber's death in 1917 were the initials restored, to a less prominent position on Lincoln's shoulder.

In less than a week in 1909, the San Francisco Mint operated its presses 67 hours to produce 484,000 Lincoln cents, the lowest circulating non-error coin mintage in the series. (By contrast, another key Lincoln, the 1914-D, has a mintage of 1.1 million.)

Between the Professional Coin Grading Service (8,900) and the Numismatic Guaranty Corporation (4,300), about 13,000 1909-S "V.D.B." cents have been encapsulated in all grades. Wholesale prices today range from about $500 in grade good to about $1,000 in grade extremely fine. PCGS-graded coins at the high end of

The Professional Coin Grading Service and the Numismatic Guaranty Corporation combined have graded and encapsulated about 13,000 1909-S "V.D.B." Lincoln cents.

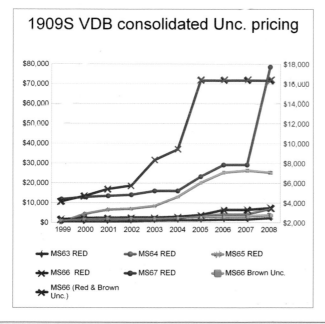

1909S VDB consolidated Unc. pricing

Legend:
- MS63 RED
- MS64 RED
- MS65 RED
- MS66 RED
- MS67 RED
- MS66 Brown Unc.
- MS66 (Red & Brown Unc.)

uncirculated (MS-67) are quoted at about $56,500; NGC-graded coins in the same grade are about $50,000. Numis-Media's market price for MS-67 is $60,000.

The more interesting grade for price analysis is MS-65 (gem uncirculated). (See accompanying chart.) In late 2007, an MS-65 1909-S "V.D.B." was worth $5,000-$7,000. Pries differ based on color (red costs more than brown).

The Lincoln cent is nearing its centennial year and will likely be replaced by at least four new Lincoln designs. More Lincoln cents have been produced than any other coin in history.

For 50 years, the original design held sway. The wheat stalks on the reverse were replaced by the Lincoln Memorial in 1959, but the obverse portrait remains more or less as Brenner originally designed it. Since its introduction in 1959, more than 360 billion Lincoln Memorial cents have been produced, accounting for 90 percent of the Mint's minor-coin production between 1793 and 1980. In any given year, the Lincoln cent accounts for more than 70 percent of the overall production at the Philadelphia, Denver, San Francisco, and West Point mints.

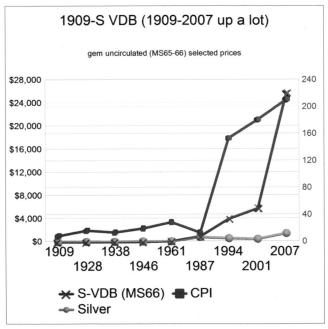

1909-S VDB (1909-2007 up a lot)

gem uncirculated (MS65-66) selected prices

When the Lincoln Memorial cent was authorized, all of the mints combined had already produced about 28 billion one-cent coins, starting with the first large cents in 1793 and continuing through December 31, 1958.

Through 1980, the last year that the Mint formally published an accounting, an eye-popping 174 billion cents were produced by all U.S. mints combined. Subtracting those issued prior to 1959 leaves an even more incredible 156 billion Lincoln Memorial cents. The coins bear two mint marks, D and S. One-cent coins produced at West Point and Philadelphia do not have mint marks. With 1980-2007 production added, more than 360 billion Lincoln cents have been coined since 1909.

Brenner was born in 1871 in Lithuania and, like many similar immigrants, came to the United States on a czarist passport. He married in 1913 in a wedding covered by *The New York Times* and produced more than 125 major commissions in his career. He is credited with starting modern presidential coin portraiture. He died after a long illness in 1924 at age 53. He is buried in Mount Judah Cemetery in Ridgewood, New York. His legacy is his coinage and art.

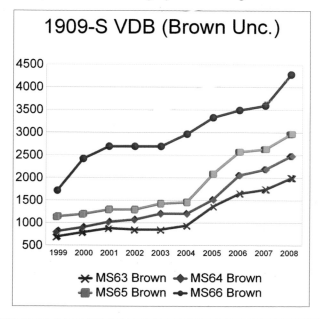

1909-S VDB (Brown Unc.)

Legend: MS63 Brown, MS64 Brown, MS65 Brown, MS66 Brown

The S mint mark is key

Warning: A 1909 cent with the initials "V.D.B." on the reverse is worth about $20 in uncirculated (MS-63) condition. About 28 million pieces were minted at the Philadelphia Mint (using no mint mark) before public outcry over the initials resulted in the Mint pulling the design and switching to one without the initials. A total of 72 million 1909 Lincoln cents without the mint mark were produced.

The San Francisco Mint, using the "S" mint mark, struck 484,000 1909 Lincoln cents with "V.D.B." on the reverse before it, too, switched over. It then struck 1.825 million 1909-S Lincoln cents without the initials.

In the 1960s, a technique was invented to drill out the rim of a genuine 1909 "V.D.B." cent, anneal it (heat it up to near the melting point of copper), insert a metal "S" into the drilled-out area, and push it through to the surface. Behold: a "perfect" 1909-S "V.D.B." cent and a change in value of more than a thousand dollars.

Chapter 6

1838-O Half Dollar

Estimated mintage: 20
Designer: Christian Gobrecht
Diameter: 30 millimeters
Weight: about 13.36 grams
Composition: 90-percent silver, 10-percent copper
Total silver weight: 0.3867 ounces

United States Mint records of the time deny this coin's existence. The 1854 *Annual Report of the Director of the Mint to the President*, and Congress, reports on the history of the New Orleans Mint from its founding in 1838. It says 205,000 dimes and 35,000 half dimes were minted, with a total face value of $22,500, but no half dollars, gold coins, or any other money. Those numbers are inaccurate. From other records, we can glean the difficult birth of one of America's rarest coins.

On April 11, 1838, two pairs of dies were shipped from the Philadelphia Mint to the New Orleans Mint in the French Quarter. They arrived May 3, 1838, and were used in January 1839 to "test the press" at New Orleans for a production run. The obverse dies were defaced on June 21, 1839; the reverse dies were still good and were held over for production.

1838-O half dollar.

Some believe the coin's mint mark was added to celebrate the first U.S. branch mint to commence operations. Regardless, the coins were struck in very limited quantity and have the unusual feature (for the time) of depicting the mint mark on the coin's obverse, above the date.

For many years, no one was quite sure about half dollars bearing that early mint mark. There are auction records as early as 1867, when Joseph Mickley's specimen sold for $2.75. In 2005, Heritage sold an example with a fabulous pedigree for $632,500. Its provenance went back to the 1953 Farish Baldenhofer sale by Stack's; then it hits a dead ends, as do so many histories of this coin.

The story of the 1838-O half dollar was published in *The Numismatist* in 1894, but few paid attention. Even into the 1950s, no one was able to nail down the mintage or number of coins that survived. John Haseltine, cataloging the Benson specimen for Bangs & Company in 1880, thought six pieces survived. Chapman, cataloging the Ferguson Haines specimen in 1888, believed only two other specimens were available. (The coin sold for $31.50.)

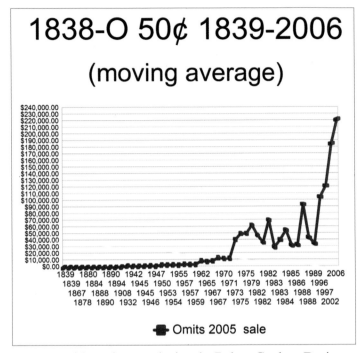

1838-O 50¢ 1839-2006
(moving average)

1839	1880	1890	1942	1947	1955	1962	1970	1975	1982	1985	1989	2006
1839	1884	1894	1945	1950	1957	1965	1971	1979	1983	1986	1996
1867	1888	1908	1945	1953	1957	1967	1973	1982	1983	1988	1997
1878	1890	1932	1946	1954	1959	1967	1975	1982	1984	1988	2002

Omits 2005 sale

David Proskey, cataloging the Robert Coulton Davis coin in 1889, noted lot 655 as follows: The mint mark was described as "O over [the] date." Significantly, he refers to a "letter from Dr. Bidell, Superintendent N[ew Orleans] Mint, 1838, which accompanied a similar Half Dollar, which it was stated that only four Half Dollars of this date and mintage were issued."

In 1903, Chapman sold a Rhode Island collector's specimen (lot 1149). He graded it very fine and stated his belief that "but four are known." Chapman guessed the coin would bring $200. He was close; the price realized was $195.

The Smithsonian Institution's national coin collection has a specimen that came from Mint coiner Rufus Tyler. So did Benjamin Franklin's grandson, who received one from Tyler in 1839 as a gift. In 1989, the last time it publicly sold, it went for more than $35,000.

In an Ed Frossard sale of the Friesner collection in 1894, the buyer, Augustus G. Heaton, received an explanatory letter with the lot: "The enclosed specimen coin of the U.S. branch mint at New Orleans presented to Pres. [Alexander] Bache [of Girard College, Philadelphia] by Rufus Tyler, the Coiner. It may be proper to state that not more than 20 pieces were struck with the half dollar dies of 1838." Bache was Franklin's grandson. He was named president of Girard College in 1836.

That coin's location was, for a long time, lost to history. In his pioneer research "Tracker: An Introduction to Pedigree Research," published in the American Numismatic Association centennial anthology in 1991, Carl Carlson makes a convincing case that the Bache coin went on to become the 1954 Anderson-du Pont specimen. Of the 20 coins believed minted, Carlson's research identifies 10 provenance trees. Since then, several other pedigrees have been recognized, if not sold. There are 11 known pieces today, and several identified but missing pieces.

Errors cropped in over the years when researchers either did not have the catalogs to cite or mis-read their notes. Howard Newcomb (1945) and Wayte Raymond (April 1946) both had 1838 proof half dollars but from the Philadelphia Mint, not New Orleans.

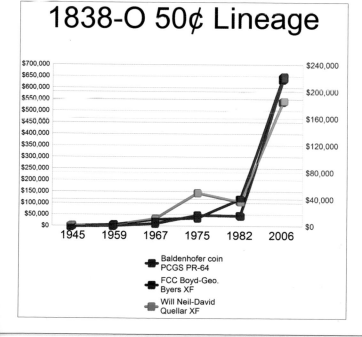

1838-O 50¢ Lineage

- Baldenhofer coin PCGS PR-64
- FCC Boyd-Geo. Byers XF
- Will Neil-David Quellar XF

Another frequent error originates from a Kreisberg-Schulman auction of February 1961. Thanks to Frank Campbell, American Numismatic Society librarian, that mystery was also solved. The auction catalog includes a proof 1838 half dollar. The confusion arises because another Kreisberg-Schulman sale, in April 1967, did have an 1838-O half dollar. According to that catalog, the coin was the Empire specimen, sold by Stack's Rare Coins in 1957.

The research also disclosed a recent finding by numismatic book dealer Karl Moulton, who found an 1838-O in a December 1880 Bangs & Company auction, cataloged by John Haseltine (son-in-law of William Idler, of 1804 silver-dollar fame). The cataloger says he knows of six 1838-O half dollars, but the coin remains an enigma. Its grade was termed "an uncirculated impression." That means it probably was not the Byers coin (XF) or the Ferguson Haines coin sold by Chapman (VF) and later termed XF by Kosoff in the F.C.C. Boyd sale (1945). Neither is it the James A. Stack (XF) specimen.

The accompany chart shows the currently assembled provenance trees of more than a dozen 1838-O half dollars with their dates of acquisition or sale. Credit goes to Carl Carlson, Stack's, and Heritage Rare Coin Galleries for their opinions, which I have synthesized. The concluding opinions are my own. For convenience, the coins are grouped first by pedigree family with grades. The prices included also provide a glimpse of the long-term market for the coins.

1838-O half-dollar provenance

Coin	Pedigree name	Source	Date sold	Price	Grade
1	Smithsonian	Mint Director Patterson	1839	$0.50	Proof (cleaned)
2	R. Coulton Davis	New York Coin & Stamp	1890	$51	"Almost proof"
2	Clapp, to Eliasberg	Stack's	1942	$1,500	Proof-60
2	Eliasberg	Bowers and Merena	1997	$121,000	NGC proof-64
3	Adolph Menjou	Kosoff	1950	$3,400	Brilliant proof
3	Cox	Stack's	1962	$9,500	
3	Century collection	Paramount	1965	$8,250	
3	Robison	Stack's	1982	$70,000	Proof
4	Mickley	Woodward	1867	$2.75	
4	Clemens	Cogan	1878	$15	
4	Frossard	Frossard	1884	$63	
4	Parmelee	New York Coin & Stamp	1890	$23.50	
4	Wilson	Elder	1908	$570	
4	Norweb	Bowers and Merena	1988	$93,500	Proof
5	Ryan	Mehl	1945	$1,875	XF
5	Neil collection	Mehl	1947	$1,600	Proof
5	James A. Stack	Stack's	1975	$50,000	XF
5	1982 ANA sale	Heritage	1982	$37,000	
5	Auction '84	Rarcoa	1984	$55,000	Proof
5	Quellar	Stack's	2002	$184,000	
6	Atwater	Mehl	1946	$2,200	PCGS proof-63
6	Hawn	Stack's	1973	$41,000	Brilliant proof
6	Auction '79	Superior	1979	$62,500	Proof-60
6	Pryor	Bowers and Merena	1996	$104,500	PCGS proof-63
6	Long Beach	Heritage	2008	$632,500	PCGS MS-63
7	Baldenhofer	Stack's	1955	$3,200	PCGS proof-64
7	Pelletreau	Stack's	1959	$4,000	
7	Jay	Stack's	1967	$14,000	
7	Clark	Stack's	1975	$50,000	
7	Bryan	NASCA	1977	Unsold	
7	Auction '82	Paramount	1982	$47,500	PCGS proof-63
7	Heritage	Heritage	2005	$632,500	PCGS proof-64
10	Haines	Chapman	1888	$31.50	VF
10	Chapman	Chapman	1903	$195	
10	Boyd	Kosoff	1945	$1,600	XF-45

Coin	Pedigree name	Source	Date sold	Price	Grade
10	Empire collection (Cass)	Chapman	1957	$4,000	XF
10	Cohen	Kreisberg-Schulman	1967	$9,250	
10	Kreisberg (mail-bid sale)	Kreisberg	1970	$12,750	
11	Guggenheimer	Stack's	1953	$3,400	
11	1971 ANA sale	Stack's	1971	$13,000	XF
11	Oviedo	Stack's	1983	$40,700	XF
11	Byers	Stack's	2006	$220,000	XF
12	Bache	Mint coiner	1839	$0.50	
12	Friesner	Frossard	1894	$113	
12	Newcomer	Mehl	1932	$2,000	
12	Anderson-du Pont	Stack's	1954	$3,500	
12	1957 ANA sale	Federal Coin Exchange	1957	$4,450	
12	1983 ANA sale	Kagin	1983	$29,700	AU
12	Robertson	Mid American	1985	$32,500	
12	1986 ANA sale	Kagin	1986	$33,000	
12	Blevin	Superior	1988	$44,000	
12	Landmark collections	Bowers and Merena	1989	$35,200	
12	Vintage Auctions	Vintage Auctions	1989	$40,700	XF-45
Unassigned	Benson	Bangs & Co.	1880	$23.50	
8	du Pont	Stolen	1967		
9	Pennsylvania estate	Fire victim (per Bowers)	1950s		

The coins' states of preservation in the chart differ, yet all started as specimens or proofs. The worst subsequent impairments resulted in extremely fine; the best is proof-64. There are minor discrepancies as to how the coins are described. In the World's Greatest Collection auction, Boyd's coin was described as VF to XF. Stack's catalogued the Byers coin as XF. PCGS has graded five 1838-O half dollars: two as proof-63, two as proof-64, and one as XF-40. NGC has encapsulated four coins: two as proof-63 and two as proof-64.

In his book *United States Dimes, Quarters and Half Dollars: An Action Guide for the Collector and Investor* (1986), Q. David Bowers discloses the probable fate of another 1838-O half dollar: lost in a fire, with its young owner, on the Philadelphia Main Line around 1960. In an article for Bowers and Merena's *Rare Coin Review* (spring 1989), researcher Tom LaMarre recalls that the October 5, 1967, robbery of Willis H. du Pont in Miami scored two 1804 silver dollars and one 1838-O "uncirculated" coin. About nine specimens, then, are numbered but unaccounted for.

There is also a confusion about one lineage. The World's Greatest Collection, which Abe Kosoff sold for F.C.C. Boyd in 1945, is credited as the source for the Guggenheimer specimen, sold by Stack's in 1953. Boyd's coin was off the market for many years but has since re-surfaced. Carlson says it went to an Eastern collector, then to Stack's 1971 ANA convention sale, and on to the Oviedo sale by Stack's in 1983. Off the market for many years again, it resurfaced in the 2006 sale of the George Byers collection with an impressive price lift to $220,000.

At one time, Colonel "Ned" Green, son of Wall Street "witch" Hetty Green, owned seven of the specimens. Researcher Walter Breen's careful tracing shows that at one time Green owned all of the following coins (some comparative prices are shown for convenience):

– The Adolphe Menjou specimen, sold by Kosoff in 1950 for an amazing $3,400.

– The James A. Stack specimen, which his estate sold through Stack's (no relation) in 1975 for $50,000.

– The Atwater specimen, later owned by Reed Hawn and sold in 1973 for $43,000.

– The Baldenhofer specimen, which found its way into the 1967 Charles Jay collection sale and sold for $14,000.

– The Boyd specimen, sold for $1,600 in 1945 as part of the "World's Greatest Collection."

– The Anderson-du Pont specimen, which brought $3,500 in 1954.

– The Empire specimen, owned by Charles Cass and sold for $4,000 in 1957.

Alas, there are no public records of the prices Green paid or the prices at which he sold the coins.

The 1838-O half dollar may not be in Mint director's reports, but it has definitely been a prominent player in the coin market.

1838-O half dollar.

Chapter 7

1913 Liberty Nickel

Mintage: 5
Designer: Charles E. Barber
Diameter: 21.2 millimeters
Weight: about 5 grams
Composition: 75-percent copper, 25-percent nickel

T his coin is a perennial favorite among collectors because it has a real story to tell. It's a story of fakery at the highest levels, deceit at the U.S. Mint, false advertising, and a king who was so wealthy that he forgot he already had bought one when he acquired another.

It's also about a young St. Louis attorney who once owned all five of them and about purchases, sales, and trades that are all fascinating. It involves a veritable who's who of 20th-century numismatics, during which time one man – dealer B. Max Mehl of Forth Worth, Texas – spent millions of dollars advertising that he would pay $50 for the coin, knowing full well his fortune was safe. And it was, until King Farouk of Egypt tried to return his duplicate, leaving Mehl with the equivalent of "tag, you're it."

Although Mehl in this instance knew where one of five 1913 Liberty nickels were, the public was blissfully unaware. So Mehl continued to advertise heavily that he would pay $50 for the 5-cent coin – building an army of future coin collectors in the process.

So look people did, buying Mehl's *Star Coin Encyclopedia* in the process and allowing Mehl to build his business into one of the most profitable mail-order-sales outlets in the world. By the time the story was over, one of these coins became the first to sell for six figures (though not at public auction). It also was the "star" of an episode of a popular television show, *Hawaii Five-0,* a police drama. The episode's plot centered on the coin's theft by a character played by Victor Buono.

There's even the story of an owner using a 1913 Liberty nickel to flip for bar bets. Another group of owners left their coin lying on the floor of a closet because they presumed it to be counterfeit. Dealer George Walton, who died in 1962 in an auto accident while en route to a coin show, had an altered date, in addition to his genuine 1913 Liberty nickel, and kept it when it was "fun" to sport a counterfeit.

1913 Liberty nickel.

More than 40 years after he died, it became known by a select few that the coin his heirs owned was the genuine one.

Welcome to the world of the 1913 Liberty nickel. All five coins' provenance goes back to Samuel Brown, who worked at the Philadelphia Mint for a decade (from December 18, 1903, to November 14, 1913) as assistant curator of the Mint cabinet. (His actual title was assistant shopkeeper, and his honorarium was $2,000 a year.) Brown was a serious enough collector that he attended the 1908 American Numismatic Association convention at the Hotel Stenton in Philadelphia (September 28 to October 2). He became a member and was assigned membership No. 808.

By the start of the Roaring '20s, Brown lived in North Tonawanda, New York. He became the city's mayor and received presidentail appointments to the 1924 and 1925 Assay Commission. But in 1920, Brown, who earlier had been a clerk to the Mint's cabinet (sometimes in a position referred to as shopkeeper at an annual salary of $1,000), took a small advertisement, about a twelfth of a page, in *The Numismatist*, the ANA's monthly journal. The ad on page 513 was simple: "Wanted 1913 Liberty Head Nickel in proof condition, if possible. Will pay $500 cash for one." It was followed by Brown's name and address.

The sum offered, $500, was a lot of money. A news item just a few pages earlier reported prices realized from Henry Chapman's October 4, 1919, auction. A 1796 half dollar, 16 stars, grade very fine, went for $166. A 1797 gold $5, 15 stars, grade very fine, was listed at $413.50. On the following page were prices realized from a Lyman Low sale of October 3, 1919. Among the results was $6.10 for a 1793 chain cent, "America" variety, grade very good.

Of course, Brown had no interest in buying additional 1913 Liberty nickels because he already had five of them. Rather, he wanted a cover story for how he acquired them and why he was selling them at $600 apiece (to make a "small" profit). Brown showed up at the 1920 ANA convention in Chicago, where he displayed the coin. August Wagner of Philadelphia next had the coins in a set for $2,000; an ad in *The Numismatist* confirms it. Wagner received offers of $600 per coin.

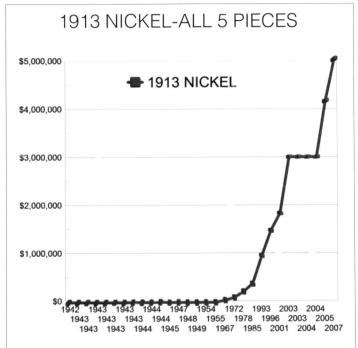

1913 NICKEL-ALL 5 PIECES

By mid-1924, the transfer was complete; Colonel Ned Green became the owner of all of the known 1913 Liberty nickels. Green owned the coins until his death in 1936. They stayed in the estate until Eric P. Newman and Burdette Johnson became the owners at a cost of $2,000 for the set of five. It took the estate about six years to sell.

It's here that the pedigrees start to get confusing, as dealer Abe Kosoff, who was involved in a number of the transactions, could readily attest. Paul Montgomery and his colleagues trace the pedigrees in their book *Million Dollar Nickels: Mysteries of the 1913 Liberty Head Nickels* (2005). Q. David Bowers also weighs in with an 18,000-word description of the 1913 Liberty nickel in Stack's January 2007 Florida United Numismatists convention auction catalog.

Newman sold the best of the five to Kosoff in 1949 for $2,350. The coin was a true gem. (Much later, the Professional Coin Grading Service graded it proof-66. The second best is a PCGS proof-64. The others go down as far as grade extremely fine for the McDermott specimen.) Kosoff marked up the coin about 5 percent and sold it to Baltimore industrialist Louis Eliasberg Sr. Eliasberg held the coin until his death in 1976. It was in the Eliasberg estate until 1993, when it was sold at auction.

Dealer Jay Parrino, who had a fine eye and good merchandising techniques, held it in inventory for several years. In 2001, he sold it at Superior Galleries' ANA convention auction, where (as lot 728, now graded PCGS proof-66) Dwight Manley was the buyer at $1.84 million. Manley held the coin for about two years and then negotiated a sale to Edward Lee, a well-known New Hampshire dealer, for around $3 million.

In 2005, Lee sold it to Legend Numismatics for $4.15 million, and in January 2007 at the FUN show, Stack's offered the coin (lot 1599) with a $3.22 million reserve. It did not sell then, but later in the year, Legend negotiated a sale to a California collector, through dealer Ron Gillio of Santa Barbara, California, for $5 million.

The 1913 Liberty nickel with the longest history and most number of sales is the Reed Hawn and Dr. Jerry Buss specimen. Newman and Johnson sold this coin, later graded PCGS proof-64, to Ohio dealer James Kelly. In 1943, Kelly sold it to Fred Olsen for $900.

Mehl sold Olsen's collection in a mail-bid sale. King Farouk won the lot, No. 1551, at $3,750 on November 7, 1944. When he bought the coin, His Majesty forgot that he was in the process of acquiring what we know today as the Smithsonian, or Norweb, specimen. Farouk returned the coin to Mehl, who returned the coin to the king, who, for some reason still unknown today, sent it to Henry Grunthal, American Numismatic Society curator. Grunthal also dealt in coins with Edward Gans (no relation to the author) in a firm known as Numismatic Fine Arts (no relation to the firm Bruce McNall founded decades later in Beverly Hills, California).

Gans cataloged the coin and reported a sale, but in fact the minimum was not met and the coin returned to Mehl again. He placed it in the Will W. Neil collection auction in 1947, and a nibble was obtained on June 17, 1947, from Edwin Hydeman, who bid $3,750 for lot 2798.

Hydeman held the coin until 1961, when Kosoff sold his collection. The 1913 Liberty nickel did not sell – a failure again to meet a reserve (a common problem with this coin through its history). Unlike many other numismatic rarities, this particular coin makes out better in private-treaty sales.

Kosoff kept the coin in his vaults for Hydeman for 11 years, when he finally brokered a deal with World Wide Coin Investments in Atlanta. Kosoff sold World Wide the "King of Coins," an 1804 silver dollar, and the "Queen of Coins," the 1913 Liberty nickel, for the then unheard-of price of $180,000. The 1913 nickel was ascribed the lion's share of the transaction at $100,000, the first coin to claim crossing that Rubicon. (The 1794 silver dollar, sold by Superior Galleries in 1973, was the first coin to realize six figures at auction.)

John Hamrick bought the 1913 Liberty nickel and promptly set out to make the coin that was already famous into a legend. It was cleverly worked into the script of *Hawaii Five-O,* which aired from 1968 to 1980 on CBS. Titled "The $100,000 Nickel," episode No. 136 aired December 11, 1973. The plot: A thief known for using sleight of hand, played by Buono, is hired to steal the coin.

With this show, the coin had finally come into its own.

Actor Victor Buono examines the 1913 Liberty nickel that starred in an episode of Hawaii Five-O. *World Wide Coin Investments, 1973*

In 1978, Dr. Jerry Buss, owner of the National Basketball Association's Los Angeles Lakers, acquired the coin. The sale of his collection in 1985 was a major event, and the price realized for the 1913 nickel was $385,000. The buyer was Texan Reed Hawn, a well-known collector whose name appears on the ownership registry of an 1804 silver dollar (Mickley specimen, sold in 1993), the 1838-O half dollar (the Atwater-Hawn specimen, sold in 1973), and other rarities. Hawn served on the Citizens Commemorative Coin Advisory Committee during the Clinton administration and has a discerning eye for great rarities in coins as well as Arabian horses.

Stack's sold Hawn's specimen in 1993 for $962,500. The buyer was Dwight Manley, who, as a youth, attended ANA summer seminars on scholarship. He later became a full-time coin dealer and then a megastar sports agent as president of United Sports Agency, which represents NBA players.

Manley held his 1913 nickel until 2003, when he negotiated a sale to Legend Numismatics for a shade less than $3 million. Legend, in turn, sold it to Donald Doyle of Blanchard & Company in 2004 for $3 million. It then went to a Blanchard customer and remains privately owned, owner undisclosed.

Simplest of the pedigrees, but also the most complicated, is the Walton family coin. It went from Newman to James Kelly in 1943 for around $900. That same year, Kelly sold it to Dr. Conway Bolt for $2,450, and in 1945, Bolt sold it for $3,750. The buyer was either Walton or a family with the last name of Reynolds, as in tobacco. For years, Walton claimed Reynolds owned it and he "borrowed" it. It is known that Walton had a counterfeit coin made – a 1910 nickel tooled into a 1913 – which he also showed on occasion.

In 1962, Walton died in an auto accident, scattering his coins on the roadside. The Associated Press filed a short story that went national: "Coin Collector Killed; Car Crash Victim Was on Way to Exhibit his Collection" was the headline in *The New York Times* of March 11, 1962 (page 76, news section). The county coroner took charge of the $250,000 collection, but the 1913 Liberty nickel Walton was known to carry with him was nowhere to be found.

His heirs found one in the closet of his home. They brought it to a well-known coin dealer in New York along with the rest of Walton's collection, which was put up for auction in 1963. Their conclusion: The coin was counterfeit, though well struck. The fact that Walton also had a tooled nickel may have contributed to this conclusion. So may have the Reynolds part of his story, too, which we know today was a cover story. In his 2007 analysis, Q. David Bowers notes the Reynolds family denies any acquaintance with the coin.

Fast forward to 2003. The ANA held its annual convention, the "World's Fair of Money," in Baltimore's Inner Harbor. Donn Pearlman – a former reporter for WBBM radio in Chicago, a former ANA board member, and now a public-relations guru – suggested exhibiting the four known examples of the 1913 nickel and sponsoring a national contest to find the missing fifth example. Pearlman was harkening back to the days when B. Max Mehl offered $50 for the coin, only with higher stakes.

Four of the five fabled 1913 Liberty nickels were scheduled to make a historic, once-in-a-lifetime joint appearance at the convention, July 30 to August 3 that year. Also scheduled to appear was Newman's specially made holder that once housed all five of the now multimillion-dollar coins, which he had retained all those years.

ANA museum curator Douglas Mudd was quoted as saying, "While the original story is simple, the who, how and why are unknown, as is the location of the fifth famed nickel that has been missing since at least the 1960s – maybe longer."

The four coins consisted of (1) Manley's specimen, (2) the specimen sold in a private transaction by Legend Numismatics in 2002 (the *Hawaii Five-O* coin), (3) the Smithsonian specimen (former King Farouk collection), and (4) the ANA museum specimen. The last coin was once owned by Milwaukee dealer James V. McDermott, who generously passed it around to strangers he met in taverns. Aubrey and Adeline Bebec purchased it from McDermott, and they generously donated it to the ANA musem.

Meanwhile, a nationwide search for the missing 1913 Liberty nickel was launched in May 2003 by Bowers and Merena Galleries, the year's official auctioneer for the ANA convention sale. The auctioneer offered at least $1 million for the lost coin.

For years, numismatists speculated that the missing quint, last seen when it was sold in 1946, vanished in the 1962 automobile accident. Research leading up to the 2003 convention, however, cast serious doubt on that story's credibility.

"I felt my numismatic life was complete just seeing one of these coins," said ANA President John Wilson. "Bringing them together is beyond my wildest dreams. On behalf of the ANA and collectors everywhere, I want to extend my sincerest appreciation and gratitude to all those who made this unbelievable exhibit possible."

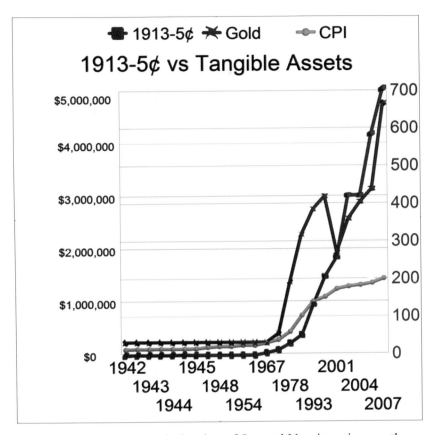

1913-5¢ vs Tangible Assets

Legend: 1913-5¢ · Gold · CPI

Laurie Sperber of Legend Numismatics was the first to offer her 1913 Liberty nickel for exhibit at the show. Beth Deisher, editor of *Coin World*, then posed the idea of bringing the other three known specimens together. Manley, the Smithsonian and the ANA then all agreed to display their respective specimens. Newman then offered his historic holder that once housed all five coins. Diamond International Galleries of Timonium, Maryland, loaned the exhibit cases for the show, and Paul Montgomery, president of Bowers and Merena Galleries, came up with the reward for the missing nickel. Pearlman pulled it all together, enlisting David Hall and Collectors Universe (PCGS' parent company) to help fund the reward.

"The first response was from David Hall, who said, 'Hell, I'd pay 10 grand just to be the first to see that 1913 nickel,'" Pearlman said. "I asked, 'Is that part of the deal?' He said, 'Yes.' So I drafted a news release that Bowers and Merena would be offering a minimum of a $1 million reward and David Hall was offering $10,000 just to be the first to see it."

The offer seemed destined for great publicity but no payout. After all, the coin had been missing for more than 40 years.

But there was a surprise ending: A newspaper reporter in North Carolina contacted Walton's heirs. They had what they thought was the counterfeit coin but were persuaded to bring it to the big show. Walton's heirs were startled when the experts – who had the four other originals with which to compare it – declared the coin genuine.

Hall was out 10 grand. But Bowers and Merena was spared a million bucks, because the coin remains a treasure in the Walton family. In 2008, it marks 63 years in the same family – a record for this and perhaps any other major rarity.

"The 40-year mystery is finally solved," Hall said. "The discovery of this famous coin is a historic event and we are thrilled to be a part of both the determination of authenticity and the celebration that is following. Participation by both PCGS and Bowers and Merena in this rare coin discovery underscores the leadership, expertise and prominence that the Collectors Universe brands bring to the world of collecting and authentication."

The accompany chart shows the provenance of the five known specimens. (Rumors of a sixth have long been discarded.) A arbitrary pedigree name has been assigned to each one. Samuel Brown, August Wagner, and Colonel Ned Green are in each chain. The subsequent owners, dates of acquisition, price when known, and a grade consensus are listed.

1913 Liberty nickel provenance

Pedigree	Owner	Buyer	Sale date	Grade	Price
1,2,3,4,5	Samuel Brown	August Wagner	1920		
1,2,3,4,5	August Wagner	Ned Green (died 1936)	1924		
1,2,3,4,5	Green estate	Newman-Johnson	1942		$400
1	F.C.C. Boyd	Kosoff-Kreisberg	1943		$900
1	Abe Kosoff	King Farouk	1944		$9,999 (estimated)
1	King Farouk	Egyptian government	1944	Proof	$2,750
1	Egyptian government	Kaplan-Kosoff	1954		$3,940
1	Kaplan-Kosoff	Emery May Norweb	1955		$3,940
1	Norweb family	Smithsonian	1978		$225,000
2	Newman-Johnson	Abe Kosoff	1948		$2,350
2	Abe Kosoff	Louis Eliasberg	1949		$2,468
2	Eliasberg estate	Jay Parrino	1996	PCGS proof-66	$1,485,000
2	Jay Parrino	Dwight Manley	2001	PCGS proof-66	$1,840,000
2	Dwight Manley	Ed Lee	2003	PCGS proof-66	$3,000,000
2	Ed Lee	Legend Numismatics	2005	PCGS proof-66	$4,150,000
2	Legend Numismatics	Ron Gillio for a California collector	2007	PCGS proof-66	$5,000,000
3	Newman-Johnson	James Kelly	1943		$900
3	James Kelly	Fred Olsen	1943		$900
3	Fred Olsen	King Farouk	1944		$3,750
3	King Farouk	B. Max Mehl	1946		
3	King Farouk	Henry Grunthal	1946		
3	Henry Grunthal	King Farouk	1946		

Pedigree	Owner	Buyer	Sale date	Grade	Price
3	King Farouk	B. Max Mehl	1947		
3	B. Max Mehl	Will W. Neil	1947		
3	Will W. Neil	Edwin Hydeman	1947	Specimen; Uncirculated	$3,750
3	Edwin Hydeman	Abe Kosoff	1961		
3	Abe Kosoff	World Wide Coin Investments	1972		$100,000
3	World Wide Coin Investments	Various, to Superior Galleries	1978		
3	Superior Galleries	Dr. Jerry Buss	1978		
3	Dr Jerry Buss	Reed Hawn	1985	PCGS proof-64	$385,000
3	Reed Hawn	Dwight Manley	1993	PCGS proof-64	$962,500
3	Dwight Manley	Legend Numismatics	2003	PCGS proof-64	$3,000,000
3	Legend Numismatics	Blanchard	2004	PCGS proof-64	$3,000,000
3	Blanchard (Don Doyle)	Midwestern collector	2004	PCGS proof-64	$3,000,000
4	Newman-Johnson	James Kelly	1943	Breen: Uncirculated	$900
4	James Kelly	Dr. Conway Bolt	1943		$2,450
4	Dr. Conway Bolt	George Walton	1945		$3,750
4	Walton family		1963		
5	Newman-Johnson	James Kelly	1943		$900
5	James Kelly	J.V. McDermott	1943	Extremely fine	$900
5	J.V. McDermott	Aubrey & Adeline Bebee	1967		$46,000
5	Aubrey & Adeline Bebee	ANA museum	1989	NGC proof-55	

Chapter 8

1946-P War Nickel

Mintage: unknown; probably fewer than 100
Designer: Felix Schlag
Diameter: 21.2 millimeters
Weight: About 5 grams
Composition: 56-percent copper, 35-percent silver, 9-percent manganese
Total silver weight: 0.0563 troy ounces

1946-P war nickel.

There's treasure to be found in pocket change – still! The coins can be worn; the important thing is that they are still around and can be found. The proof: war nickels, that well-known series of silver-based 5-cent coins first struck in 1942 with oversized mint marks on the reverse. Until recently, collectors thought the series ended in 1945.

Sparking the excitement was the discovery of a 1946 silver war nickel in pocket change in the San Francisco Bay area. It was authenticated and encapsulated by the Professional Coin Grading Service with a grade of fine-12.

Burton Blumert of Camino Coin Company in Burlingame, California, reported the discovery. He's a longtime dealer whose other accomplishments include launching the first coin-dealer Teletype network two generations ago and later founding the National Association of Coin & Precious Metals Dealers. The NACPMD later merged with the Industry Council for Tangible Assets, but not before it began lobbying Congress to the benefit of coin collectors.

Blumert said a dealer friend, Carter Collins of Collectible Coins in Mill Valley, California, was searching through a coffee can full of war nickels to fill a client's order when he saw the unusual coin that had the right color, wear and style of a war nickel but the "wrong" date, 1946, instead of the 1942-1945 dates.

Collins brought the oddity to the attention of Blumert, who was convinced it was genuine but wanted further confirmation. Blumert asked Fred Weinberg of Encino, California, a well-known error specialist, to examine the coin. After a brief look-see, Weinberg was also convinced and recommended that the coin be encapsulated by PCGS, which would also opine on its genuineness and grade. The PCGS Web site confirms that the service has encapsulated only one 1946 nickel.

The coin, which was placed in a PCGS holder mislabeled MS-12 (for mint-state 12), is a strong grade fine – well worn from a lifetime of circulation but nonetheless bearing the silver-gray color that is the hallmark of war nickels.

The origins of war nickels began in 1941 when the United States was under attack in the midst of a world war but with an economy still suffering the effects of the Great Depression.

Raw-material shortages and rationing were the watchwords of the day. The fall of the Malay Peninsula in Southeast Asia meant a critical shortage of tin and rubber in the United States. Copper, required for shell casings, was also increasingly difficult to come by.

America had a strong tradition of nickel in its 5-cent pieces and copper in its cents, but when these metals became critically scarce during World War II, a change had to be made.

Yet, it was done reluctantly. Many in Congress expressed concern for how the public and special-interest groups, such as vending-machine operators, would react. Nickel, a key ingredient in munitions and armament manufacture, was virtually impossible to secure in large quantities. There was seemingly impasse at every turn, but if the war was to be won, sufficient supplies of these critical materials had to be found. Time was of the essence.

Not long after the disaster at Pearl Harbor, Congress began work on a war-powers bill – comprehensive legislation that would affect every American. Among the many proposed regulations was a fundamental change in the coinage system. Ultimately, for the first time since 1815, production of the cent was suspended. When it returned, copper had been eliminated from its alloy content.

Also affected was the 5-cent piece. Its nickel composition, actually only 25 percent of the total alloy, and its copper content (the remaining 75 percent) became temporary casualties of war.

In addition to these substantive changes, there was one proposal that was turned into law but never into reality – the reissuance of a 3-cent coin, last struck in 1889. The coin, its sponsors contended, would have eliminated the need for substantial quantities of metal required for other critical industrial projects.

Precisely how America got its wartime coinage – or some parts of it – is a fascinating story involving complicated legislative proposals, debates on the floors of the House and Senate, and even a degree of wonderment as to what names the new coinages should have.

The 5-cent came first for congressional consideration because it involved the most critical of all war materials, nickel. A secondary concern was copper, which was by no means plentiful but was more available thin nickel.

As Representative Charles McLaughlin of Nebraska explained in debate on February 24, 1942, Title XII of the War Powers Act "changes the existing composition of the 5-cent piece and makes it half copper and half silver." Why silver? For one thing, the

Burt Blumert discovers the error.

government had a massive stockpile of the metal, much of which cost less than 50 cents an ounce. Some had been purchased for as little as 31 cents an ounce. And the metal was not critical to the war effort.

The legislation's framers were not clear if the 50-50 composition would prove satisfactory in production. So the legislation provided for a "certain amount of tolerance for an additional alloy," McLaughlin said.

There was also some concern for the vending-machine industry, which was, as now, a dominant user of the nation's coinage. It was essential that the coin "be available for use in food vending machines and machines in which the coin could not be used if it were required to be composed entirely of silver and copper in equal proportions," McLaughlin told the House.

Representative Jesse Wolcott of Michigan was concerned that the coin would have a disproportionate value. "What will be the actual value of the nickel when this new formula is in effect?" he queried. "Something over 4 cents," Representative Clarence Hancock of New York replied. McLaughlin agreed.

Wolcott inquired, "Does not the gentleman think that will induce the hoarding of nickel to the point where perhaps we shall have to coin ... more nickels to effect the savings [of metal]?" McLaughlin replied, "The Treasury Department is not of the opinion that that fear is well founded."

The stakes for the new coin were enormous to the vending-machine industry and the rest of the nation. Originally, the idea was to simply take nickel out of the coins and allow silver and copper to take its place.

"On this basis," McLaughlin said, "it is estimated for the fiscal year 1941, there would be a saving of 870,000 pounds of nickel and the same amount of copper. Nickel is indispensable in armor plate for tanks and battleships, machinery bearings, bomb racks ... and naval vessels. The amount of nickel saved in one year would be sufficient for the production of 16,000 tons of armor plate and enough for 1,000 heavy tanks."

The problem with the original proposal, however, was that the alloy had no magnetic properties. The coin's resistivity – the means by which vending machines accepted or rejected them – was not the same as the previous nickel's. As a compromise, the Mint director was permitted to "vary the proportions of silver and copper and … add other metals if such action would be in the public interest," provided the Treasury secretary and War Production Board chairman approved.

On March 7, 1942, the bill was the subject of a humorous speech that only a Saturday session could allow. Representative William Nelson of Missouri proposed that the new 5-cent coin be called a "Paddy." Claiming that he was echoing the remarks of R.L. "Bob" Hill, president of Rotary International and a University of Missouri alumnus, Nelson said War Production Board Chairman Donald M. Nelson had the nickname "Paddy" when he was a student at the school. "So," the representative said, "I think that the new nickel-less nickel ought to be called a 'Paddy' after the person who first proposed it." Needless to say, the proposal never caught on.

Even as the nickel shortage was being brought to a successful resolution, the equally serious copper shortage was causing the Mint to curtail its production of the cent. (The 1943 copper cent error was a result of this.) The coin's composition before the war was 25-percent nickel, 75-percemt copper. The nickel was a sop to Senator Joseph Warton of Pennsylvania immediately after the Civil War.

With nickel and copper in short supply, the copper cent was eliminated (a steel substitute was supplied), a 3-cent piece authorized (but never produced), and the 5-cent's composition was changed to 35-percent silver, 56-percent copper, 9-percent manganese. Although the congressional act called for 50-percent silver and 50-percent copper, the Mint director exercised his authority to change the composition if public interest warranted.

War nickels of 1942-1945 featured a large mint mark above Monticello's dome on the reverse.

To distinguish the coins further and to allow for their eventual withdrawal from circulation, large mint marks – P, D and S – were placed above Monticello on the reverse. The coins contained 0.05626 troy ounces of silver, which, at 40 cents an ounce, gave the coins an intrinsic value of about 2.2 cents. By 1961, when the Treasury stabilized silver prices at $1.29 an ounce, war nickels were worth 7 cents apiece intrinsically. At the height of the silver boom in 1980, when the price topped $48 an ounce, each war nickel was intrinsically worth $2.70.

Approximately 870 million war nickels were produced from 1942 to 1945 using about 50 million ounces of silver from the strategic reserve. (That same reserve was used until recently to produce American Eagle bullion coins.)

Off-metal error coins are more common than generally believed. Among them are the 1946 silver-planchet war nickels. In his book *Walter Breen's Complete Encyclopedia of U.S. Coins* (1988), Breen catalogs the error as No. 2703 and terms it "extremely rare." He notes that at least four had been authenticated as of publication of his book. All of them, like the recently discovered Collins coin, were from the Philadelphia Mint.

Unlike some modern error coins or even the 1933 Saint-Gaudens gold $20 coins that have been pursued by government authorities, the Collins coin's fine-12 grade makes clear that this coin had a long life in circulation and was evidently put there through the proper channels. Jefferson's hair is smooth on the coin, and the steps of Monticello are smooth.

Blumert and Weinberg say it's hard to value the coin, though they offer parallels to the 1943 copper cent or the 1944 steel cents. The 1944 steel has ranged from $10,000 to $12,000 in recent sales; the 1943 copper is multiples of that level.

How the error was produced is unknown. Blank planchets from 1945 were probably tossed into the production hopper and then struck into coin in 1945. As a shiny new, uncirculated piece, it must have looked remarkably like the nickel-copper coins otherwise produced in 1946.

It also shows that error coins are still out there undiscovered, years after they were produced and entered circulation. It also shows that a coin doesn't have to be in top uncirculated condition to command a significant price premium.

The 1943 copper cent and the 1944 steel counterpart are better-known examples, but the American Numismatic Association museum in Colorado Springs, Colorado, also has off-metal issues for cents of the early 1940s, when Colombian centavo planchets were mistakenly made into Lincoln cents.

The moral is that the so-called junk box at your local coin dealer's store could contain a hidden treasure if you take the time to learn what to look for and then look at the coins.

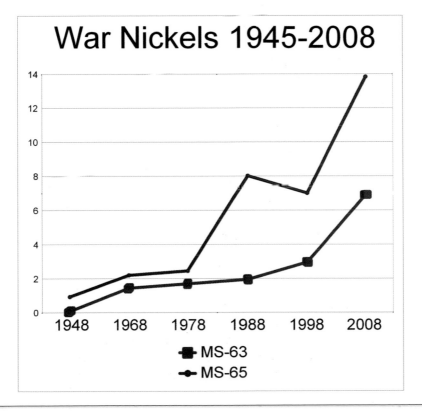

War Nickels 1945-2008

MS-63
MS-65

Chapter 9

1804 Silver Dollar

Mintage: 19,570*; about 15 known
Designer: Robert Scot
Diameter: 39-40 millimeters
Weight: about 26.96 grams
Composition: 89.24-percent silver, 10.76-percent copper
Total silver weight: 0.7737 ounces
*Official U.S. Mint records

I t is among the most frequently counterfeited of American coins and remains an enigma more than two centuries after its date. It bears the date of the Jefferson administraton but was produced in the age of Jackson and onward to the Buchanan administration and the outbreak of the American Civil War.

Welcome to the world of the 1804 silver dollar.

It's a coin of legend, mystery, armed robbery, complicity in fraudulent acts, and greed. At least one specimen found its way into the collection of Henry Linderman, probably while he was U.S. Mint director, and wound up in a Lyman Low auction catalog in 1887. After litigation with the government, J.W. Scott listed it in his sale of February 28, 1888. The coin, known today as the Linderman-du Pont specimen, brought $470. The Davis-Wolfson specimen also sold in 1888 and yielded $660.

About 15 specimens are known. They were produced at three separate times using different dies – and all many years after the date impressed on the coins. The Mint report for 1804, and succeeding Mint reports, show 19,570 silver dollars being struck. The following year, 1805, weighs in with 321 dollars produced. Serious collectors today know that no silver dollars were produced from late 1803 until 1836, but the records say something else. In fact, the 1966 Mint report (table C19, "Annual Silver Coinage, Philadelphia Mint, Number of Pieces") still carried the same information, long since proven false.

The 1804 silver dollar originates from a diplomatic mission in the 1830s to open up Siam (modern-day Thailand) and Muscat (today part of the United Gulf Emirates) to the West. On June 20, 1834, President Andrew Jackson, having previously made a recess appointment, formally nominated Roger Taney to be Treasury secretary.

At around the same time, the Senate acted on two separate treaties, as its executive journals document: "Resolved (two-thirds of the Senators present

1804 silver dollar.

concurring), That the Senate do advise and consent to the ratification of the treaty of amity and commerce between the United States of America and His Majesty Seyed Syeed Bin, Sultan of Muscat, made at the city of Muscat, in the Kingdom of Aman, the twenty-first day of September, in the year of our Lord, one thousand eight hundred and thirty-three."

Then, "The treaty with the King of Siam was read the second time and considered as in Committee of the Whole; no amendment having been made thereto, it was reported to the Senate accordingly. Mr. Wilkins submitted the following resolution for consideration: Resolved (two-thirds of the Senators present concurring), That the Senate do advise and consent to the ratification of the treaty between the United States of America and His Majesty the King of Siam, concluded at the royal city of Siayuthia (commonly called Bankok), the twentieth day of March, in the year of our Lord one thousand eight hundred and thirty-three."

A single envoy, Edmund Roberts, was appointed to handle these far-flung countries.

On December 6, 1836, in his last annual address to Congress, Jackson reported, "Commercial treaties, promising great advantages to our enterprising merchants and navigators, have been formed with the distant governments of Muscat and Siam. The ratifications have been exchanged but have not reached the Department of State. Copies of the treaties will be transmitted to you, if received before, or published, if arriving after, the close of the present session of Congress."

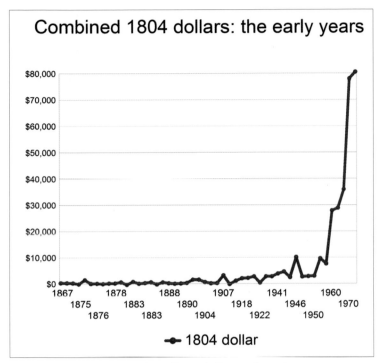

Combined 1804 dollars: the early years

Legend: 1804 dollar

Y-axis: $0, $10,000, $20,000, $30,000, $40,000, $50,000, $60,000, $70,000, $80,000

X-axis: 1867, 1875, 1876, 1878, 1883, 1883, 1888, 1890, 1904, 1907, 1918, 1922, 1941, 1946, 1950, 1960, 1970

All research on the 1804 silver dollar, at least in modern times, inevitably returns to the seminal volume *The Fantastic 1804 Silver Dollar* by Eric P. Newman and Kenneth E. Bressett (1962). They quote, as do many successive catalogers, from a letter dated November 11, 1834, from Secretary of State John Forsyth to Mint Director Dr. Samuel Moore. Forsyth, confirmed June 27, 1834 (and serving until the change of administrations on March 4, 1841), wrote that Jackson had "directed that a complete set of the coins of the United States be sent to the King of Siam and another to the Sultan of Muscat."

There are other provisos, but it appears that the Mint director caused a "complete" set of coins be produced for both commercial treaties. The results were two 1804 silver dollars extant today: the king of Siam specimen and the Watters-Childs specimen, whose provenance includes the iman of Muscat. Sets prepared for the emperor of Japan and the king of Cochin China

Scholars believe the 1804 silver dollars were struck specially for inclusion in proof sets presented to foreign dignitaries.

(Indochina) were evidently returned to the Mint after the special diplomatic agent's death from dysentery.

Two other versions of the 1804 dollar were produced well into the late 1850s. Newman and Bressett weave the fascinating tale of deceit, nepotism and fraud involving the coins. Newspapers have been fascinated with the story from the time the coins began to sell at auction at multiples of the then living wage.

Newspapers have published numerous reports of supposed 1804 silver-dollar finds. Consider the following excerpt from a story that appeared June 7, 1888, in the *Providence Journal* and was reprinted July 1, 1888, in *The New York Times*, but remember that no 1804 silver dollars were struck before 1834:

"Mrs. Constant Tourgee, who is visiting her niece at … Pawtucket, has one of the rare silver dollars … of 1804 whose whereabouts has not been publicly known until very recently. … Upon her 18th birthday (she is now in her 76th year), her father gave her this dollar, which he received at the close of the war of 1812, as part payment for services in that war."

Phoney!

Media interest in the coins' auction records stretches back more than a century. "The Parmelee Coin Sale," whose 1804 silver dollar cited its provenance from an earlier Sanford sale and its acquisition by Byron Reed for $570, was reported in *The New York Times* of June 27, 1890. Reed's collection was willed to the City of Omaha, so that coin is out of reach and has been for over a century.

On March 18, 1893, the *Times* reported the purchase of an 1804 silver dollar for $1,200. There was debate in the article about how many of the coins were extant; the writer reported four to eight or even 12. (Contemporary accounts now show 15.)

The Stickney collection sale, conducted June 24, 1907, in Philadelphia by Henry Chapman, also made the *Times*. Stickney claimed he obtained his 1804 dollar from Paterson DuBois of the Mint in 1843. At that time, "It was not known that the date was scarce," the *Times* reported. "He simply desired to fill out his set of dollars up to date." The paper said Stickney exchanged "some Pine Tree Massachusetts silver and the gold Immune Columbia," which "was not supposed to be particularly rare, but it has since developed" to be unique.

The Stickney specimen, lot 849, brought $3,600 in the Chapman auction – or 80 percent more than the Dexter specimen had sold for in 1903 ($2,000).

The Stickney coin has a long history. It went from chief coiner Adam Eckfeldt to the Mint cabinet around 1838. In 1843, the Mint traded the class I, lettered-edge variety coin to Stickney for items the cabinet lacked. The Mint retained its class II new reverse example (plain edge struck over an 1857 Swiss shooting thaler), in addition to its class I coin, which Breen describes in his encyclopedia as a "badly cleaned proof."

Colonel James Ellsworth was the buyer in 1907 – ony the second owner since 1843 – and he held it until Wayte Raymond purchased his entire collection for $100,000 in 1923. Raymond, in turn, sold it

Some past collectors actually owned more than one of the 15 extant 1840 silver dollars.

to William Cutler Atwater, who owned it from 1923 to 1946, when his collection was cataloged and sold by the diminutive, but overly large numismatic promoter, B. Max Mehl of Fort Worth, Texas.

Mehl auctioned off the Atwater collection in a sale that numismatic literature cataloger John Adams grades "A+." The coin was acquired by a dealer for a customer at $10,500. The ultimate buyer's name: Louis Eliasberg, who just happened to be starting his quest to obtain one of every U.S. coin. (He eventually completed this quest.) When his estate finally sold the coin in 1989, the price realized was an incredible $1.815 million. (The coin was graded proof-63.)

Condition is sometimes critical when studying 1804 silver dollars. For example, William Cutler Atwater owned two specimens, both proofs. Using today's standards, one was a proof-63, the other a proof-62. The price difference between the two could be substantial. In 1946, when Mehl sold Atwater's collection in a mail-bid sale, the lower grade went for $2,875 (very respectable) and the better grade went for $10,500. The latter was an 1804 silver-dollar record that stood until 1960.

Lorin Parmelee was another collector who owned more than one 1804 silver dollar. His better-known piece stayed in his collection until 1890, when it sold for $570. Today, this coin, referred to as the Parmelee-Reed specimen, is the one owned by the City of Omaha. But Parmelee is also involved in the pedigree of the Cohen-American Numismatic Association specimen. Parmelee sold the coin privately in 1878 for $600.

Two coins track particularly well. First is the Dexter specimen, which Breen calls "brilliant proof, dipped" in his masterful study. Today, it is graded proof-64. The coin's provenance starts with its sale in Berlin in 1884 for $216. It next turns up in an American sale by Chapman in 1885, where it sold for $1,000.

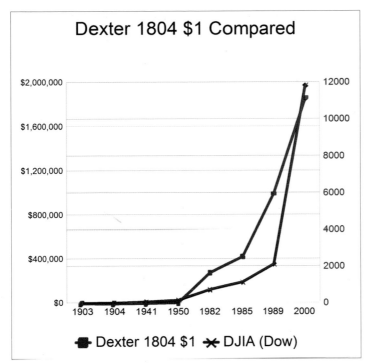

Dexter 1804 $1 Compared

Dexter 1804 $1 ■ DJIA (Dow) ✳

In 1903, it acquired the Dexter name; James Vila Dexter owned it from 1885 to 1903. It was then sold by Lyman Low to H.G. Brown for $2,000. In 1904, it sold again, to William Forest Dunham ($1,100), showing, indeed, that rare coins need some time to appreciate in value and may indeed decline in the short-term. A holding period is always wise.

Dunham's sale in 1941 at $4,250 brought the coin to Charles M. Williams, who held it from 1941 to 1950. When the coin sold again in 1950 ($10,000), the buyer was a shrewd and experienced collector, Harold S. Bareford, whom we met in an earlier chapter. It turns out that besides having a knack for gold coins, Bareford had eclectic collecting interests, including the proof-63 Dexter 1804 silver dollar.

The Bareford coin was sold by Stack's in 1981 for $280,000. That works out to a return on original capital of about 87 percent annually. A comparison to other investments that might have been made during the period shows coins more than held their own.

Ed Milas of Rarcoa was the buyer at the Bareford auction. He was then a seller in 1985 at $425,000; the buyers were Leon Hendrickson and George Weingart, who re-sold it the same year for $500,000. In 1989, Hugh Sconyers was the buyer ($990,000) for the American Rare Coin Fund Limited Partnership. That group sold at a hefty profit in 2000 ($1.84 million).

The other 1804 silver dollar that tracks especially well is the Adams-Carter specimen. It starts with John Haseltine's sale in 1876 at $395. It then goes to Phineas Adams in a set in 1876 at $1,880 and then to a Chapman sale of 1913 ($340). Other landmark sales included the Jerome Kern collection sale, held by Mehl in 1950 ($3,250); the 1984 Amon Carter collection sale (Stack's, $198,000); the L.R. French sale (Stack's, 1989) at $242,000; a 2001 sale conducted by Bowers and Merena ($874,000); and the 2003 ANA convention sale by Bowers and Merena ($1,207,500).

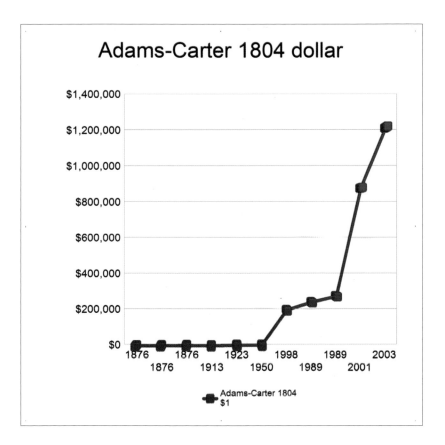

Adams-Carter 1804 dollar

Chapter 10

1894-S Dime

Mintage: 24
Designer: Charles Barber
Diameter: 17.9 millimeters
Weight: About 2.5 grams
Composition: 90-percent silver, 10-percent copper
Total silver weight: 0.0724 ounces

T he story of this coin is one of intrigue, mystery, scandal, ice cream, and a little girl. First, the little girl named Hallie, whose father was superintendent at the San Francisco Mint and newly appointed for fiscal year 1894.

An embezzlement scandal at the Carson City Mint had just taken place, duly noted in Treasury Department document No. 1829, the Mint director's annual report for the fiscal year ended June 30, 1895. Although the Mint report normally covers only part of the calendar year (July 1 to June 30), all of the action concerning the 1894-S dime took place in the early part of the year.

John Daggett was appointed superintendent and began service August 1, 1893. Although popular lore suggests there are no Mint records to support the striking of the 1894-S dime – similar to the 1838 New Orleans Mint report – chart 53 in the 1894 Mint director's report shows that from January 1 to June 30 that year, $2.40 worth of dimes were struck at San Francisco. The figure repeats in the 1895 and subsequent reports.

Mint records give no reason why only 24 dimes were struck in a year when $10.8 million in gold $20 and $250,000 in gold $10 pieces were manufactured by June 3, 1894. No half dimes or 20-cent pieces were struck because these denominations had long since become extinct. In the 371-page report, the Mint director showed substantial melting of non-current coin and a variety of other activities.

Kevin Flynn's remarkable book, *The 1894-S Dime: A Mystery Unraveled, 2nd Edition, 2006,* suggests all 24 dimes were produced on June 9, 1894. (Flynn's book includes copies of the original documents and is a treat that should not be missed.)

Mint appropriations and expenditures are in tabular form in the report. Among four mints and six assay offices, $1,119,569.37 was anticipated. Philadelphia accounted for the 37 cents; every other facility

1894-S dime.

ended in an even amount. The unexpended balance of appropriations for San Francisco included 50 cents in wages and $2,037.98 in contingent expenses (totaling $2,038.48). The stock of silver bullion on deposit with the Mercantile Safe Deposit Company in New York, as reported on June 30, 1894, was 154,674 fine ounces valued at $0.6323 an ounce. Precious-metals stocks were about evenly divided between gold and silver – $627.2 million in gold and $624,347,757 in silver.

The Treasury itself held $17,738,968 in subsidiary coinage (silver 3-cent coins, half dimes, dimes, quarters, and half dollars) and had 41 million silver dollars to boot. The San Francisco Mint melted 2,012,451 dimes and other non-current coins with a total face value exceeding $3 million.

Page 139 of the Mint report discloses that 40 dime dies were sent to San Francisco from the Philadelphia Mint, but this covers July 1, 1893, to June 30, 1894. These dies produced about 2,491,425 coins, or about 62,500 coins per die. (By contrast, the following year's Mint report shows 30 dies for 1,120,000 coins, about 37,000 coins per die.) No dimes were struck from July 1, 1894 (after the 1894-S dimes were struck), to December 31, 1894. All of the 1895-S dimes recorded were produced in the first half of the new year. Flynn quotes from original documents that 10 die pairs were prepared for 1894 dime production in San Francisco. They were returned to Philadelphia in January 1895.

What's clear from this is that after the defalcation at the Carson City Mint – a grand jury was convened as outlined in the 1895 Mint report – there was no balancing-the-books reason to strike an 1894-S dime.

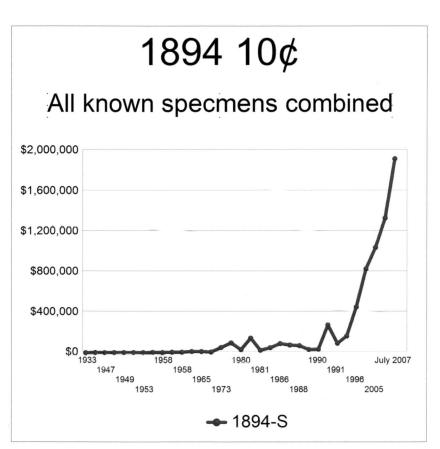

1894 10¢

All known specmens combined

1894-S

Records of the 1894 Assay Commission, which met in February 1895 and is documented in the following year's Mint report, show that 3,981 silver pieces worth $1,973.85 were set aside for assay. Only subsidiary silver coinage and silver dollars are included in this. (Gold coins are assayed, too, but not base-metal coins.) There are only so many numerical ways to reach 85 cents without use of a nickel. You could have a quarter and six dimes (possible, given general assay requirements) or three quarters and a dime (much more probable). Inevitably, then, at least one of the 1894-S dimes minted was set aside and melted. Flynn shows convincing evidence that at least two and possibly three 1894-S dimes are receipted for. To meet the 85-cent requirement, three more – six coins total – were sent to the melting cauldrons among 111 coins melted that year.

The way the Assay Commission worked is that the coins were deposited in the pyx and then some were withdrawn to be counted, weighed and then melted. (It worked the same way when I served on the commission 80 years later, in 1974.) Perhaps more coins than usual were melted because of a metal-fineness problem at the San Francisco Mint, which the assay report recites for March, April and May 1894. In any event, that accounts for many of them.

Most prominent of the 1894-S dime stories is that the superintendent ordered a handful of dimes produced, gave three to his daughter Hallie (then about age 10), and told her to hold onto them because they would have substantial value some day. In a 2007 Stack's Rare Coins auction catalog, Q. David Bowers hypothesizes that the coins were test strikes for a production run that never came. Flynn disagrees and goes with the theory of avarice on the part of Mint officials.

The number of dies suggests that a production run was planned but ultimately abandoned. Dr. Milton Friedman, in his book *Monetary History of the United States 1867-1960* (1963), may have inadvertently shown the reason based on statistics emerging from the Panic of 1893.

President Grover Cleveland, in an 1893 message from the executive mansion, put it this way: "The financial disturbance which swept over the country during the last year was unparalleled in its severity and disastrous consequences. ... Among those who attempted to assign causes for our distress it was very generally conceded that the operation of a provision of law then in force which required the Government to purchase monthly a large amount of silver bullion and issue its notes in payment therefore. … This led to the repeal on the 1st day of November, 1893, of this statutory provision."

As the wholesale price index declined from 1892 to 1896, the implicit price index declined, the velocity of money plummeted, and income fell precipitously. There simply was no reason for dimes to be produced in quantity; the 40 dies were sent as a precaution.

Regardless, at least two of the 1894-S dimes reached circulation and stayed there for many years. They survive today – one in grade about good-3 (Romito specimen) and the other in good-4 (Friedberg specimen).

That is a nice segue into the story – probably apocrypha – that Hallie's father gave her three dimes, one of which she spent on ice cream that June day. Forgetting that Mark Twain claimed that he spent the coldest winter of his life one summer in San

1894-S Dime

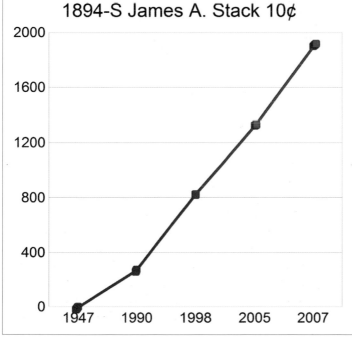

Francisco, the fact is that today there are two 1894-S dimes in well-worn condition.

Robert Friedberg, with his brother Jack, held the coin concession at Gimbels department stores and founded The Coin & Currency Institute, which his sons Arthur and Ira Friedberg manage today. In 1957, Friedberg bought the G-4 specimen over the counter at Gimbels.

Its subsequent history shows that even a well-worn coin can have substantial value. It sold in 1969 at a Harmer Rooke auction for $7,400. In 1980, Steve Ivy conducted the American Numismatic Association convention auction, and this coin went for $31,000. The following year, Bowers and Merena offered it at the 1981 ANA convention auction, and it brought $25,500 – a decline in a down market. But in 1989 at Bowers and Merena's Four Landmark Collections auction, it went for $33,000 to a private collector.

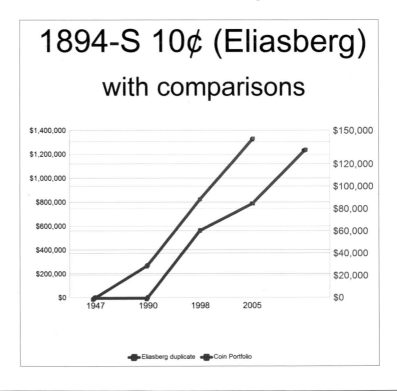

1894-S 10¢ (Eliasberg)
with comparisons

The accompanying chart shows clearly how bright a future this coin has. In 1996, the Eliasberg estate received $451,000 for its proof-65 specimen. The James A. Stack specimen (sold for $275,000 in 1990) then went up in a David Lawrence auction in 1998 and brought $825,000. In 2005, Bradley Hirst, the buyer, sold off his Barber-dime collection, and the 1894-S brought a new record of $1,322,500. In 2007, a private-treaty sale saw that coin brokered (again by David Lawrence) at $1.9 million.

Finally, on October 17, 2007, Stack's sold a lost specimen in its 72nd anniversary sale. The coin was formerly in the Samuel Gillespie collection. Grading proof-64 by the Professional Coin Grading Service, the coin brought down the house with a price of $1,552,500.

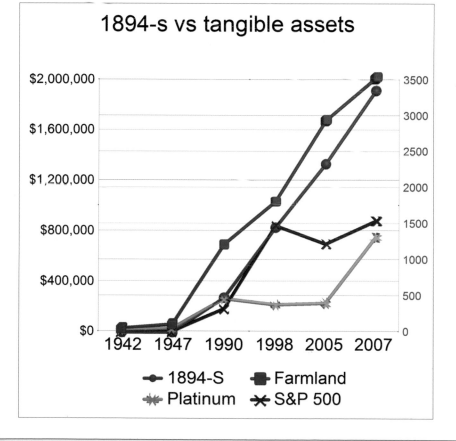

The accompany chart shows the performance of a generic 1894-S dime compared to the return on farmland, platinum and the Standard & Poor's 500.

Also charted are the pedigrees of 11 different coins. On that point there is still substantial disagreement.

Flynn lists nine bloodlines. He omits the Adolphe Menjou specimen, which Abe Kosoff sold in 1950. Author Walter Breen lists 12, including a dubious one (Mitchelson) alleged to be in the Connecticut State Library, but recent visitors say it is a myth. Breen calls it "unverified," but also omits the Menjou specimen. John Feigenbaum of David Lawrence Rare Coins, an acknowledged expert on Barber coinage, tracks 11 different lines on the PCGS CoinFacts Web site, expanding on his father's 1991 book. He also grades the coins, which is important because some of the grades have changed over the years.

The accompanying chart lists public sales of 1894-S dimes. The last four sales – two in 2005 and two in 2006 – all topped $1 million. If only Hallie had held onto that other dime instead of buying an ice-cream cone.

Public sales of 1894-S dimes

Coin	Owner	Sale	Date sold	Price
1 (proof-60)	Waldo C. Newcomer	Mehl auction	1933	$1,000
1	F.C.C. Boyd	"World's Greatest Collection" (Kosoff-Kreisberg)	1945	$2,350
3	Louis E. Eliasberg Sr.	Stack's auction	1947	$2,150
1	Will W. Neil	Mehl auction	1947	$2,325
4	Hallie Daggett		1949	$2,750
5	Hallie Daggett		1949	$2,750
11 (brilliant proof)	Adolphe Menjou	Kosoff auction	1950	$1,850
5	F.S. Guggenheimer	Stack's auction	1953	$2,100
6	Dr. Charles Cass	Empire Collection (Stack's)	1957	$4,750

Coin	Owner	Sale	Date sold	Price
8	(Unsold)	New Netherlands Coin Co. auction	1958	$3,200
6	Q. David Bowers		1958	$6,000
7	Bowers and Ruddy	Fixed price list	1958	Offered at approximately $6,000
1	Edwin Hydeman	Kosoff auction	1961	$13,000
1	A. Hinman	Century Collection (Paramount)	1965	$12,250
8	Harmer Rooke		1969	$7,400
5		MANA auction (Kagin's)	1973	$52,000
4	Bowers and Ruddy	Rare Coin Review No. 21	1974	$97,500
8		ANA convention auction (Ivy)	1980	$31,000
1	Leo Young	Auction '80 (Rarcoa)	1980	$145,000
8		ANA convention auction (Bowers and Ruddy)	1981	$25,500
5	Jerry Buss	Superior auction	1985	$50,600
1		Pacific Coast auction	1986	$91,300
6	Emery May Norweb	Bowers and Merena auction	1987	$77,000
5	Michelle Johnson	Blevins auction (Superior)	1988	$70,400
8		Landmark auction (Bowers and Merena)	1989	$33,000
9	Laura Sperber		1990	$35,000
3	James A. Stack	Stack's auction	1990	$275,000
6		55th anniversary auction (Stack's)	1991	$93,500
4	John Deland	Superior auction	1992	$165,000
2	Eliasberg Estate	Bowers and Merena auction	1996	$451,000
3		David Lawrence auction	1998	$825,000
4		FUN convention auction (Heritage)	2005	$1,035,000
3	Bradley Hirst	Richmond auction (David Lawrence)	2005	$1,322,500
3		Private sale (David Lawrence)	2007	$1,900,000
10 (proof-64)		72nd anniversary auction (Stack's)	2007	$1,552,500

Chapter 11

1933 Gold $20

Mintage: 445,500
Designer: Augustus Saint-Gaudens
Diameter: 34 millimeters
Composition: 90-percent gold, 10-percent copper
Total gold weight: 0.9675 troy ounces

A double eagle with a mintage in the hundreds of thousands is one of the rarest U.S. gold coins and, in 2008, probably the most valuable coin in the world. At least it was the most expensive when it sold at public auction in July 2002 for just over $7.59 million. (The "just over" was its face value, which the sellers required for separate consideration.)

The coin is the 1933 double eagle, or gold $20 piece.

This one coin does not mean that other coins of the same date, denomination and mint mark have the same value. Indeed, the government is still litigating the issue with the Israel Switt family, which recently turned in 10 of them – count 'em – to try to "legalize" the coin. The Secret Service and other government agencies have seized more than that number since the coin was minted at the beginning of the Franklin Roosevelt administration.

The hazards of holding gold were learned by millions of Americans in 1933 when they awoke to find that Roosevelt had essentially ordered gold nationalized and Treasury Secretary Henry Morgenthau had prohibited private gold ownership of all but "rare and unusual coin."

By the time the Gold Reserve Act of 1934 passed, title to all gold bullion, gold coin, and gold notes (including Federal Reserve notes) was taken from the American people, not to be in their hands again for two generations, until 1974. More than 400,000 double eagles dated 1933 were produced, many of them between FDR's inauguration on March 4 and the confiscation order in April of that same year. Some evidently were produced after the order, in May.

Historically, the U.S. Mint claimed that none of the coins was placed in circulation and that none was authorized for release. But the 2001 case involving a 1996 seizure of a coin owned by British dealer

1933 Saint-Gaudens gold $20.

Stephen Fenton proved just the opposite. It showed a pattern of bureaucratic deceit that spanned over five generations and of conduct that was contemptuous of the legal system, not to mention the collecting public.

The coin in question came from the King Farouk collection. In an undated letter from Treasury Secretary Henry Morgenthau Jr. to Secretary of State Cordell Hull, the Treasury chief represented the coin as the "only one of its kind in the hands of the general public."

Evidently, King Farouk's agents located the coin for him in the 1940s, and through diplomatic channels, he applied for it to be exported from the United States to his palace collection in Egypt. Farouk was not sophisticated about coins, but he liked them and collected them. His request went to Mint Director Nellie Tayloe Ross.

Ross, former governor of Wyoming, was an FDR appointee who ran one of the government's largest manufactories. She received the coin along with a request that it be authorized for export as a "rare and unusual" coin. The request came in wartime, when Egypt was a badly needed ally in North Africa.

Origins of the legal prohibition against owning a 1933 gold $20 date back to 1917, when Congress passed the Trading With the Enemy Act, which gave the president (then Woodrow Wilson) authority to ban the holding and disposition of gold, silver and a plethora of other items. FDR, an assistant secretary of the Navy in the Wilson administration, was familiar with the law.

The act was aimed at limiting trading with Imperial Germany and to give Wilson diplomatic maneuvering room to try to prevent armed battle or at least prevent American goods and assets from helping to finance Germany's armed struggle. But the unintended consequence became apparent a generation later.

In 1933, FDR issued Executive Order 6120 (based on the 1917 law) prohibiting private gold ownership except for "rare and unusual coin," which permitted numismatists to hold up to four examples of each date and mint mark. (The Treasury secretary at the time was William Woodin, himself a well-known collector of coins.)

At the time of Roosevelt's decree, the Mint evidently had already produced 1933 gold $20 coins but had not released them into circulation. An unknown quantity left the Mint – to this day it is unclear whether they left in other coin bags or were secreted out – and eventually, some went into collectors' hands. They looked like every other double eagle, except for the date.

King Farouk's coin is unique, in one sense. Fenton's counsel, Barry Berke, a partner in the New York law firm of Kramer, Levin, Naftalis, & Frankel, proved this in 2001 when he made civil discovery demands on the U.S. government in the litigation over the Fenton coin, which the government tried to seize

Fenton obviously suspected the coin was Farouk's, and the information must have been from more than a catalog description since Sotheby's 1954 Palace Collection auction offered the coin as part of a larger single lot. Fred Baldwin cataloged the coin as lot 185 together with a 1925-D and -S, 1926-D, 1927-S, 1928, 1929, 1930-S, 1931-P and -D, and 1932 double eagles – all grouped as a single lot with the 1933. All were graded "mostly extremely fine," after the European fashion, meaning they were uncirculated.

Fabulous in composition, this 17-coin lot wound up being sold as a 16-coin lot when the 1933 was withdrawn at the request of the Egyptian government, which acted after American diplomatic interests tried to recover the coin that had been legally but probably improperly exported to King Farouk.

The insular world of rarified numismatic sales knew that, in the late 1930s and early '40s, a number of specimens were traded on the sly, often at relatively high prices. The beginning of the end came when a specimen appeared as lot 1681 in the Colonel John W. Flanagan sale, sold March 25, 1944, by Stack's Rare Coins. Flanagan purchased the coin for $2,200. At around the same time, L.G. Barnard purchased a specimen from J.F. Bell. Stack's publicized the sale, calling the coin "excessively rare and in great demand."

The Secret Service seized the Flanagan coin – no compensation was offered – and the coin was reputedly melted. At the time of the coin's proposed sale, Stack's claimed in the auction catalog to know of eight or 10 pieces that had been sold privately. One cataloger queried as to whether they may have been "all different."

David W. Akers, a respected expert on gold coins, picks up the story: "According to [dealer] Abe Kosoff, Treasury Department agents then asked various coin dealers for the names and addresses of collectors to whom they had sold 1933 double eagles. Kosoff, and possibly others, preferred to contact their customers privately, return their money, and then turn over the returned coins to the agents."

Fast forward to 1952, when Colonel Gamal Abdel Nasser led a coup d'état against Egypt's King Farouk, deposing him and sentencing him to a life in exile. (The king died in Italy in 1965 at the relatively young age of 45). Farouk did everything to excess. His fast cars, fast women, palaces, and fabulous collections of coins, stamps, antiquities, and other objects were worthy of an Ottoman sultan, of which he was the last. (As late as 2007, his three daughters were still litigating with the Egyptian government over a palace that had been seized a half century earlier.)

Nasser's provisional government seized all of these assets and ordered that they be sold for the benefit of the Egyptian people. Included in the items seized were about 8,500 coins, which were offered for sale in 2,798 lots as the Palace Collections of Egypt.

John Jay Pittman, later an American Numismatic Association president, went to Egypt for the sale together with Abe Kosoff, Hans M.F. Schulman, and many others. Kosoff and Schulman had an unusual credit arrangement, since they had sold Farouk many coins, still unpaid for, that were being auctioned. Pittman had to pay pure cash.

Pittman reflected years later how astonishing it was to see a complete collection of double eagles with date and mint-mark runs from 1850 to 1933. According to Polly Pittman, his daughter, the 1933 coin was removed from the lot at her father's suggestion because of its problematic history, which was

The author is shown here, in 1973, with John J Pittman and Rep. Wright Patmanm, D-TX & Leonor K. Sullivan, D-MO.

apparent by 1954. The U.S. government had, after all, seized nine coins from private collectors and destroyed them. John Pittman wanted to buy some of the Farouk coins but not the problems associated with the 1933 double eagle.

Many of the Americans who purchased the larger Farouk lots bought, sold and traded among themselves so that each got some portion of what they wanted in the first place – a task made easier by the removal of the 1933 double eagle.

Pursuant to the Freedom of Information Act and the Federal Rules of Civil Procedure, Fenton's lawyers were entitled to all of the information the government had – pro and con – on the case. The rules prevent a trial by ambush or surprise. Fenton's lawyers demanded documents that had been stored for decades. One of the surprising finds were Treasury Department documents dating back to Ross' tenure as Mint director (1933-1953) that referred to the 1933 double eagle and an export license issued for Farouk.

One can only imagine the diplomatic intrigue that was going on. Farouk was a playboy but a potential ally in the struggle for Middle East hegemony. The export license itself has never been found, but documentary evidence refers to it and shows the Treasury Department issued it. Thus, the evidence acknowledged that the U.S. government authorized the coin's sale and export to Farouk. Before that, Ross had sent the coin to Theodore Belote of the Smithsonian national coin collection to examine it and determine if it was "rare and unusual," the criteria for permitted ownership. He nodded in the affirmative, and Ross authorized the issuance of export license TGL-11-1709 in March 1944.

I didn't know until recently that Hugo Ranta, assistant general counsel for the State Department, in a December 23, 1953, memo to a Treasury official, termed it "politically inadvisable" to ask for the return of the 1933 $20 from Egypt. It turns out it was legally inadvisable, as well.

Dr. Leland Howard, acting Mint director in 1944, later tried to gloss over this action, but the fact remains that an export license was issued to Farouk, the coin traveled to Egypt, was curated into his collection, and eventually was seized by the junta that kicked Farouk out of office.

Farouk's collection was then sold by Sotheby's on behalf of the provisional government, and the U.S. government formally asked for the coin's return. The coin was withdrawn from the sale, but its fate remained unknown until it surfaced in Fenton's hands, though rumors of its existence pervaded Europe in the 1970s.

Another collector who was less lucky than Fenton was James A. Stack (no relation to the Stack's Rare Coins family), whose coin was seized by the Secret Service. That case was litigated in New York in the early 1950s.

Also unlucky was L.G. Barnard, who lost a case in 1947 in which the government sued to reacquire the coin. Barnard had purchased it at the J.F. Bell collection auction, conducted by Stack's in 1944. At that time, of course, private gold ownership was illegal, and the coin itself was suspect. The Barnard case was litigated in Tennessee, the Stack case in the same U.S. District Court in New York where the 2001 Fenton case was resolved.

Today, as Barry Berke showed, skilled counsel caused a result different from Barnard and Stack — based in large apart on the export permit, which in essence made the government guilty of laches, or lulling someone into a disadvantageous position by virtue of the passage of time, inaction, or, as the case here shows, affirmative action. The still-compelling and unanswered question is whether the lawful government of Egypt has unasserted its rights in this coin.

In 1975, I first wrote extensively about the 1933 double eagle: "There is still hope that the 1933 coin may once again be owned – legally. Congress, when it passed the legislation authorizing private gold ownership at year's end, specifically included language that would negate all of the legal impediments and restrictions to the 40-year-old prohibition. Quite possibly, this could be interpreted as including the ban on coinage and hence ownership of the rare double eagle."

In legalizing private gold ownership anew, public law 93-373 provided, "(b) No provision of any law in effect on the date of enactment of this Act, and no rule, regulation or order in effect on the date subsections (a) and (b) become effective may be construed to prohibit any person from purchasing, holding, selling or otherwise dealing with gold in the United States or abroad."

If interpreted literally, its meaning is clear: All of the executive orders banning gold are tossed out the window, assuming that they were legally issued in the first place. (Professor Henry Mark Holzer wrote compellingly in the *Brooklyn Law Review* in 1977 that the ban on gold ownership itself was an illegal action by FDR.)

Some 40 years ago, I remember asking Hugo Ranta, former Treasury Department assistant general counsel, if he believed that the government's theory behind the 1933 double eagle extended to these other coins and that the government could seize them. He answered in the affirmative.

When I put the question to Aubrey Bebee, who owned major rarities of this caliber (see the 1913 Liberty nickel), and told him that the government thought it could seize the coinage, he said, "Let them just try!"

After years of litigating, the government capitulated and struck a deal to auction the 1933 double eagle and split the proceeds with Fenton, who jumped at the chance to have the government imprimatur on the sale.

Months of feverish excitement and hype led to the joint auction on July 30, 2002. The 56-page auction catalog contained a single unnumbered lot – the fabled 1933 double eagle.

When the smoke cleared at the 6 p.m. sale, held at Sotheby's east-side New York auction room, 1334 York Avenue, a new world's record price of $7.59 million was bid for the coin. It was hammered down by David Redden, Sotheby's vice chairman and a veteran auctioneer. The entire event took about 18 minutes.

Everything about the sale was unusual, from the single-lot, large-size catalog to the attendance. Upwards of 800 people packed the auction room. News cameras, U.S. and international press, and dealers and collectors all gathered to see history made by this coin of mystery. The first bidder at the July 30 sale was Barry M. Goldwater Jr., a former member of Congress and son of the late Arizona senator and presidential candidate. Goldwater started the bidding at $2.5 million on behalf of the National Monetary Mint, as announced by Redden.

It was quickly eclipsed in a series of rapid bids. Goldwater stayed competitive until $4.5 million. So did bidder No. 111, who stood at the rear of the room to maintain some anonymity. The bidding then shifted to others, including several anonymous telephone bidders. Presale estimate was $4 million to $6 million.

Unlike many other auctions, where the cadence is in increments of $100 or $250 and the duration can be just seconds for a lot, this was a unique event that Redden seemed determined to expand to fill the enormity of the occasion. The audience responded with a reverence that has been seen on other historic occasions, such as when a Brasher doubloon from the Friedberg family collection was offered at auction in 1979 or when an 1804 silver dollar hits the block.

Holding paddle 101 is former eight-term California Congressman Barry M. Goldwater, Jr., son of the former Arizona senator and 1964 presidential nominee. He bid on the 1933 $20 gold piece past the $4-million mark with just a little movement of the paddle. An anonymous bidder won the price at over $7-million, and was presented this bill of sale from Mint director Henrietta Fore.
Author's photos.

Bidding moved steadily in $100,000 increments. About eight floor bidders were registered, with several more bidding by telephone through Sotheby's personnel.

Several others holding paddles were well-known personalities. Goldwater had paddle No. 101. Steve Tebo of Colorado, now a real-estate developer, had paddle No. 102. Larry Stack of Stack's Rare Coins held paddle No. 105, and dealer Kevin Lipton of Beverly Hills, California, held paddle No. 108.

As the sale progressed and seconds ticked into minutes, there was palpable excitement as Redden hastened the cadence. Selby Kiffer, a Sotheby's employee, was on the telephone with an absentee bidder, who ultimately prevailed. Redden declined to disclose his name, even as Mint Director Henrietta Holsman Fore signed the title documents to transfer the 1933 double eagle to the winning bidder.

An ordinary bill of sale accompanies most auctions, but this one was a unique engraved bill of sale and transfer of title prepared for the Mint and engraved by the U.S. Bureau of Engraving and Printing. It was signed by Fore and David Pickens, the Mint's associate director of sales.

The sale was a significant event in modern numismatic history. It seems destined to be looked at the same way as the 1973 sale of the first $100,000 coin, which took rare coins to a new level.

1933 gold $20 time line

Date	Event
March 4, 1933	Franklin Roosevelt inaugurated.
March 5, 1933	Last shipment of gold coins from the U.S. Mint.
March 6, 1933	Presidential proclamation 2039 declared a bank holiday. Payment of gold coin prohibited.
March 15, 1933-March 24, 1933	First 100,000 1933 gold $20 coins struck.
April 5, 1933	Executive order 6102 issued, requiring return of gold coins with specific exceptions.
April 7, 1933-April 27, 1933	A total of 200,000 1933 gold $20 coins struck.
May 8,1933-May 19, 1933	A total of 145,500 1933 gold $20 coins struck.
January 30, 1934	Congress passed the Gold Reserve Act.
February 2, 1934	Thirty-four 1933 gold $20 coins were extracted from assay holding and added to vault F, cage 1 or kept in the cashier's vault.
February 1934	Twenty 1933 gold $20 coins were segregated for Mint laboratory testing and melted during testing.
February 14-15, 1934	The Assay Commission met and examined and tested 446 1933 gold $20 coins. Nine were destroyed in testing.
February 20, 1934	The Assay Commission returned 437 gold $20 coins to the Mint. They were stored in the cashier's vault.
March 20, 1934	George McCann named Mint cashier.
October 2, 1934	McCann sent two 1933 gold $20 coins to the Smithsonian collection.
February 6, 1937-March 18, 1937	1933 gold $20 coins were sent to the refinery for melting.
Early February 1937	Israel Switt purchased an unknown number of 1933 gold $20 coins.
February 15, 1937	Switt sold one of his 1933 gold $20 coins to James Macallister.
February 1941	Smith & Son advertised a 1933 gold $20 in The Numismatist.
February 1944	A Stack's Rare Coins advertisement in The Numismatist announced the Colonel James W. Flanagan collection auction.
February 23, 1944	B. Max Mehl sold a 1933 gold $20 to King Farouk of Egypt.
February 25, 1944	An Egyptian royal legation delivered a 1933 gold $20 to the Mint with a request for an export license.
February 29, 1944	The U.S. Treasury issued the legation export license TGL-170 for the 1933 gold $20.
March 6, 1944	A letter from the Smithsonian associate director to the Mint director confirmed that the 1933 gold $20 destined for King Farouk was shown to T. Belote, who answered affirmatively that the coin was of special interest to collectors prior to April 5, 1993, and December 28, 1933.

Date	Event
March 22, 1944	The U.S. Secret Service became aware of 1933 gold $20 coins being advertised for sale. An investigation began.
March 23-25, 1944	Stack's conducted its auction of the Flanagan collection, which contained a 1933 gold $20 (lot 1681).
March 24, 1944	Secret Service agents Jack Haley and Harry W. Strang seized the Flanagan 1933 gold $20 from Stack's. The same agents seized a second 1933 gold $20 from dealer Max Berenstein.
March 25, 1944	Haley and Strang interviewed J.F. Bell, F.C.C. Boyd and Ira Reed in New York City. Bell immediately surrendered a third 1933 gold $20 to the agents.
March 29, 1944	In Philadelphia, Secret Service agents conducted follow-up interviews with Reed and Macallister. Macallister informed agents he purchased five 1933 gold $20 coins from Switt, a gold dealer with a history of violations of the 1934 Gold Reserve Act.
March 30, 1944	Strang and fellow agent George Drescher interviewed Switt. In the interview, Switt admitted to one-time possession of nine 1933 gold $20 coins. He told agents he sold five of them to Macallister, two to Reed, and two to Kosoff. Switt professed no recollection of his source for the coins but admitted he had been to the Philadelphia Mint frequently in his capacity as gold dealer.
March 30, 1944	Leland Howard, acting Mint director, sent a memo to the Secret Service chief recounting events leading to the granting of the export license to King Farouk. Howard explained his awareness of illicit removal of 1933 gold $20 coins from the Mint in response to a "routine inquiry regarding the number of such coins that had been placed in circulation." In the memo, Howard recounted his first realization that no 1933 gold $20 coins had been placed in circulation. He said the Mint understood the situation only after the export license had been issued.
April 6, 1944	The Secret Service chief received written confirmation from the Treasury Department that its records "do not show that any payments of 1933 Double Eagles were authorized to be made by the United States Mint, Philadelphia, to any Federal Reserve Bank or Branch."
May 4, 1944	Referring to the King Farouk 1933 gold $20, the Treasury Department general counsel advises, "It would be proper to attempt by diplomatic representations to have the coin returned to the United States."
June 18, 1944	Collector F.C.C. Boyd surrendered a 1933 gold $20 to Agent Strang, the fourth coin known to have been turned over to the Secret Service.
June 19, 1945	The Secret Service seized a fifth 1933 gold $20 coin, from T. James Clarke through his attorney.

Date	Event
June 20, 1945	The Secret Service seized two more 1933 gold $20 coins (Nos. 6 and 7), from James A. Stack and Charles M. Williams.
August 12, 1947	The United States recovered a 1933 gold $20 (coin No. 8 to be seized) from L.G. Barnard at the conclusion of litigation.
September 1949	The Treasury Department drafted a letter to King Farouk demanding return of the 1933 gold $20. The letter was submitted to the State Department for review. The State Department advised that it was "politically inadvisable" to raise the subject with Egypt. The letter was not sent.
1952	Louis Eliasberg surrendered a 1933 gold $20 to the United States (No. 9). "[When] I heard there was a cloud to the title, I surrendered the coin," Eliasberg said.
July 23, 1952	A coup d'état ousted King Farouk of Egypt.
February 26, 1953	Sotheby's was appointed official adviser to the Egyptian government in the sale of property belonging to deposed King Farouk.
December 1953	The U.S. State Department instructed the U.S. Embassy in Cairo to request the return of the King Farouk 1933 gold $20.
January 27, 1954	The U.S. State Department instructed the U.S. Embassy in Cairo to "request that coin be withheld from sale and that it be returned to the United States Department of Treasury."
February 24, 1954	Sotheby's conducted session 1 of its auction of the "Palace Collections of Egypt" (King Farouk collection). Lot 185 was to contain 17 gold $20 coins, including the 1933, but the coin was withdrawn at behest of the U.S. Government.
March 31, 1954	The U.S. Embassy in Cairo reported the return of the 1933 gold $20 was "under consideration" by the Egyptian government.
Late summer 1995	Stephen Fenton purchased a 1933 gold $20, along with other U.S. gold coins, in London.
February 8, 1996	U.S. federal agents arrested Stephen Fenton and Jasper Parrino at the Waldorf=Astoria Hotel in New York while Fenton and Parrino were attempting to consummate the sale of the 1933 gold $20. The coin was seized.
January 25, 2001	The U.S. government and Fenton reached an out-of-court settlement. The government retained ownership of the coin, but the sale of Fenton's specimen was authorized.
July 30, 2002	The only 1933 gold $20 "issued and monetized" by the U.S. government was sold at an auction conducted by Sotheby's New York City.
2006	The Israel Switt family turned in 10 1933 gold $20 coins to the Mint to authenticate and legalize. Shortly thereafter, the family commenced suit against the United States.

Chapter 12

1993 Thomas Jefferson Silver Dollar

Mintage: 600,000 authorized (599,818 struck: 332,891 proof, 266,927 uncirculated)
Designer: James Farrell after Gilbert Stuart (1805)
Diameter: 38.1 millimeters
Composition: 90-percent silver, 10-percent copper
Total silver weight: 0.7734 troy ounces

On April 13, 1994, the 251st anniversary of his birth, America's first true Renaissance man, Thomas Jefferson, was honored with a new commemorative silver dollar in impressive ceremonies held on the "Little Mountain" – Monticello – several hours south of Washington, D.C., in rural Charlottesville, Virginia.

The new coin – bearing an unusual, little-remembered portrait of Jefferson that is arresting in style and design, and a distinctive frontal view of Monticello – turned out to be a popular issue. Of 600,000 coins authorized, a 99.9-percent sellout resulted. 599,818 proof and uncirculated versions combined.

The coin commemorates the 250th anniversary of Jefferson's birth and memorializes his home. Congress directed that it go on sale May 1, 1994.

"I am as happy no where else and in no other society, and all my wishes end, where I hope my days will end, at Monticello," Jefferson wrote on August 12, 1787. The Monticello that he wrote of is not the flat object on the reverse of the nickel that bears his sobriquet. It is a living estate in Albemarle County, Virginia.

That Jefferson had substantial numismatic knowledge can be seen easily in the 17 volumes of his collected works. But that is but one facet of a multi-talented man who mastered several Indian dialects as well as Latin, Greek, Italian, French, German, and Anglo-Saxon. As an undergraduate at the College of William and Mary in Williamsburg, Virginia, his academic interests also included natural history, mathematics, history, geography, civics, economics, and philosophy.

Small wonder that in 1962, when President and Mrs. John F. Kennedy held a dinner at the White House honoring many Nobel Prize laureates, the 35th president's remarks centered on the third president. "I think this is the most extraordinary collection of talent, of human knowledge, that has ever been gathered together at the White House, with

1993 Thomas Jefferson silver dollar commemorating the 250th anniversary of his birth.

the possible exception of when Thomas Jefferson dined alone," Kennedy said.

Here were individuals whose respective disciplines made them men and women of achievement. These were the best, the brightest; individuals who had, in the words of Alfred Nobel's will, "contributed most materially to the benefit of mankind in the year immediately preceding" in the fields of physics, chemistry, medicine, literature, and peace.

Even 136 years after his death in 1826, Jefferson still held sway. He does no less today.

Jefferson was a genius, a master of many disciplines, including numismatics. The records of the American Philosophical Society record that at the start of his second term as president, in 1805, he donated 150 Roman bronze coins to the APS. His gift was said by him to "be worthy" of inclusion in the organization's cabinet.

Jefferson was an aristocrat with a fine mind, fortunate to have fine teachers who expanded his horizons. William Small, at the Collage of William & Mary, brought him the teachings of the Scottish Enlightenment and the philosophy of integrating the study of history, law and the sciences.

Jefferson was born April 2, 1743, on the old-style calendar (today celebrated as April 13). Congress directed that the silver dollar commemorating his birth be minted in 1994 but dated 1993. Part of the proceeds from the coin's sales were earmarked for the restoration of Monticello. The house is presently administered by a trust set up by the family that preserved it from ruin 70 years ago.

From 1769 to 1809, Jefferson was constantly building on the house. In the Thomas Jefferson Memorial Association's guidebook to this unique American treasure, Frederick D. Nicholas and James A. Bear Jr. write, "No other house in America so well reflects the personality of its owner." The residence was "strictly Jefferson's own creation."

Work began on the mansion in 1767 and continued irregularly but more aggressively after Jefferson's marriage in 1772 to Martha Wayles Skelton, a wealthy widow. Still, Jefferson's long absences in service of his state and nation precluded the supervision that he as architect wanted.

In 1782, when French General Marquis de Chastellux visited, he was impressed with the "house of which Mr. Jefferson was the architect, and often one of the workmen." He described as "rather elegant and in the Italian taste. … we may safely aver that Mr. Jefferson is the first American who has consulted the fine arts to know how he should shelter himself from the weather."

Jefferson's Monticello is familiar to even a schoolchild because of its depiction on the 5-cent piece, starting in 1938. It appears to be a two-story building with a dome. The dome, after the Temple of Vesta design, is a distinctive feature, but the building is deceptive, an optical illusion as to height. As Paul Wilstach noted in the April 1929 *National Geographic*, "Being an artist and imaginative, Jefferson loved to create … illusions and in yet another way he made his house look smaller than it actually is" by hiding two of the four floors.

The basement cannot be seen from the traditional frontal view; the second and third floors are effortlessly seamed together. The fourth floor is "artfully concealed by the pediments of the two porticos and by the balustrade, which edges the roof line."

Congress mandated that the 1993 silver dollar bear a portrait of Jefferson on the obverse and a "frontal view" of Monticello on the reverse. Wilstach notes the irony: "When we come to enter we discover that there is no back to Monticello. … There are, indeed, two fronts, as was the case with nearly all major plantation houses. These were the approach front, to which callers and guests came, and the opposite or private, front, where, especially screened by the portico, the family gathered." (The public today enters through the approach front.)

Jefferson's portraiture on numismatic designs dates at least to his presidency. According to some

The Fine Arts Commisson viewed these sketches in 994 for the 1993 dated coin.

The Fine Arts Commisson viewed these sketches in 994 for the 1993 dated coin.

U.S. Mint records, dies for the Jefferson peace medals (after the bust by Jean-Antoine Houdon) were cut by Robert Scot in the latter part of 1801. Robert Julian and other numismatic scholars, including Michael Hodder, suggest that John Reich was the true author.

In 1938, anxious to change the 25-year-old Buffalo nickel design at the first legal opportunity, the Treasury Department opened a competition to American sculptors to produce designs that would be judged by an advisory committee. Records of the Commission of Fine Arts in Washington disclose that the competition was brought to the commission's attention, as required by law, on February 3, 1938. The contest terminated April 15 of that year.

Subject matter required an "authentic portrait" of Jefferson on the obverse and a "representation of Jefferson's historic home near Charlottesville" on the reverse. A $1,000 prize awaited the winner.

Some 390 plasters were received in response, depicting, in the words of the *Washington Post* newspaper, unique visions of Jefferson. Judging began April 20. Felix Schlag's design was chosen four days later.

The designs went to the Commission of Fine Arts for review, as mandated by statute, and there was opposition to the "modernistic" reverse showing a three-quarters view of Monticello. In his book *The U.S. Mint & Coinage (1966)*, Don Taxay quotes at length from a July 17, 1938, criticism by Charles Moore, commission chairman. The document is apparently no longer in the commission's archives.

Note cards kept by the commission, recently made available under the Freedom of Information Act, show only the February 1938 notification and then a July 28, 1938, memo indicating the model submitted by the Mint director was "approved with recommendations." The changes included revising Monticello into a tomblike view and using more classical lettering.

Perhaps it was perceived as beautiful at the time, but there was criticism of the change. The Commission of

Fine Arts archives record receipt of protests on August 10, 1938, all of which were forwarded to the Treasury Department for response. It was to no avail, and by mid-September 1938, the coin was in production.

Nearly a half century later, in August 1992, Congress passed the Thomas Jefferson Commemoration Commission Act," which authorized a number of programs to commemorate the anniversary of Jefferson's birth. But surprisingly, no one moved to support a coin, in large measure because 1993 already had a full plate with the Madison commemorative coin, honoring Jefferson's friend and neighbor who is widely known as the principal draftsman of the Bill of Rights. (As it turns out, Jefferson was the architect of his friend's home, Montpelier, too.) But this didn't deter Senator John Warner of Virginia, a longtime Jefferson buff who strongly believed that there ought to be

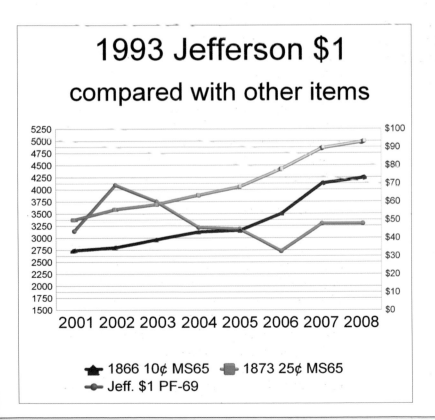

1993 Jefferson $1

compared with other items

1866 10¢ MS65   1873 25¢ MS65   Jeff. $1 PF-69

a distinctive numismatic tribute to this founding father in a commemorative, rather than a circulating, coin. A fund-raising goal provided the impetus.

Senate bill No. 959 (and its companion, House of Representatives bill No. 5056) was introduced April 25, 1991. It was reintroduced on January 21, 1993, the day after President Bill Clinton was inaugurated. Interestingly, Clinton's journey to his White House inaugural began by bus from Monticello – no doubt inspired by his middle name, Jefferson.

Warner's bill looked as if it would go nowhere, but in the waning hours of the 103rd Congress' first session, an onslaught of five commemorative coin bills moved to the forefront. Warner viewed the Jefferson coin bill as an "accompaniment" to the Jefferson commission bill signed into law by President H.W. Bush the previous August 17. "It is important to realize the continued great popularity of Jefferson and Monticello not only in our country but throughout the world," Warner said. "In the past three years alone, Monticello has been visited by 10 heads of state.

"I believe that no other American is more deserving of being honored with a commemorative coin than Thomas Jefferson: the third President of the United States, Vice President to John Adams; the first Secretary of State; Commissioner to France; author of the Declaration of Independence; Governor of Virginia, and author of the preamble to the Virginia Constitution for Religious Freedom."

On November 10, 1993, a hearing was held by the House Banking, Finance & Urban Affairs Subcommittee on Consumer Credit and Insurance, which now handles all coinage matters. Included in the hearing, chaired by Representative Joseph Kennedy II of Massachusetts, was the Jefferson commemorative and three bills honoring America's service men and women.

Things began moving at a frenetic pace, and in a rare Sunday session on November 21, it appeared the commemorative freight train was pulling out of the station at record speed. It suddenly became a veritable Christmas tree ornamented with a variety of bills that now included coins for Jefferson, the Vietnam War memorial, women in the military, prisoners of war, and, later, the 200th anniversary of the U.S. Capitol. The deluge occurred even as Kennedy introduced a "sense of the House" resolution – a non-binding legislative rule – to limit commemorative coin programs to two per year and refer them all to the Citizens Commemorative Coin Advisory Committee.

Along with the mintage limit and design specifications, the bill specified the obligatory statutory inscriptions and an "inscription of the year '1993,'" even though it was clear at the time that production could not begin until early 1994.

The Treasury secretary would select the designs after consultation with the executive director of

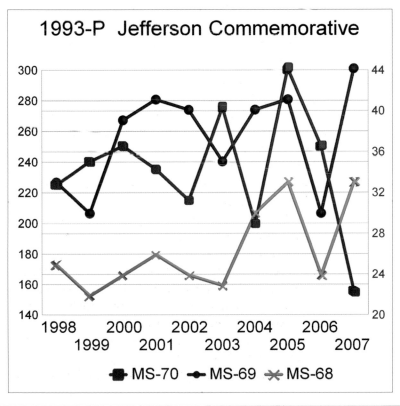

1993-P Jefferson Commemorative

Legend: MS-70, MS-69, MS-68

the Thomas Jefferson Memorial Foundation and the Commission of Fine Arts. The newly created Citizens Commemorative Coin Advisory Committee was also required to approve the pieces.

Unusually, the coin's sales period was set in the statute as "beginning on May 1, 1994 and ending on April 30, 1995." That raised the question of whether the coins would have to be dated 1994 or 1995, if manufactured in either of those years, in addition to the legislatively mandated 1993 date. Congress has the ability to suspend the provision of this or almost any other law, but if it doesn't do so, then the other operative laws apply. The phraseology typically used is "notwithstanding any other provision of law." That wasn't done in this case.

Hence, it could be correctly argued that the Jefferson coin should have been dual-dated if struck in years other than 1993. But the Mint's position evidently was that the coins could be dated 1993 regardless of the year in which they were actually struck.

When Clinton signed the measure into law, he shifted the drama to the Citizens Commemorative Coin Advisory Committee, which met in Washington for the first time in December 1993 on the same day of the president's signing. Time was short compared with most contemporary production schedules. The law was passed December 14, 1993, with sales to begin the following May 1. A mere 135 days from authorization to mandatory sales were trying under any circumstance. The Mint acknowledged that "because the time frame for production of this coin is very short, the Mint's engraving staff, utilizing resources from the Thomas Jefferson Memorial Foundation and the Mint's own archives, developed the designs."

The Mint's marketing office and the Jefferson foundation agreed on some design aspects, but the advisory committee made several substantive recommendations for change. The first matter considered was which portrait of Jefferson to use. One version showed him in Colonial-style garb, the other in a far different style. Each was based on a known portrait of Jefferson.

There are but 26 portraits of Jefferson (not including silhouettes) known to have been done during his lifetime. Jefferson purchased the Houdon marble sculpture, the model for the Jefferson nickel, from the sculptor in France for 1,000 livres on July 3, 1789. The Mint said a "depiction of Jefferson in a frockcoat and pigtail would be more familiar to the American public due to its use on the Jefferson nickel" but sided against it on grounds of marketability.

The sketch prepared was after Houdon's portrait showing Jefferson as a mature man of 46. The portrait was not one of Jefferson's favorites. He preferred one from his later years, painted by celebrated portraitist Gilbert Stuart when Jefferson was 62. It was created at Stuart's studio at Seventh and F streets N.W. in Washington. Jefferson paid Stuart $100 "for drawing" his portrait on the afternoon of June 7, 1805. Jefferson wrote to the artist, thanking him for "taking the head a la antique."

Jefferson described the portrait as a "profile in the medallion stile" executed in "water colours," though at a later time he also described it as a "sketch of me in medallion form … on paper with crayons." Both descriptions are correct. The original portrait was executed in gouache – opaque watercolor – over a lightly indicated crayon on handmade laid paper.

This portrait hung in the White House until Jefferson left office on March 4, 1809, after which it became part of his collection at Monticello. When Jefferson's holdings were disposed of after his death, this portrait was reserved for his granddaughter Ellen Wayles Randolph Coolidge. In 1960, it was donated to the Fogg Art Museum at Harvard University. In 1813, Jefferson listed this work as the "approved portrait" of him. In 1815, he wrote to Horatio Gates Spafford that the drawing was "deemed the best which has been taken of me." Nonetheless, the portrait is not especially familiar to many today, though it was illustrated in great-granddaughter Sarah N. Randolph's *Domestic Life* of Jefferson, published in 1871.

At 4 p.m. January 20, 1994, a half-hour conference call was held, linking executive deputy Mint director Philip N. Diehl and advisory committee members Elvira Clain-Stefanelli, David L. Ganz, Reed Hawn, Danny Hoffman, Elsie Sterling Howard, and Thomas V. Shockley III. The meeting's minutes report that Diehl "opened by stating the purpose for the teleconference was to review the proposed obverse and reverse designs for the Thomas Jefferson 250th anniversary silver dollar." They also report, "Members had been sent the proposed and alternate designs, which had received the approval of the sponsoring organizations."

Several alternative designs were floated, as well as criticism of some of the artistic elements of the proposed and alternate designs. One uniform comment was that all of the designs seemed cluttered, either with verbiage or detail, and that a cleaner look seemed preferable. Some of the criticism was minor. On one view of Monticello, the central step (at the right pillar) lacked perspective; others commented on the size of Jefferson's head (too large for the coin). But the bulk of the criticism focused on the depiction of Monticello.

Although Jefferson's portrait has been criticized, I found it attractive almost immediately. I sent a fax to my fellow committee members: "Given this as a choice, the Jefferson portrait utilized (which my law partner [Teri Towe] immediately recognized as coming from the portrait located at Harvard, a copy of which, he advises me, is at the State Department), is arresting. It is similar in style to that of Elizabeth Jones for the Olympic $5 gold piece (Nike) and is Greek in culture and depth. It is, in a word, beautiful."

The result is a coin that may well redefine the way Americans think of their nation's third president. Certainly, the James Ferrell rendering is a beautiful, artistic, sensitive, and exquisitely detailed portrait.

The reverse was intriguing for many reasons but also the subject of some criticism. My comments to the advisory committee were, "The reverse as proposed is neat. I like positioning off to the side. But I would eliminate [the word] Monticello ... as unnecessary and give some depth by using the same perspective for the center stair as is done for the side stair – if that is the reverse we use."

But at least initially, I had a different idea as to what ought to be used: "As nice as that reverse is, a different view (done by Felix Schlag, originally for the 1938 Jefferson nickel, and rejected by the Fine Arts Commission as too avant-garde) shows a frontal view of Monticello, angled to the side. I attach two copies, one enlarged, the other placed side-by-side with the other."

The problem, as I explained it, was, "I am not convinced the Schlag view is frontal, but if the Mint believes that it is, the design is superior in every respect and shows the rich details of Monticello, which Jefferson (as architect) designed."

Sketches of the various possibilities and some computer-generated recreations were also included for each of the committee members.

Although the committee's deliberations are private, it is fair to characterize them as candid and vigorous. The committee, for example, agreed that the concept of Monticello angled to the side was beautiful. But the original version supplied by the Mint, which placed Monticello off-center, used a drawing that appeared wooden and lacking the vitality of Jefferson's mansion – not to mention that the doors and windows were improperly scaled and foreign to the way the building really looks.

The solution was to keep the concept but use the other sketch of Monticello – in essence, blending the two designs. That is precisely what the advisory committee members ultimately recommended and the Mint adopted. On January 27, 1994, the Mint's graphics department sent faxed examples of the revised reverse design to all panel members. The result was one beautiful coin. For the purist, the sketches showed seven steps up to the portico. The design also marked an integration of incused lettering and raised letter-

Olympic $5 gold piece
(Nike)

> **Encapsulated 1993 Thomas Jefferson silver dollars**
>
> Numismatic Guaranty Corporation:
>
> - 1,435 mint state (about 1,000 in MS-69).
> - 22 proofs (17 proof-69).
>
> Professional Coin Grading Service:
>
> - 2,857 mint state (about 2,500 in MS-69).
> - About 1,100 proofs (850 proof-69).

ing on the reverse and the first time that "E Pluribus Unum" has appeared in a straight line on a coin.

I attended a black-tie dinner held throughout the main floor of Monticello's main building to mark the 250th anniversary of Jefferson's birth. My dinner partner was a member of the Rockefeller family, which had participated in the restoration and revitalization of the home.

An extraordinary evening and an extraordinary man, that Jefferson. He invented the American coinage system. His "Notes on Coinage" (1785) formed the basis for our contemporary money, cent to dollar.

Jefferson viewed his high government service as important but not among his three greatest accomplishments. His tombstone, located near Monticello, was inscribed as he dictated:

"Here was buried
Thomas Jefferson
Author of the
Declaration
of American Independence
of the
Statute of Virginia
for
Religious Freedom
and Father of the
University of Virginia
Born April 2, 1743, O.S.
Died July 4, 1826"

He wrote this "because by these, as testimonials that I have lived, I wish most to be remembered."

The accompanying charts show values for the 1993 Jefferson silver dollar. The Mint's issue prices were $27 for the uncirculated version and $31 for the proof. Only the highest grades of each have yielded a reasonable return. In the modern commemorative series (since 1982), the real value added can be seen in MS-69, proof-69 and MS-70 for the most part. The sole exception is low-mintage items, such as the Jackie Robinson gold $5, the brilliant-uncirculated Capitol silver dollar, and similar instances where the supply will never equal demand.

This analysis may well make the case for buying modern issues in the aftermarket after they have been encapsulated, graded and discounted off their original issue price.

Unlike many of the coins in the Salomon Brothers marketbasket or the other major rarities, the 1993 Jefferson dollar is not a truly rare coin, though demand outstripped supply.

1993 Thomas Jefferson silver-dollar values

Source: NumisMedia, October 2007.

Coin	MS-66	MS-67	MS-68	MS-69	MS-70
1993-P brilliant uncirculated	$26	$28	$33	$44	$156
1993-S deep-cameo proof	$25	$26	$31	$51	$2,000

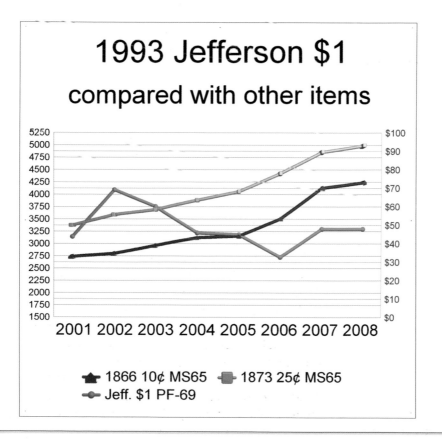

1993 Jefferson $1 compared with other items

- 1866 10¢ MS65
- 1873 25¢ MS65
- Jeff. $1 PF-69

Glossary

$20.67 Fixed price of gold, 1837-1933.

$42.22 The official price of an ounce of gold in 2008, as it has been for more than 30 years. That means a gold $20 has $40.84 worth of gold in it at the official price, not more than $900, as the free market says.

0.900 fine A 0.900-fine coin contains 90-percent gold or silver and 10-percent base metals.

24k 24-karat; pure gold, as expressed in parts per 24. A 22-karat (22/24ths) coin has a fineness of 0.91666, typical of British gold coins. American gold coins are generally 21.6 karats (0.900 fine).

Adjustment marks Commonly found on older gold and silver coins, these are evidence of an overweight planchet having been filed down to reduce a coin to legal weight.

Ag The chemical symbol for silver.

AG-3 Grade about good, 3 on the 1-to-70 grading scale. Only bare design details are visible.

Aliquot A small representative sample taken from a gold bar for assay.

Alloy A mixture of two or more metals. Gold is mixed with a base metal or other precious metals to lower the purity, influence the color, or add durability. American gold coins typically are an alloy of 90-percent gold and 10-percent copper, silver or other metals.

American Eagle bullion coins U.S. Mint gold, platinum and silver coins issued in proof and uncirculated versions. Gold and platinum coins are issued in tenth-ounce, quarter-ounce, half-ounce, and one-ounce sizes.

ANA American Numismatic Association, the national coin club, founded in 1891 and chartered by Congress in 1912. It headquarters are in Colorado Springs, Colorado.

ANACS Formerly the American Numismatic Association Authentication and Certification Service and later the Amos Numismatic Authentication and Certification Service. ANACS is a commercial authentication and grading service, which, for a fee, will tell you if your coin is genuine and opine about its grade.

Ancient coin A coin made in Rome, Greece, Byzantium, or other countries generally before A.D. 500.

Annealing The process by which blanks are heated in a furnace to soften them before they are struck into coin.

ANS The American Numismatic Society, founded in 1858, the oldest educational organization of its kind in the United States. Its headquarters are in downtown New York City.

Anthony dollar Susan B Anthony dollar, produced from 1979 to 1981 and again in 1999.

Arrows Arrows around the date on 1853 and 1873 U.S. coins, and continuing for several years after, indicate a change in the coins' weight. The dime's weight, for example, dropped from 2.67 grams to 2.49 grams in 1853. Arrows in the talons of an eagle on a coin are a symbol of war.

Ask The price at which a dealer or other seller is willing to sell a coin.

Assay The melting of one or more coins to analyze their weight and metal composition.

Assayer A tester, who is often an officially recognized individual or company, of precious metals to determine their purity.

AU Grade about uncirculated or almost uncirculated, 50 to 58 on the 1-to-70 grading scale. Better than XF but not quite uncirculated. All letters and devices are in nice visible shape with minor scuffs or wear on extreme high spots of the coin.

Au The chemical symbol for gold.

Barber coinage Coins designed by father and son William and Charles Barber, two great engravers at the Philadelphia Mint in the 19th and 20th centuries. Their coinage designs are universally referred to by their last name – Barber dimes, Barber quarters, and Barber half dollars, all 1892-1916.

Bareford, Harold A New York attorney (died 1978) who collected coins in the 1940s and '50s with spectacular results.

Base metals Generally refers to the coining metals copper, nickel, aluminum, and zinc.

Bid The price at which a dealer or other buyer is willing to buy a coin. Opposite of ask.

Blank A coin before it is struck; a planchet empty of design. It may or may not have the milled edges of a finished coin.

Brilliant uncirculated Describes a circulation-strike coin that has not seen widespread or general circulation. It has a nice shiny surface.

Britannia British gold bullion coin first issued in 1987. This 22-karat (0.9166-fine), legal-tender piece was the first new gold coin issued by the British Royal Mint since the sovereign was reintroduced in 1817.

Bronze A copper alloy.

Bullion A generic term for gold and silver. It originally came from the old French word *bouillon*, which means boiling.

Bureau of Engraving & Printing The government agency that prints U.S. paper money. It has production facilities in Fort Worth, Texas, and Washington, D.C.

Bust A Roman- or Greek-style facial portrait facing left or right. The style is commonly used in portraits on coinage.

Centenario A Mexican gold bullion coin with a face value of 50 pesos and a gold content of 1.2057 troy ounces.

Chevronetz A Russian bullion coin containing 0.2489 troy ounces of 0.900-fine gold and with a face value of 10 roubles. Issued in the 1970s.

Circulating coins Cents, nickels, dimes, quarters, half dollars, and dollars used in daily commerce. U.S. gold pieces were circulating coins until 1933.

Clad coinage Dimes, quarters and half dollars of copper-nickel composition in sandwich form, authorized by the Coinage Act of 1965.

Coin gold A gold alloy, usually with a minimum fineness of 0.900, used in making coins, usually with silver or copper to improve durability.

Coin silver Silver that is 0.900 fine, by U.S. statutory definition.

Coinage Act of (date) The Coinage Act of 1792, Coinage Act of 1837, Coinage Act of 1873, and Coinage Act of 1965 are the major coin legislation passed by Congress. There have been many other coinage laws – more than 200, in fact – since 1792.

Coining press The machine that strikes coins at speeds upward of 700 pieces per minute for the presidential dollars to only several strikes per minute for proof coins.

Colonial coinage Coinage of various Colonies, including Massachusetts Bay, New York, New Jersey, Rhode Island, Connecticut, Delaware, Maryland, Virginia, the Carolinas, and Georgia.

Commemorative A legal-tender coin struck primarily for collectors. Used examples are occasionally found in circulation.

Comstock Lode Located near Virginia City, Nevada, the greatest silver find of the 19th century.

Conjugate To join two heads together on a coin design. An example is the 1990 Eisenhower commemorative silver dollar, which depicts Ike as a general and president.

Continental currency Coinage of the 1776 era.

Corona An Austrian gold coin (100 coronas, or 1 crown) that became popular with investors between 1950 and 1974. The 0.900-fine coin contains 0.99802 troy ounces of gold. It was first struck from 1908 to 1915 under the Austro-Hungarian Empire. It was minted regularly as a non-legal-tender re-strike with a low premium from the 1950s until the mid-1970s, when it was largely replaced by bullion coins.

Cowrie shell A seashell used as a form of exchange.

CPI Consumer Price Index, as calculated by the U.S. Commerce Department's Bureau of Labor Statistics since 1913.

Crane & Co. The Bureau of Engraving & Printing's principal supplier of paper for the printing of U.S. paper money.

Date The digits appearing on most coins to indicate the year a coin was made, though not always. Bicentennial coinage dated "1776-1976" was struck starting in July 1975.

Device Designs on a coin other than portraiture, such as a mint mark, wildlife, scenery, and more.

Die The metal punch or device that is used to produce a coin on a press. The deeper the design is cut into the die, the higher the relief on the coin.

Dollar The basic U.S. currency unit. It is an international currency; more than two-thirds of all U.S. $100 bills circulate abroad.

Dore Impure gold bullion, yet to be refined.

Doubled die Refers to doubling of an image or lettering on a coin. It is usually caused by a mistake in die production.

Double eagle A U.S. gold $20 coin struck for circulation.

Eagle A U.S. gold $10 coin struck for circulation. The generic term "eagle" for the denomination should not be confused with modern American Eagle bullion coins.

Edge lettering Lettering incused, engraved or struck on a coin's edge.

Edge The outside rim of a coin; its third side after obverse and reverse.

EF Grade extremely fine, also expressed as XF, 45 on the 1-to-70 grading scale. An EF coin shows hints of mint luster, nice details, and little wear. It's better than a VF but not as nice as an AU or unc.

Effigy A portrait on a coin, usually on the obverse. It can be singular or conjugated.

Error A coin or other numismatic item on which a mistake has been made.

Euro The basic currency unit of the European Economic Union.

Exergue The space on a coin or medal below the central design and often containing the date of issue.

Exonumia Tokens and medals. It is a modern word coined (so to speak) by Russell Rulau, former editor of *World Coin News* and author of several books on tokens.

F Grade fine, 15 on the 1-to-70 grading scale. A grade fine coin has more details than one grading very good but fewer than a very fine coin. On 19th-century U.S. coins, all seven letters of the word "Liberty" are readable.

Face value A coin's legal-tender value, or denomination. It is often used in reference to bullion coins, which have nominal face values but are traded for their precious-metal content.

Fair market value The price that a willing buyer and willing seller reach.

Fair-2 A coin grade that is a little better than poor (PO-1) but not as nice as AG-3 (about good).

Field The portion of a coin not covered by the principal design on the obverse or reverse.

Fine ounce A descriptive measurement for gold with a minimum purity of 0.995 fine.

Fine weight The actual precious-metal weight of a bar or coin.

Fineness The purity of precious metal in a coin, expressed in parts per thousand. Most U.S. coins are 0.900-fine silver or gold. British sovereigns are 0.9167 fine.

Flan The blank metal disc or planchet onto which a coin design is imprinted.

Fort Knox A U.S. bullion depository in Kentucky. It was completed in December 1936.

G Grade good, 4 on the 1-to-70 grading scale. A grade good coin will have basic design elements with many mottos and devices visible but not strong on details.

Gold The most widely traded precious metal in bullion form. Latin name is *aurum*. Its chemical symbol is Au. Its melting point is 1,063 degrees Celsius.

Good The grading term for a poor-condition circulated coin. Yes, the term is confusing.

Groat British silver coin in circulation from 1279 to about 1955 (value: 4-pence).

Guinea British gold coin with a nominal value of 1 pound (20 shillings). It was first issued in 1663 and named for gold from Guinea in West Africa. It was unofficially revalued at 21 shillings by the Great Recoinage of 1696.

Half cent The smallest denomination struck by the U.S. Mint, produced from 1793 to 1857.

Half eagle Traditionally, a U.S. gold $5 coin struck for circulation. Some modern U.S. gold $5 commemorative coins have also been struck.

Hallmark A symbol of fineness and manufacture.

Hub A piece of metal bearing a coin's design in exact size of the coin. It is cut by a Janvier engraving machine, heat treated to harden it, and then sharpened and improved by an engraver. It is then placed in a hydraulic press and is slowly pressed into a blank piece of soft die steel until a negative replica is made (master die).

Incused design A design recessed into the coin's surface.

Initials They usually indicate the engraver or sculptor who designed the coin and reproduced it in die form. "V.D.B.," for Victor David Brenner, on the cent is an example.

Inscription Verbiage appearing on coins either because it is required by law ("statutory inscriptions") or because it is customarily used. "Liberty" is a statutory inscription on American coinage.

Janvier engraver This machine cuts a coin design into soft tool steel, tracing the exact details of the model and producing a positive replica of the model called a "hub," which is used to make dies. The 12-inch model can thus be reduced to a 1-inch die.

Krugerrand South Africa's gold bullion coin produced since 1967.

Legal tender Coins or other money that can be used for all debts, public or private, under compulsion of law.

Legend The inscription surrounding the effigy on a coin, such as "In God We Trust" on the cent.

Maple Leaf Canada's gold bullion coin.

Maria Theresa thaler A trade coin made by the Austro-Hungarian empire in 1780 and still minted today as a non-legal-tender trade coin.

Marketbasket A combination of items representative of a market as a whole or a segment of it and designed to obtain price averages of several rather than all. The Dow Jones industrial average is one such basket; the Salomon Brothers coin portfolio is another.

Medal A commemorative that is not a coin and generally larger than a coin.

Melted Coins are destroyed for many reasons, including a precious-metal value that exceeds face value. Millions of gold and silver coins were destroyed this way when bullion prices rose above nominal value.

Metal composition The raw materials, or metals, that were used to produce a coin. The metal composition of clad coins, for example, is clad layers of 75-percent copper and 25-percent nickel bonded to a pure-copper core.

Millimeters Metric measure used for coin sizes. The cent is 19 millimeters in diameter; the Morgan silver dollar is 38.1 millimeters.

Mint mark A small mark on a coin, usually a letter, identifying where it was produced. Examples on U.S. coins include a "W" for West Point, "D" for Denver, and "S" for San Francisco.

Mint set Uncirculated coins produced and marketed in a set by the U.S. and other world mints and sold to collectors. In 1970, the D-mint-mark half dollar (produced at Denver) was included in mint sets but not for general circulation.

Mint state Grade uncirculated, 60 to 70 on the 1-to-70 grading scale.

Mint Where coins are made. In addition to the main mint in Philadelphia, the United States has branch mints in Denver, San Francisco and West Point, New York.

Mintage Number of pieces coined.

Modern commemoratives The term commonly refers to U.S. commemorative coins produced since 1982.

Modern issue Contemporary precious-metal coins minted by official agencies in unlimited numbers for investment purposes.

Motto A phrase on coinage such as "In God We Trust" and "E Pluribus Unum."

MS-65 Grade uncirculated, gem quality.

Napoleon A French 20-franc coin containing 0.1867 troy ounces of 0.900-fine gold.

National motto For the United States, "In God We Trust."

NGC Numismatic Guaranty Corporation. A commercial authentication and grading service

that, for a fee, will tell you if you coin is genuine and opine about its grade.

Nickel The U.S. 5-cent coin with a composition of 75-percent copper, 25-percent nickel. The composition was first used for the 5-cent in 1866.

No motto The term refers to U.S. coins without the motto "In God We Trust" in their design and usually designates a design variation from other coins of the same type. Examples include the Saint-Gaudens gold $20, which was introduced in 1907 without the motto. The motto was added to 1908 and later gold $20 coins by congressional mandate.

Numismatic products Coins and coin-related products produced by or for the U.S. Mint specifically for sale to the public.

Obverse The front, or face, side of a coin.

Olive branches They symbolize peace when found in the talons of the eagle on U.S. and other coinage designs.

Onza Mexico's gold bullion coin containing one ounce of 0.900-fine gold. Fractional versions are also produced.

Panda China's gold bullion coin. Launched in 1982, it is 0.9999 fine and is produced by the China Mint Company in Beijing.

Pattern coins A trial strike of a proposed coin design. Patterson DuBois noted in an early article that patterns are "half-forgotten witnesses … [to] the impractical schemes of visionaries and hobbyists – a tale of national deliverance from minted evil, the tale of what 'might have been.'"

PCGS Professional Coin Grading Service. A commercial authentication and grading service that, for a fee, will tell you if your coin is genuine and opine about its grade.

Penny Colloquially, a U.S. cent, but more accurately, a British coin.

Pennyweight Originally, the weight of a silver penny in Britain in the Middle Ages. It is still widely used in North America as a unit of weight in the jewelry trade. Twenty pennyweights equal one troy ounce.

Perth Mint Australia's oldest operating mint was established in Perth, Western Australia, in 1899 as a branch of the Royal Mint to refine metal from the state's eastern gold fields.

Philharmoniker An Austrian gold coin of 0.9999 fineness, first issued in 1989.

Planchet A blank metal flan from which a coin is struck. Planchets accidentally shipped with coins are collectible in their own right as type I (without rim) and type II (with upset rim) errors.

Platinum Chemically described as the 78th element in the periodic table. It has a high density, 21.5 grams per cubic centimeter, and a melting point of 1,772 degrees centigrade (3,224 degrees Fahrenheit). Platinum is also the most valuable "impurity" of most nickel deposits. The platinum-group metals ruthenium, palladium, osmium, and iridium are byproducts of nickel mining. Discovered by Italian scientist Julius Scaliger in 1557, large quantities of the metal were not available until about 1750, when the Spaniards found platinum in Peru. They named it platinum from their word "plata," which is Spanish for silver.

PO-1 Grade poor, the worst on the 1-to-70 grading scale.

Pocket change Coins typically found at the end of a day in your pocket or purse.

Precious metal In numismatics, the term generally refers to the coining metals of gold, silver and platinum.

Presidential dollars U.S. coin series started in 2007 to honor the nation's deceased chief executives.

Privy mark A mark on a coin that indicates the mintmaster in charge of its production.

Proof set Proof coins produced and marketed in a set by the U.S. and other world mints and sold to collectors.

Proof A high-quality coin struck primarily for collectors. Proof coins are struck from highly polished planchets using highly polished dies, usually on a hydraulic press. They are sometimes struck more than once to bring up the relief. The specially treated dies produce a mirrored background, sharp relief, and a frosted image on the finished coin.

Pure gold Gold having a purity of 24 karats, or 0.9999 fine.

Quarter eagle A U.S. gold $2.50 coin struck for circulation.

Regulation An administrative rule issued by a governmental department, frequently based on laws. The Treasury Department usually administers coin-related regulations.

Restrike A numismatic item that is reproduced, usually for collectors. Sometimes original dies are used, and sometimes new dies are made from an original hub. The 1827 quarter and 1804 silver dollar are two examples of collectible restrikes.

Reverse The back of a coin.

Rim The raised area of a coin bordering the edge and surrounding the field.

Sacagawea dollar A golden-colored U.S. coin (manganese-brass composition) honoring the guide to Lewis & Clark, struck since 2000.

Saint Nickname used by dealers and collectors for 1907-1933 gold $20 coins, designed by Augustus Saint-Gaudens.

Salomon Brothers survey An annual report comparing coins and other tangible assets with stocks and bonds. It was in vogue from about 1978 to 1990.

Screw press An old coining press that used a giant screw that moved up and down to apply pressure to produce the coin.

Scrip Privately issued pieces that are not legal tender but are redeemable for goods or trade.

Secondary device A design element on a coin that is not part of the primary design.

Silver dollar A U.S. coin struck from 1794 to 1935 (90-percent silver) and again from 1971 to 1978 (80-percent silver, proofs only). The term is also commonly but erroneously applied to any U.S. dollar coin, including those of clad composition.

Silver The most widely used precious metal in commerce and industrial applications. Its Latin name is *argentum*. Its chemical symbol is Ag, its relative density is 10.5, and its melting point is 960 degrees Celsius.

Sovereign British gold coin with a face value of 1 pound sterling, a fineness of 0.9166, and a total gold weight of 0.2354 troy ounces. Sovereigns were first issued in 1489 for Henry VII.

Saint-Gaudens, Augustus The great American sculptor and designer of the gold $10 and $20 coins struck from 1907 to 1933.

State coinage Coinage issued by 12 of the 13 original Colonies from 1776 to 1789.

State quarters Common reference to the U.S. Mint's 50 State Quarters, which began in 1999.

Statutory inscriptions Mottos or other verbiage that appear on a coin because the law so requires.

Stella A U.S. gold $4 pattern, 1879-1880.

Sterling In silver, 0.925 fine, typical of the British pound sterling.

Surcharge An amount added to the selling price of a commemorative coin that benefits an organization related to the coin's subject. The surcharge amount and the beneficiary organizations are specified in the coin's authorizing legislation.

Tael Traditional Chinese unit of weight for gold. One tael equals 1.20337 troy ounces and 37.4290 grams.

TAMS Token & Medal Society, a group of exonumists.

Tetradrachm Ancient Greek coin (value of 4 drachma).

Token A privately issued, non-legal-tender object similar to a coin that can be redeemed for goods or services. It can be made of metal, cardboard or any other suitable media.

Trade coin A coin not necessarily legal tender whose design, weight and purity are intended as a bullion substitute. The U.S. Trade dollar (1873-1885) is one example; the Maria Theresa thaler (1780) is another.

Travers, Scott Contemporary coin dealer and author.

Trial of the pyx A common reference to the annual U.S. Assay Commission, which was mandated by the original Mint Act of April 2, 1792, and continued uninterrupted until 1980. Designed to maintain oversight over a narrow aspect of the executive branch, the commission examined a sampling of the nation's coins to certify to the president, Congress and the American people that they met the requirements for purity, weight and value.

Trimes U.S. 3-cent coins composed of 75-percent silver (1851-1853) and 90-percent silver (1854-1873). During World War II, they were authorized again but never produced.

Troy ounce The traditional unit of weight for precious metals, attributed to a weight used in Troyes, France, in medieval times. A troy ounce (31.103 grams) is slightly heavier than an avoirdupois ounce (28.350 grams) Twelve troy ounces equal one troy pound.

Unc. The abbreviation and a common reference for grade uncirculated, or mint state.

Uncirculated A coin that has not yet entered general circulation and is usually in brilliant, shiny condition. Uncirculated coins have a satin finish versus the mirrored background and frosted image of proof coins.

U.S. Mint The government agency – a Treasury Department branch – responsible for production of the nation's coinage.

Upsetting The milling process that gives a coin its rim or edge.

VF Grade very fine, 20 to 30 on the 1-to-70 grading scale. A grade VF coin has more design details than a grade F coin but less than an EF coin. A VF coin is long on wear, but all letters and devices are clearly visible, including some fine detail.

VG Grade very good, 8 on the 1-to-70 grading scale. A grade VG coin has more design details visible than a G coin but less than an F. For 19th-century U.S. coins, three letters in the word "Liberty" are usually visible on a VG coin.

Vreneli Swiss gold coin with a portrait of a girl on the obverse. The coin first appeared in 1897 and was minted until 1949. It was legal tender, with a face value of 20 francs, until 1935. The 0.900-fine coin contains 0.1867 troy ounces of gold.

Wampum Beads made from conch shells used as mediums of exchange well into the 19th century.

Weight For a coin, it is usually given in grains or grams and refers to the piece's total weight, including all precious and base metals.

Whitman albums Coin holders produced by Whitman Publishing since the 1930s. They are usually in a fold-out format and contain individual spaces for each coin in a particular series.

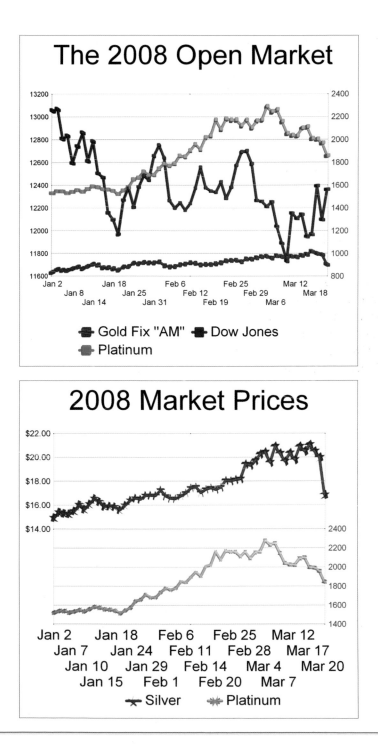

The 2008 Open Market

Gold Fix "AM"   Dow Jones
Platinum

2008 Market Prices

Silver   Platinum

Selected Bibliography

Adams, United States Numismatic Literature. Vols. 1 & 2. 19th- and 20th-century auction catalogs. (Crestline, 2001 and 1990.)

Associated Press, "Coin Collector Killed," *The New York Times,* March 11, 1962, p. 76 (online edition courtesy of Bergen County Cooperative Library System).

Auction '79.

Auction '84.

Auction Prices Realized (Krause Publications, various editions, 1982-2002).

AuctionValue.com.

Berman, Neil S., and DiGenova, Silvano, *The Investor's Guide to United States Coins* (2007).

Berman, Neil S., and Schulman, Hans M.F., *The Investor's Guide to United States Coins* (1987).

Bowers, Q. David, *Silver Dollars and Trade Dollars of the U.S.,* Vol. 1 (Bowers and Merena, 1993).

Bowers, Q. David, *Louis Eliasberg: King of Coins* (Bowers and Merena, 1996).

Bowers, Q. David, *A Buyer's Guide to Silver Dollars and Trade Dollars of the U.S.,* 3rd ed. (Ed. John Dannreuther), (Zyrus Press, 2006).

Bowers, Q. David, *The Numismatist's Weekend Companion,* Vol. 4 (1992).

Bowers and Merena, and Bowers & Ruddy Galleries, various auction catalogs.

Bowers, Q. David, *Abe Kosoff: Dean of Numismatics* (Bowers and Merena, 1985).

Bowers, Q David, *United States Dimes, Quarters, and Half Dollars: An Action Guide for the Collector and Investor* (1986).

Breen, Walter, *Walter Breen's Encyclopedia of United States and Colonial Proof Coins, 1722-1989* (1989).

Bressett, Kenneth E., "Ownership Changes & Experiences in The Fantastic 1804 Dollar: 25th Anniversary Followup," p. 167, America's Silver Coinage, 1794-1891 (Coinage of the Americas Conference at the American Numismatic Society, November 1, 1986), (1987).

Bressett, Kenneth (ed.), *The Official ANA Grading Standards for U.S. Coins* (6th ed., 2005).

Burd, William A., "The Inscrutable 1894-S Dime," *The Numismatist,* (1994).

Carlson, Carl W.A., "Tracker: An Introduction to Pedigree Research in the Field of American Rare Coins," in The ANA Centennial Anthology (eds. Carlson and Hodder, 1999), pp. 349-364.

Carothers, Neil, *Fractional Money: A History of Small Coins and Fractional Paper Currency of United States* (John Wiley & Sons, 1930).

Catalog of the Numismatic Collection of Charles Benson Esq. of Philadelphia. John Haseltine, Bangs and Company, December 16, 1880.

Coin World Staff, *Coin World Almanac*, millennium edition (2000).

Flynn, Kevin, *1894-S Dime: A Mystery Unraveled* (2nd edition, 2006).

Frankel, Allison, *Double Eagle*, pp. 78-79 (2006).

Friedman, Milton, and Schwartz, Anna Jacobson, *A Monetary History of the United States, 1867-1960* (Princeton University Press, 1963).

Ganz, David L., *Smithsonian Guide to Coin Collecting* (manuscript, 2008).

Ganz, David L., "Proof of Value of Coin Collection," *95 Proof of Facts*, 3rd edition, pp. 155-465 (2007).

Ganz, David L., *The World of Coins & Coin Collecting* (1980, 3rd edition, 1998).

Haseltine Type Table Catalog (Mehl reprint, 1927).

Heritage Auction Galleries Web site.

Heritage Auction Galleries, various catalogs.

Hodder, Michael, and Bowers, Q. David, *The Norweb Collection* (1987).

Kosoff, A., *The Edwin M. Hydeman Collection of United States Coins* (March 3-4, 1961).

Kosoff, A., *Abe Kosoff Remembers* (Durst, 1981).

Mehl, B. Max, *The Will W. Neil Collection* (1947).

Montgomery, Paul; Borckardt, Mark; Knight, Ray; *Million Dollar Nickels: Mysteries of the 1913 Liberty Head Nickels Revealed* (2005).

Newman, Eric P., and Bressett, Kenneth E., *The Fantastic 1804 Silver Dollar* (Whitman, 1962).

Numismatic Guaranty Corporation census Web site.

Numismatic Gallery(A. Kosoff), *The World's Greatest Collection of United States Silver Coins* (1945).

Numismatic Gallery (A. Kosoff), *The Adolphe Menjou Catalog of United States Coins* (June 15-16, 1950).

NumisMedia, *Wholesale Dealer Price Guide (Moderns)* (various).

NumisMedia, *Wholesale Market Dealer Price Guide* (various)

Professional Coin Grading Service population Web site.

Yeoman, R.S., *A Guide Book of United States Coins* (various editions, 1947-date).

Stack's Rare Coins 67th Anniversary Sale, the *Queller Family Collection of U.S. Half Dollars, 1794-1963*, October 15-16, 2002.

Stack's Rare Coins, 72nd Anniversary Sale, *United States Coins*, October 16-17, 2007.

Stack's Rare Coins, *The George "Buddy" Byers Collection of U.S. Half Dollars*, October 17, 2006.

Stack's Rare Coins, various catalogs.

Superior Galleries, various catalogs.

Superior Galleries, "The King of Siam Proof Set," brochure (1990).

Superior Galleries, *The Dr. Jerry Buss Collection*, January 28-30, 1985.

The Numismatist, various issues.

Travers, Scott, *The Coin Collector's Survival Manual* (multiple editions).

Travers, Scott (ed.), *Official Guide to Coin Grading* (PCGS, 2004).

Treasury document 1729, *Annual Report of Director of the Mint for the Year 1894* (Washington: Government Printing Office, 1894).

Treasury document 1829, *Annual Report of Director of the Mint for the Year 1895* (Washington: Government Printing Office, 1895).

U.S. Coin Digest. David Harper, editor. (2008).

Vartan, Vartanig G., "Wall St. Bulls Prevail; Brokers Jubilant as Rally Lifts Dow And Customers Crowd Boardrooms." *The New York Times*, October 12, 1965, p. 67.

Vermeule, Cornelius, *Numismatic Art in America* (1971).

Vintage Auctions Inc., *The 1989 Pittsburgh Pre-ANA Coin Convention* (1989).

Worden, Leon, "Coins + PR = Donn Pearlman. He Spreads the News," *COINage* magazine (October 2006).

www.bustdollars.com (October 8, 2007).

About the Author

David L. Ganz is a past president (1993-1995) of the American Numismatic Association and has written about coins and coin collecting for more than 40 years. A lawyer by profession, practicing as senior partner in the New York City firm of Ganz & Hollinger, P.C. since 1980, he started writing the "Under the Glass" column for *Numismatic News* in 1969 and has written thousands of articles since 1965 for nearly every hobby periodical. Some of his most recent coin books include *The Official Guide to America's State Quarters* (Random House, 2000), *The Official Guide to U.S. Commemorative Coins* (Bonus Books, 1999) , and *The World of Coins & Coin Collecting* (1st edition, Scribner's, 1980; 3rd edi-

tion, Bonus Books, 1998). His article "Planning Your Rare Coin Retirement," found in the 1982 *A Guide Book of United States Coins* (Red Book), was the first expanded hobby analysis of the Salomon Brothers study. He has written "Coin Market Insider's Report" for *COINage* magazine monthly for more than 30 years and earlier wrote "Coin Market Perspective" in *Coins* magazine for more than a decade. He is a former seven-year mayor of Fair Lawn, New Jersey, and since 2003 has been an elected at-large freeholder (county supervisor) in Bergen County, New Jersey, where he has chaired the Committee on Budget & Finance and managed a $460 million budget for the past five years. My website: www.GanzHollinger.com

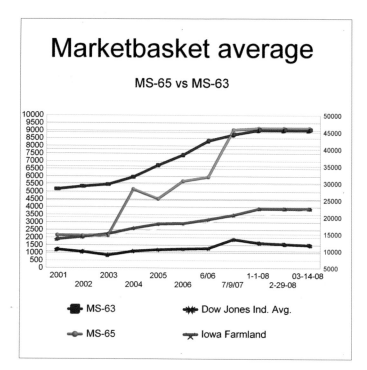

Marketbasket average

MS-65 vs MS-63

Legend: MS-63, MS-65, Dow Jones Ind. Avg., Iowa Farmland

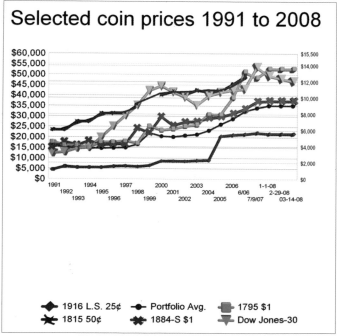

Selected coin prices 1991 to 2008

Legend: 1916 L.S. 25¢, 1815 50¢, Portfolio Avg., 1884-S $1, 1795 $1, Dow Jones-30

1794 Silver Dollar
A 125 year auction history

Legend:
- 1794 Dollar (x-Adams, 1876)
- 1876-1941 (same coin)

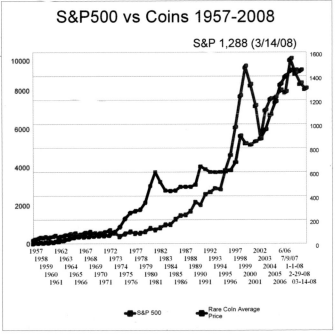

S&P500 vs Coins 1957-2008

S&P 1,288 (3/14/08)

Legend:
- S&P 500
- Rare Coin Average Price